LIVINGSTONE'S
AFRICAN JOURNAL
1853–1856

Also edited by I. Schapera

Livingstone's Missionary Correspondence, 1841–56
David Livingstone: Family Letters 1841–56 (2 vols.)
Livingstone's Private Journals, 1851–53

LIVINGSTONE'S
African Journal
1853-1856

EDITED
WITH AN INTRODUCTION
By
I. SCHAPERA

VOLUME II

1963
CHATTO & WINDUS
LONDON

Published by
Chatto & Windus Ltd
42 William IV Street
London W.C.2

*

Clarke, Irwin and Co Ltd
Toronto

CONTENTS

CONTENTS

CONTENTS

MAP

Plate facing page 459

BACK AMONG THE BALONDA

Cabango

20th May '55. Cabango. Reached this a few days ago, and will leave tomorrow. I am unable to write, in consequence of a blow recieved on the eye by a branch of a tree in riding through forest. With pain I managed to make a map of this part of the country and from Cassange, and sent it with a note to Sir R. Murchison. Also a letter for my wife, one for Mr Maclear, and one for Mr Gabriel.[1] We proceed in the first place to a town called Bango.[2]

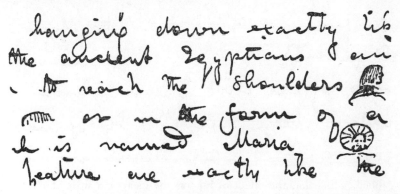

23d May. Looking back towards Loajima, I may fill up what I was prevented from doing by inflammation of the cornea. We remained a day (1st May) constructing a bridge accross the Loajima, and this we were able to do by the help of a tree which had fallen into the river, its roots resisting the force of the current. The river is very deep, but only about 25 yds wide. On the 2d May we marched forward by a bend in the course to Tamba,[3] where we found great abundance of native corn, fowls, mandioc, &c.

[1] The letter to Murchison (17.v.55) was published in *JRGS*, 1856, pp. 80–1; that to Mrs Livingstone (20.iii.55) in part by Blaikie, *Life*, 172–3 (copy in *Fam. Letters*, ii. 258–9); and an abstract of that to Gabriel (2.iii.55, with postscript 18.v.55) in *JRGS*, 1855, pp. 235–7, and *PP England*, 1856, LXII, 111–12. There is a copy of the one to Maclear (18.v.55) in the Rhodesian National Archives.

[2] See below, p. 246.

[3] Presumably on or near the Tamba R., which joins the Mombo in lat. 9.38 S, long. 20.39 E (GSGS 2465, SC 34).

People seem industrious, and all are extremely fond of plaiting their hair, of which they have a great profusion, in various fantastical forms. Some, for instance, have it in strings hanging down exactly like that of the ancient Egyptians and long enough to reach the shoulders, or in curves, or in the form of a glory which is named Maria[1] [see facsimiles]; & many in feature are exactly like the forms pain[t]ed in Egyptian sculpture, and others in Prichard's work of tribes farther north.[2]

They tatoo different parts of the body, more especially the abdomen, back, loins, & upper part of the arm, by cuttings of $\frac{1}{2}$ inch in length. In a row of these of different figures some black substance is

rubbed, which has the effect of raising the cicatrix a little above the rest of the surface [see facsimile]. The figures are of all sorts and ill formed. The colour of the people here is more of an olive yellow colour, and they having never before been visited by slave dealers were timid and civil. All, however, in these parts look at us with an air of superciliousness which is unpleasant.

Having remained two days here buying provisions, because they are reported to be scarce in front, we turned back to our route and travelled along the Tamba for four hours. It is usual in all these parts for persons to bring presents to the stranger when they wish to make more than by a speculation at purchasing. But this is nothing else but a real deal, for after giving the food they leave the basket and wait for a return, but when given it is by no means unusual for them to object

[1] '. . . of the glory round the head of the Virgin' (Travels, 449, and illustration).
[2] J. C. Prichard, Researches into the Physical Ethnography of the African Races (3rd ed., 1837), plates I–III (depicting N.E. African native types).

to the articles and request an exchange. I have been frequently taken in, but now make a regular rule to ask what my donor wants before recieving the gift. We not only look at the 'given horse in the teeth', but sometimes refuse him altogether. (Old man & his fish.)

Nearly all file their teeth to a point, which makes them extremely ugly. There is a slight change in the female dress here. It is the beginning of Matiamvo fashion, there is more covering behind.

7th. 6½ hours' march brought us to the Maomba, a considerable stream, over which we were ferried in a canoe. It runs into the Shima close by our ford.[1] It is about 30 yds wide and contains hippopotami, which do also the Quilo, Loange, Chikapa, & Loajima. It was running N.W., and had mobola, a Zambesi fruit, growing on its banks.

Here, as also on the banks of the Quilo and Chikapa, the geological structure is on the top of the bank an ironstone conglomerate, which in many parts looks as if it had been smelted, from having rounded masses as in slag and a smooth scale on the surface. The pebbles in it are of all sorts, and generally small. This mass is succeeded by metamorphosed sandstone of a pale red colour and very hard, then whinstone, and beneath all a granular rock with a few pebbles which I take to be what Murchison calls his 'bottom rocks'. In some parts there is a portion of white rock like limestone to be seen, and in others a solution of the iron seems going on, for it is seen dissolved in the springs with a surface like tar. Banks of white round gravel stones too.

The banks of the rivers (the slopes) generally are deeper from the surrounding level than where we crossed them in going north, and all along there are springs oozing out and forming circumscribed bogs. Around the eye of these a clump of trees is supported, and their various forms and dark foliage looks extremely pretty on a ground of yellowish grass. Between the rivers the surface is level and covered with grass, bushes, and stunted scraggy trees. Near the rivers the rank luxuriance of the country alone can be seen, and all along their slopes the grass is about a foot higher than our heads, and very dangerous for the eyes. There is no coffee, but many coffee-looking trees ('coffee's brothers').

In passing along the rather dreary intervals which separate the rivers, it is impossible not to be painfully struck with the absence of all animal life. Not a bird to be seen, except occasionally a tomtit & a

---

[1] The 'Shima' is obviously the Luachimo, which the 'Maomba' (Mahombo or Mombo) joins from the south in lat. 9.36 S, long. 20.40 E (GSGS 2465, SC 34). In *Travels*, 453, and *JRGS*, 1856, p. 81, the ford is located in lat. 9.38 S, long. 20.13.34 E; but see above, p. 237.

black bird peculiar to the country (a kind of small crow).[1] There are remarkably few small animals too. Everything of flesh has been hunted to extermination. Only near the rivers we are gladdened by the voice of birds, & even there they are not numerous or varied. There are few insects also, scarcely a mosquito or common fly. Only ants abound, and these are in great numbers and varieties. The solemn stillness is peculiarly painful, and makes me long to hear the singing of birds & see the beautiful antelopes feeding on [the] banks of the Zambesi, & the stately giraffe, ponderous elephant, and sleek eiland (O how beautiful) on its plains. Here there is an air of stillness, and a great stillness of the air besides. It is still, hot, oppressive scenery, except when we come to rivers.

A fowl and basket of meal were given for a yard & half of cloth. We have now plenty of meal, and I have discovered that the manioc and lotsa meal, which when eaten alone produce most distressing heartburn, agree well with the stomach when eaten in conjunction with jingoba nuts. I did not know this when going north, and the meal diet punished me sorely. Both kinds are nearly pure starch, and a continuation of this diet affects the eyes of the people, as in experiments of animals fed on pure gluten or amylla.

A sudden cessation of the rains happened about the 28th April. Since then the cold is severe in the mornings, viz. 58°, 59°, 60°. Water 58°. Sometimes, protected from the air, thermometer stands as high as 64° [or] 62° at 6 o'clock in the mornings. It feels cold, for when the sun is well up the thermometer is always above 80°, evenings 78°.

9th. Proceed to Ngomba[2] in 3½ hours. Saw fresh tracks of eilands in the way. A girl turned aside, sick, in the path, and though we waited next day till search was made she was lost; perhaps slept some time, then waking in the dark went farther and farther astray.[3]

The uneasiness of the trader is perpetually shewing itself, and upon the whole he has reason to be on the alert day and night. His carriers are of the Songo tribe, and of course partake of all the vices of heathenism, thieving perpetually the goods entrusted to their care and

[1] Identified in *Travels*, 454, as *Dicrurus Ludwigii*, i.e. square-tailed drongo (Roberts, *S. African Birds*, 275).

[2] Possibly the Gambo, joining the Luachimo from the south in lat. 9.20 S, long. 20.49 E (GSGS 2465, SC 34).

[3] 'A poor little slave-girl', she was presumably one of the women a *pombeiro* with DL was taking to sell in Mwata Yamvo's country for ivory (*Travels*, 447, 455).

thereby causing a great diminution of the trader's gain. He cannot openly accuse them, for they might plunder and leave him in the lurch in revenge. He may manage them after getting his goods safe in a house in Cabango.

11th. We were kindly met in the way by the traders of Cabango, of whom Mr Faria[1] is the chief, and reached Kanesi, another stream flowing north-east. This and another,[2] the Fombeji, come accross the path before we reach Cabango. These would be invaluable in a country where irrigation was employed. They were each at least ten yards wide and two deep, & running fast with fine clear water.

Cabango is situated on the banks of the river Chihombo, and is the dwelling place of Muanzanza,[3] one of Matiamvo's subordinate chiefs. His village consists of about 200 huts, and he is an agreable and amiable negro. Ten or twelve square huts built of grass and poles constitute the traders' portion of the buildings, and the persons employed are half-blood Portuguese from Ambaca. They are agents for Cassange traders, and keen hands enough they are. They treated me as kindly as their means allowed, Pascoal & Faria, by kind instructions from Mr Neves their employer, being the most conspicuous in their attentions.

A person having died in the village, we could transact no business with the chief untill the funeral obsequies were finished. These occupy about four days, and during these there is a constant succession of dancing, wailing, and feasting. Drums are beat during the whole night, and the whole of the relatives, dressed in fantastic caps &c, keep up the ceremonies with spirit according to the amount of brandy, beer, and beef, expended. When these are large the remark is made afterwards, 'What a fine batuque[4] that was'. A figure consisting chiefly of

[1] In September 1853 Feliciano da Costa Faria, lieutenant of militia at Golungo Alto, had been granted leave of absence to go trading in the interior (*Boletim official*, no. 414).

[2] MS has 'two others', but cf. *Travels*, 455: 'We crossed two small streams, the Kanesi and Fombeji, before reaching Cabango'. 'Kanesi' may be the Tchinege, joining the Chiumbe from the SSW in lat. 9.28 S, long. 21.05 E (GSGS 2465, SC 34). 'Fombeji' is not named on that map; it can hardly be the Fumbige (see above, p. 221).

[3] According to Carvalho (*Ethnographia da Lunda*, 70, 101, 560), the holder of this official name ranked as an 'uncle' (mother's brother) of Mwata Yamvo. He is called Manzaza by Graça, who lists him among the chiefs paying tribute to Mwata Yamvo ('Expedição', 468).

[4] 'A song-and-dance with stomping and hand-clapping' (Taylor, *Portuguese-English Dictionary*, 98).

feathers and beads is paraded on these occasions. It seems to be regarded as a divinity.[1] Much time is spent in these funerals and in weddings, which, too, are conducted with great ceremony.

The negro character did not appear to me in a favourable light, perhaps because I viewed it chiefly as accustomed to the pusillanimous treatment of slave dealers who, afraid of their own people, submit to any exaction the chiefs demand. When I required a guide to conduct us to Katema, Muanzanza agreed to give one for a certain amount of cloth, much less than usual because my friends represented my not being a trader as a reason for leniency. The amount (16 yards of blue print) being given, it was objected to and another sort demanded. This being settled, a counsellor proposed the traders' amount as a proper levy. This was put an end to by Mr Faria snatching up the cloth and threatening to put us in the path himself. Muanzanza sent for it afterwards, but we had to give prepayment to the guide and his father or owner of other two pieces of cloth & some beads. Mr Faria kindly went with us to this man's village and settled all.

The guide went one day, and when I gave another man a few beads for a present of manioc he pretended to be offended, because he had not got the same, and would go no farther. There is no honour among them in regard to keeping engagements with Europeans. He seemed not the least ashamed at breaking his engagement, and no disgrace will be attached to the deed by Muanzanza. We did then what I wished to do before paying, go on in the direction of Katema & enquire the path of the villagers. A path, though no better than a sheep's walk, is much easier than going straight in one direction, though this certainly is shorter. The beaten path leads through otherwise impassable forests to fords of rivers, and avoids untreadable bogs. On this account we always try to get a guide.

Cabango lat. 9° 31' south, long. 20° 31' or 32' east.[2]

As a cargo of goods had come by Mr Pascoal the chief seemed to expect a present, and Mr Faria gravely presented a common chamber utensil, the which Muanzanza recieved with abundant expressions of

[1] '... seems to be regarded as an idol' (*Travels*, 456). In a brief account of the Lunda 'mourning dance', Turner says that the masked figure, which he describes and illustrates, 'is thought to portray the shade of the dead man' (*Lunda Rites and Ceremonies*, 1953, pp. 33–5, 36).

[2] The longitude (repeated in *Travels*, 456) is almost certainly wrong; in the latitude given, the Chiumbe flows northward in approx. 21.05 E. Cabango, also named in 1890 by Carvalho (op. cit., 101, 560), appears on the Portuguese map of Angola, 1912, in lat. 9.33 S, long. 21.04 E.

gratitude as 'Zambi, Zambi' (god, god).[1] They are highly valued as being deep and containing more food or beer.

Several of the children of the late Matiamvo live here. They come to beg, but never offer any food as the people in the south do, but having told one, a young man named Liula (Heavens),[2] of this niggardliness, he brought some bananas with nuts and manioc. I think if traders would humour them less they would appear more amiable, but the former are so completely at the mercy of their own people they are glad to submit to anything for peace with the inhabitants. The latter, knowing their position, are not slow to take advantage of it.

The people of Matiamvo have no staple trade except ivory and slaves. They spend their time in everlasting talk, funeral ceremonies, and marriages. They seem generally in good spirits, laughing merrily the whole day long. This occupation of the mind and flow of animal spirits must be the reason why they are such an indestructible race. The perpetual influence on their minds, too, of the unseen gods must tend in the same direction by producing the mental quietude of [a] species of fatalism. The strong religious feeling of the negro is manifested in Congo and other parts where the church ceremonies are kept up, an unmeaning gibberish being substituted for the chaunting of the priests.

Prospects of the negro

It is probable that there will be a fusion or mixture of the black and white races in this continent, the dark being always of the inferior or lower class of society. It is proceeding in Angola. There seems an utter hopelessness in many cases of the Interior, except by a long-continued discipline and contact with superior races by commerce. Such as Sekeletu's people are inured to bloodshed and murder, and care for no god except being bewitched, desire of fame by killing people of other tribes, praise for valour when that is exercised only on the flying and defenceless. No motive can be brought before them equal to these, and then except by the grace of God they go on in their sins untill they perish. Their smoking the Cannabis sativa perpetually is much against any clear thought on any subject beyond the earth.

The great thing in working for such people is to remember that we are forwarding that great movement which God is carrying on for the

[1] The Lunda word Nzambi, 'God', is also used 'to give thanks to this supernatural power and invoke its favour' (Carvalho, *Lingua da Lunda*, 339).

[2] This name does not appear in the (admittedly incomplete) list of Mwata-Yamvo Naweji's sons given by Carvalho, *Ethnographia*, 579.

renovation of the world. We are parts of [the] machinery he employs, but not exclusive parts, for all who are engaged in ameliorating the condition of our race are fellow-workers, co-operators with God— sanitary reformers & clergy of all sorts, the soldiers at Sebastapol and sailors on the coast of Africa, inventors of telegraphs and steam engines, promoters of emigration and of prison reform. We shall not see the fruition of our hopes in any department, but we can work with the assurance that the 'good time is coming yet'.

It is a pity that the Bible was not translated in the Negro language instead of the Sichuana, for it is questionable whether the latter are one of the imperishable races. They easily succumb before the white man, and perhaps in future years the Sichuana Bible will take its place beside Elliot's Choctaw Bible in the library of one of the American colleges, a monument of industry and zeal in a language which no mortal understands and which no human organs can now articulate.[1] At present the course of events seems to militate against the Kuruman mission's being permanent, and all the labour expended on the station may end in its being a comfortable Boer's establishment. The Hottentots have not been much diminished.

Report of Matiamvo's country

After leaving Cabango on the 21st we crossed several little streams, and in one of them saw tree ferns, which I believe are supposed to inhabit the New Continent only. One, close to the ford of the little stream, was about four feet in height and about 10 [inches] in diameter. (Also grass trees forty feet high, of two varieties.) I took two leaves which were in a state of fructescence and put them in my hat. The heat has spoiled them.

In six hours we crossed the Chihombo, waist deep & rapid. It abounds in hippopotami, and buffaloes exist on its banks. Sleeping at a village on the Mumpua, we were left by our guide next morning, but proceeding in a south & by east direction we got on very well to the village on the Modieje.[2]

[1] John Eliot's translation, published 1663, was into the language of the (now extinct) Massachusetts Indians, and not into 'Choctaw' (cf. Fam. Letters, ii. 263 n.). DL was unduly pessimistic about the future of the Tswana peoples; they now number more than 850,000 (Schapera, The Tswana, 1953, p. 11). Moffat's translation of the New Testament into their language appeared in 1840; he completed that of the Old Testament in 1857 (cf. above, p.24).

[2] Murieje, lat. 9.58 S, long. 21.13 E. The 'Mumpua' is not named on GSGS 2465, SC 34.

23d. One of the men became sick.

24th. Remain on account of the sick companion. No inhabitant near, but two villages about 3 miles off.

Having a little leizure I may put down some of the information I recieved at Cabango respecting other tribes. Matiamvo is situated E.N.E. of Cabango and is distant 19 days march with negroes carrying cargoes. As they go on an average about $3\frac{1}{2}$ hours per day, this would give $66\frac{1}{4}$ hours, and at 2 miles an hour 132 miles.[1] He cannot be more distant. Cabango then being in long. $20°\ 32'$, $+132$ ($=2°\ 12'$)$=$ $22°\ 44'$ E. (rather, $22°\ 32'$),[2] and about $9°\ 20'$ lat. south. He is said to be mild in his government, which otherwise is despotic. From all accounts the population nearer his seat of government is more dense than in the parts of Lunda through which we have come, that being rather sparse. Food is very abundant, and the country in parts hilly.

In going to Matiamvo from Cabango, at the distance of six days the river Casai is crossed ($=42$ miles), then 2 days ($=14$ miles) beyond the Caunguesi, another considerable river flowing into the Casai;[3] then six days ($=42$ miles) beyond it the Lolua, which also flows into the Casai, swelling it into a river about $\frac{1}{2}$ a mile wide. These distances may be represented as, from Cabango to Casai 42 miles, from Casai to Caunguesi 14 miles, from Caunguesi to Lolua 42 miles, from Lolua to Matiamvo (5 days) 34 miles, $=132$ miles.

Another independant chief in this country, named Mai,[4] is visited by traders. His town is 32 days journey from Cabango ($=224$ miles, or in lat. $5°\ 45'$ south). The town is pointed out as N.N.W. from Cabango, and Luba, another independant sovereign, is 8 days[5] ($=56$ miles or lat. $4°\ 50'$) in the same direction. Mai is situated west of the Casai, and near his town the river contains a very large waterfall. Five days west of Mai the confluence of the Casai and Quango occurs ($=40$ or 50 miles). The Casai even beyond that is obstructed by many waterfalls or cataracts, and cannot be navigated. This I had hoped

[1] DL's multiplication is wrong; the figures should read '$66\frac{1}{2}$ hours' and '133 miles' respectively.

[2] Interlineation in MS; my parentheses.

[3] The Caunguesi (Kaongeshi) joins the Kasai in lat. 7.05 S, long. 21.40 E (GSGS 4646, SB 34). The distances given above in parentheses are interlineations.

[4] Traditionally the younger brother of Ilunga, progenitor of the Mwata Yamvo dynasty (see p. 228), Mai himself founded a chiefdom, known after him as Bena Mai or Mai Munene, in the region of the Kasai-Chicapa confluence (Carvalho *Ethnographia*, 98; Turner, 'Lunda Love Story', 25).

[5] '... eight days farther' (*Travels*, 458).

might not be the case, but my hopes were vain. The river, however, recieves a large branch from the N.E., called the Lubilash,[1] which contains large waves.

This information was procured from an old man who came from Mai and intended to return immediately. He was clothed in the cloth made of the inner bark of a tree. Guns and Portuguese traders are not admitted into the country by the chief. If a native Portuguese goes there[2] he must clothe, like the common people in Angola, with a loose robe. He trades in shells chiefly, beads, &c. His people kill elephants by means of spears, traps, & poisoned arrows.

In going to Mai 2 rivers alone are crossed, viz. the Loajima and Chihombo. The Casai is still east of the town, but near it. This part of Londa, the Songo and Chiboque lands, seem the highest, and all drain towards the north to be absorbed into the Casai and Zaire. The Zambesi is known to some of Matiamvo's people as on one side of his country and passing to the south. It is reported small there.

Here the more kindly spirit of the southern Londa people appears, for an old man brought a large present of food and volunteered to go as guide with us. They will be spoiled by slave traders.

The Chief Bango and his people

28th May 1855. We are now in the town of Bango or Mbango[3] on the banks of the Loemba, one of the feeders of the Casai. The population seems large, and the cultivation of manioc greater than any we have seen in Lunda.

Having left the Loash, where we were detained a day by sickness, we were conducted to another village, and as usual they made every effort to induce us to remain and trade in food. We went forward, and after a long ride through forest came to the Lofuje,[4] a fine stream about 15 yds broad. Crossing it we came next morning to villages, but the people refused to shew the path unless we should remain and buy food for a day. We left them, and the path we took led into an inextricable thicket. Returning to another we had seen we found it do the

---

[1] Known in its lower course as the Sankuru; main tributary of the Kasai, which it joins in lat. 4.16 S, long. 20.23 E (GSGS 4646, SB 34).

[2] 'Neither guns nor native traders are admitted into the country, the chief of Luba entertaining a dread of innovation. If a native trader goes thither ...' (*Travels*, 458).

[3] Not identified; presumably a minor Lunda chief.

[4] Lufige; joins the Luembe in lat. 9.59 S, long. 21.30 E (GSGS 2465, SC 34).

same, and were obliged to ask the villagers again. They still refused, &
we were forced to remain. Although I offered a large payment in
addition to a handsome present if one would accompany us, they
refused to do more than merely point in the direction and describe the
way we ought to take. We found by following their directions a faint
path, which led into a better one in dense tangled forest, in which it
was impossible to ride and through which our carriers could not have
come except by a very tedious process involving great labour.

Five hours of this brought us to the village of Nyakalonga, a
daughter of a former Matiamvo.[1] She recieved us very kindly, and only
requested us to wait an hour or two that meal might be brought for sale.
She presented meal, ground nuts, a fowl, & manioc roots fermented &
raw. She could not send people with us beyond Bango, but sent her son
that distance without payment. The stream at her village was quite
impassable there, the bog being soft & shaky, & when the crust was
broken through was about 6 feet deep. In the evening we reached
Bango.

28th.[2] The chief Bango came at midday with a present of meal and
pallah meat.[3] I gave an equivalent, & told him the objects of our journey, &c. He appeared pleased so far as that went, but objected to a
crack in the pannikin which formed part of the present. I exchanged it.
He then wished double the amount of cloth, but to this I objected, as
it was not trade. When told we would move off in the morning, he
gave us to understand that he had still large demands to make, but my
men are, I am happy to observe, determined to move in spite of Bango.

The lat. is 10° 23',[4] and counting the time we occupied in the way
between this and Cabango, about 60 miles distant, we make about 10
or 10½ geographical miles per day, & our rate is not more than 2 per
hour.

30th May 1855. Left Bango on better terms than his words led us
to expect. His village consists chiefly of huts of his wives. We were

---

[1] '. . . a sister of the late Matiamvo' (*Travels*, 461). I have found no other reference to her, but Nicalonga village, lat. 10.18 S, long. 21.13 E (Angola, 1917),
possibly bears her name.

[2] *Sic.* The context suggests that it should be '29th'.

[3] '. . . and the meat of an entire pallah' (*Travels*, 462), i.e. of an impala buck,
Aepyceros melampus.

[4] Given in *Travels*, 686, as 10.22.53 S (misprinted as 12.22.53, ibid. 462), with
long. 20.58 E. The Luembe, in that latitude, is in long. 21.32 E (GSGS 2465, SC
34). Bango village is nowadays located in lat. 10.28 S, long. 21.14 E (Angola,
1917).

detained by the sickness of a man, and when Bango visited us he only begged a little powder, and was abundantly satisfied with about ½ a pound, giving a guide & speaking in friendly terms. His people are scattered over the country, each in his own little village. This arrangement pleases the Africans vastly, and any one who expects to have a village gives himself airs in consequence, like the heir presumptive of an estate.

We travelled over 5 hours of the usual flat country, which is covered at this season with yellowish grass [and] dried bushes, some of which are green; others are shedding their leaves, the young buds pushing the old foliage off; and parts are burned in order that the young herbage which springs up by the moisture in the soil may attract the game. Buffaloes come to feed on it, and pallahs, waterbucks, & eilands. We see flesh of these animals among the people. The flats are relieved by occasional vallies, distant 5 or 6 miles from each other, in which there is a stream or bog, and clumps of trees, tall and green with large leaves and closely planted together. In some of these clumps I saw palm-like trees (grass trees) which I did not know, and in some of the hollows or vallies were seen palms with three rows of leaves longitudinally on the tree, giving it a sort of triangular form. Dates also begin to appear. Manioc grows to a great height, 8 ft., & the roots are often seen as thick as a man's arm. We passed also today Cape heaths 10 ft. high, and the wood stalks were 2½ inches in diameter.

30th. Saw the first kite today, whether going north or south I don't know, but they are now absent from the Kuruman and Bakwain countries. Swallows appeared on the rivulets west of Cabango, and at that place of the white-bellied sort. Here we have black-bellied specimens in abundance, and larger than the white. (Winter extends up as far as Cabango, probably by the south wind.)

Valley of the Loembwe

Having reached the Loembue, flowing N.N.E., we find it much larger than we expected, and must go along it in a S.S.W. direction for a ford. It abounds in hippopotami, and is at present pretty full of water, the morasses on its banks being impassable. There are fishing weirs formed accross it, and though we found it about 4 ft. deep and 60 yards wide, it is not so all the year round. The valley in which the river winds is about ¼ mile wide, and when seen from the high bank is extremely beautiful, and an estate of a few miles of such rich land and fine scenery would cost in England many a pound.

But the general flatness of the country, and the gloomy forests still as death, impart a tameness & superstitious frailty to the character of the people. There are hunters among them, some who have travelled far, but the general character seems wanting in energy. They are, however, terribly keen traders, and every art is tried to detain us for a single night at their villages in order that they may have the pleasure of trading in meal, manioc roots, & ground nuts. Some few specimens of copper are offered of this shape [*see facsimile*]. Two men volun-

teered to guide us this morning, and after marching a few miles wished to turn off the path, but having refused they went about 10 miles and then desired us to go directly westward to their place to buy provisions. They preferred allowing us to go on without them, although they knew they were sure of a handsome reward in the evening. The paths are very difficult to follow, the long grass being interlaced accross them so as even to confuse an ox and cutting the feet of the men unmercifully. Yet we met a woman and girl & a little child wending their way home with loads of manioc. The sight of a white man infuses a tremor into their dark bosoms, and they seem relieved when fairly past without my springing upon them.

In every part of the country bundles of sticks are placed at different spots as offerings to the gods for success or in fear, and this afternoon we passed a small frame house with the head of an ox in it as an object of worship. Feathers are hung up in their gardens. Little mounds with medicine smeared over them, and idols with pots of medicine in little sheds. The dreary uniformity of gloomy forest and gameless flats has a depressing influence on the minds of the people. They never or rather rarely travel, they have no mountains from which to gaze and wonder what lies beyond the distant line of blue. They want stimulus, hence they wear out their dreary lives in gloomy superstitious observances.

At Bango we had a specimen of the feelings of the negro. An old woman continued to belabour a good-looking young man for hours with her tongue. Irritated at last he uttered some words of impatience, when another man sprang at him, 'How dare you curse my mother?' They caught each other, and a sort of wrestling, pushing & dragging match ensued, which ended by one falling under the other. Both by this time being stark naked picked up their duds and made off, each to his own quarters, with threats to bring his gun. Only one, however, appeared, and the old woman continued her scold by our camp untill my men were fairly tired of her tongue.

1st June. Came to a valley in a forest having many idols, clay lions, &c. They requested us civilly to remain that they might sell meal, and we rested at midday for the purpose. On parting, two young men were sent as guides, who continued with us next day though often told by the villagers we passed that we would not pay them.

2d. Having slept at a village, the headman came in the morning after I was mounted, with 3 large calabashes of beer as a present. I thanked him but declined his gift, as I must have stopped an hour & paid him double. He then took away our guides and sent a young man to lead us instead, calling after him, loud enough for us to hear, 'Lead them to the impassable part of the morass that their oxen may be stuck fast'. We went on without minding our charitably disposed headman, and our guides soon appeared.

These morasses or bogs are exceedingly trying to both cattle and men. The surface is covered with a kind of wiry grass, which is rooted in clods floating on soft slush. If one can manage to tread on these they bear him up, but one often steps on the side instead of the crown, & the foot slips off and down a foot or two, sometimes three, into the slush. I never get over one of these bogs without many such mishaps, and the people the same. In the centre there is usually a fine stream of water flowing, and in its vicinity there seems to be a very thin covering of grass spread over the surface, which quivers under the feet and except at certain spots allows one to drop up to the middle or higher. The oxen, having four feet, find it much more difficult to select clods than we for our two, so they are always with one or two feet deep in the mud, and when they drag out the hind down go the fore, or frequently all four together, leaving him lying on his belly; and so fatigued do they become by about $\frac{1}{4}$ of a mile of this, they often lie down disheartened and can be raised only by the people biting their tails. We crossed four such bogs on the 2d, one of which was called Bombue.

At a large village we were peremptorily ordered to stop by the headman, an old man devoid of teeth, but when he saw we held on our course with a smile he bestowed as hearty a curse as any in his vocabulary, and left.

Kawawa

We reached Kawawa's village in the evening of the 2d, and found a village of 40 or 50 huts, with the batuque being beaten over a man who had died the day preceding. Some women were making a furious wail at the door of the hut in which the body of the deceased lay, as if addressing it. Drums were beating, and these they continued to belabour during that and the following night untill sunrise. It resembled the monotonous thumping of a steam engine on board ship. A person dressed in a great number of feathers left the people engaged in the dance or wail in the morning, and returned from the deep forest in the evening. He is intended to represent one of the departed, or a god. The drums are beaten with the hands, & the loud wailing must try their lungs. The service of the devil is rather hard.

On Sunday morning we were honoured with a visit from Kawawa, who is a person of some power in these parts.[1] He presented 2 baskets of meal and a goat, and professed to be much pleased with my arrival and the prospect of the white man's path being through his town. I gave in return for his present two large cloths 6 ft. square, $\frac{1}{4}$ lb of powder, a good quantity of beads, and an iron spoon. This is a very handsome present in these parts, and he was evidently pleased with it. He visited us again and enquired with some curiosity for a sight of European articles—an iron pot, a revolver, watch, burning glass, &c. I promised a sight of the magic lantern pictures in the evening, and went to visit him. He has a fine large court house, well built and large, though of the beehive shape. He brought a jug,[2] of the shape of an old man holding a can of beer in his hand, as the greatest curiosity he had to shew. A case was then brought before him, probably promoted by himself. A man & his wife were accused of having bewitched the man whose wake was being held when we reached the village, and before he heard the case defended he said, 'You have killed one of my children; bring all yours before me, that I may choose which of them shall be mine

---

[1] Graça ('Expedição', 467) mentions 'Cauau' as one of the chiefs paying tribute to Mwata Yamvo; Verhulpen (Baluba, 147) says that the first 'Kawewe' was a Lunda nobleman who broke away from Chinyama's Luvale. There is a village named Cavava, presumably after him, in lat. 10.59 S, long. 21.31 E (Angola, 1912).

[2] '. . . of English ware' (Travels, 468).

instead'. The wife eloquently defended herself outside, but it would avail little, for this is one of the means resorted to [to] furnish victims for the slave market.

In viewing the pictures all were delighted except Kawawa, who exhibited symptoms of dread and several times rose up as if to rush away, but was prevented by the dense crowd around. Some of them understood the explanations well and expatiated eloquently on them to the more obtuse.

We informed him that we should leave next morning, and he promised a lad to guide us. When I sent to let him know that we were ready to start, he replied that 'if an ox came in his way ought he not to eat it?' I had given one to the Chiboque, and must give him the same, together with a gun, gunpowder, and a black robe such as he had seen one of my men spread out to dry the day before; that if I refused an ox I might give one of the men, and a glass or other instrument by which he might see whether Matiamvo's heart were favourable to him or whether he wished to cut off his (K.'s) head.[1]

When we were nearly ready, Kawawa came in the coolest manner possible and told me he had seen our goods the day before & must have all he asked. I replied the goods were my property & not his, and we would go in spite of him. He ordered his people to arm when we were starting. Many of my people were panic stricken & did not stir when I mounted. As the way lay through dense forest I did not see this, and one ran after me say[ing] the people had begun to plunder. Turning back I jumped off the ox and made a rush at them with a revolver in hand. They dispersed quickly from the luggage, and my own [men], knowing that they had disobeyed orders, caught up their burdens with great alacrity when they saw their leader get a punch on the head with a pistol.[2] A few followed us, looking out of the forest after us, but no shot was fired.

It is extremely unpleasant to part with these potentates so, after spending a day or two in the most amicable intercourse. But they have not the smallest idea of European power or of the rights of strangers. Kawawa came to plunder us with the same sort of feeling as Dr

[1] '. . . I must give one of my men, and a book by which he might see the state of Matiamvo's heart towards him, and which would forewarn him, should Matiamvo ever resolve to cut off his head' (*Travels*, 468).

[2] 'I shouted to my men to take up their luggage and march; some did so with alacrity, feeling that they had disobeyed orders by remaining, but one of them refused, and was preparing to fire at Kawawa, until I gave him a punch on the head with the pistol, and made him go too' (*Travels*, 469).

Richardson's dog did against a bear, utterly fearless because entirely ignorant of the power of the larger animal.[1]

Our man was determined to have his orders obeyed, and sent four men to precede us at the ford of the Casai, about 10 miles distant, and that we should not have the use of the canoes untill we had delivered up all the goods demanded as *tribute*. We were duly informed of the decision of this negro, who spoke as if he felt the white man was quite helpless at a river a good 100 yards broad and deep. The canoes were hidden among the reeds, and by the unasked loan of one, after dark, in the space of two hours oxen, donkies, and men, were all snug by our bivouac fires on the south-eastern bank of the Casai, the latter laughing uproariously at the disgust of our enemies when they would come and find nothing of the white man but some beads to defray all damages.[2] The canoe having been left on their own side of the river would puzzle them as to who had been the paddler. This was the last we had of Kawawa.

Where slave traders have frequently been, the negroes do not seem to have the smallest idea of presents being reciprocal, and in the most absurd manner say, 'We shall come tomorrow to recieve the articles you have brought us'; and when presents are [given] object to some as too little or not of the proper colour or too little &c. And when they go away it is [with] grumbling that they will come again for more, never however thinking they ought to give anything in return. Here it is different. A present of food is given, and this is the ancient law towards strangers. It is not difficult to make them return to it. When I have recieved the insolent message, 'I shall come to recieve, &c', I replied, 'You need not unless you bring, &c', and always succeeded.

---

[1] This may refer to the Arctic explorer Sir John Richardson (1787–1865), but I have not located the source of the allusion.

[2] 'I left some beads, as payment for some meal, which had been presented by the ferrymen' (*Travels*, 470).

XII

RETURN TO BAROTSELAND

The Lotembwa

Crossing a large plain containing much of the larger game we came to the Lotembua, or rather its source,[1] a flat a mile broad covered with coarse grass and water about 3 feet deep. I suppose it dries up, & the main source is Dilolo. We shall cross it again.

Here we had another specimen of impudence. Sebatochue, by whom we had been betrayed at Ionga Pansa's,[2] came in the evening & boldly seated himself at our fire. He soon found out his mistake & fled, as he thought, in danger of his life. We invited him back to hear our complaint sent to his chief, in company with a present and excuse for passing without visiting him, but he would not trust himself near us again. His chief, Kangenke, treated us well in going north, and expelled this man for betraying him. He was now in company with Bangalas, who are the slave traders in those parts. Our present to Kangenke was in gratitude for his goodness.

10th June '55. We forded the Lotembua plain on the 8th, when, having been thoroughly wetted in the lower extremities and chilled for many days past, I was seized by vomiting of blood and heat of body, which induced me to drink about seven pints of water in the course of the night. The water is 47° in the mornings, and the air 50° and being loaded with moisture is very cold to the feelings. If we march before the dew is off the grass all are wetted, for the grass is long. The sun is very hot by day, between 80° & 90° in the coolest shade, 76°–78° in the evenings, & sometimes as low as 40°–42° in the mornings.

The plains which are annually filled with rain water are not destitute of insects, especially ants, which seem capable of establishing themselves everywhere in Africa. Here they manage, during the period when all their horizon is submerged a foot deep, by ascending to little houses of refuge built on grass stalks higher than the line of inundation. These must be the result of experience, for if they had waited till the water actually invaded their terrestrial habitations they would want materials for the upper [quarters],[3] unless they dived for

[1] In approx. 11.16 S lat., 21.45 E long. (GSGS 2465, SC 34).
[2] See above, pp. 113–14.
[3] Word supplied from *Travels*, 328.

every mouthful of clay. Some are about the size of a bean, others as large as a man's thumb, and all are formed [of] tough black soil.

Caterpillars mount the stalks of grass in large numbers, and are food for flocks of birds on these occasions.

Saw a beautiful frugiferous pigeon at Cabango. The bill is shaped exactly like that of the dodo, & the hind toe remarkably thick and large compared with the others. It was of a green colour, & small; would eat nothing but figs or other wild fruits.

Many swallows were observed near water, and on the plains the water of which had not yet dried there were swifts, large white-bellied with forked tails, little black ones, and two brown martins. We raised a caprimulgus.[1] They are not migratory here at least. Though this is winter and cold at nights, insects may be seen, butterflies in numbers, dragon-flies, &c. The swallows do not seem in pairs. Bee eaters are seen everywhere; one, a firey red shouldered & light blue above the tail with dark head, is very pretty. Larks of jet black, and yellow shoulders, enliven the mornings with their songs, but do not continue long on the wing. Some vultures shew that there is carrion to be found. Several ardea and other water birds and occasionally wild ducks appear, but they only remind one of approaching the Zambesi, where every fowl abounds.

Flocks of forked-tailed white-bellied swallows appear, but don't seem in pairs. The Great Senegal swallow was observed near the Leeba in pairs. The Buceros is in flocks, and so are shrikes, though other birds seem to be breeding.

(31st July.[2] I have been observing a number of swallows all the way down the Leeambye. There are great numbers of a white-bellied swallow, not forked-tailed. On the wing it seems to have a white band accross the forehead & a black one round the front of the neck. The black swift with white rump has nests on the banks, & other swallows both on banks and under horizontal branches of trees. And this is midwinter.)

Whether the non-intercourse with European traders nearer the coast has been caused by the petty jealousies of the tribes themselves, or by kidnapping practiced by intervening nations, who invariably in Africa try to keep all advantages to themselves, either by preventing traders passing their territory or refusing their fellow-countrymen

---

[1] 'caprimulgus or goatsucker' (*Travels*, 471); nightjar. Buceros, mentioned below, is the hornbill.

[2] As the date shows, a later insertion (at the foot of the page).

going seawards, the effects of this narrow policy is painfully visible in the appearance of the inhabitants who are situated far from markets. The women at Kawawa's and many other parts of Lunda are nearly quite naked. A patch of cloth or skin about three inches broad is esteemed apparel, and nothing could exceed the eagerness with which they offered to purchase strips of calico. They were delighted with about two feet for a fowl and basket of meal, and, when we could no longer purchase, with true maternal feelings they held their little naked babies before me, entreating me to sell only a rag for them. As we had but a small stock I had to refuse. Firewood they say is their only clothing by night, and the only heat the little ones derive is by clinging close to the parents. Powder is sold by a little measure which indicates a good shot, and a shot is deemed a fair price for a fowl. If trade could be extended to them, they would be stimulated to industry in raising wherewithal to buy clothing. At present they raise abundance of ground nuts, manioc, &c, and would soon convert the former into oil if they could only sell it.

A most eligible site for a commercial and missionary settlement would be the right bank of the Leeba near the confluence with the Leeambye, or, more easterly, the confluence of the Kabompo with the Leeambye as it comes from the north. It is a considerable river on the eastern side of Matiamvo, and as it flows south recieves the river of the Babiza, then parts with the large branch Loenge or Bashukulompo, which again joins it near Tete.[1] There would [be] water carriage over extensive territories, and ultimately the result would be glorious for Africa. I pray God that the good men and true of our benevolent England may be inclined to look to this desirable point. It surely is of as great importance as any in the Niger. There is fever, it is true, and I find it is fatal even among natives, but there are few other diseases—no consumption, scrofula, hydrocephalus, or glandular diseases, no mental affections. Drs Conolly & Winslow[2] would have neither hospitals not patients here.

The fever generally puts on an intermittent, or the safest, form. I

[1] The description is inaccurate: the Bisa (see below, p. 361) live in N.E. Rhodesia, and their 'river' is presumably the Luangwa, which joins the Zambesi at Zumbo, long. 30.27 E; the 'Loenge or Bashukulompo', i.e. Kafue (known over much of its course as Lwenge) joins the Zambesi farther west, in long. 28.56 E; Tete is in long. 33.36 E.

[2] John Conolly (1794–1866) and Forbes Benignus Winslow (1810–74) were both pioneers in the humane treatment of lunatics, and had published works on insanity (DNB.).

have had [it] 27 times,[1] and I attribute the frequency in my attacks to the hardships it was necessary to undergo in exploration. Few could remain month after month sleeping on the ground and fed only on the manioc roots or meal nearly pure starch, which affects the eyesight if no animal food can be obtained, or a meal made from fine bird-seed,[2] which is better than the other but cannot be compared to wheaten or oaten meal. In some parts of the country we could get nothing but the manioc and ground nuts. Few could bear this and frequent wettings without suffering in health. My experience is therefore no criterion by which to judge of what others, better provided, might suffer or bear. I think some wheat necessary to support the stamina [of] every Englishman. The native Portuguese are all puny and weak who live on country food. The finest children I saw in the country were those who had a proportion of maize or wheat in their diet.

Lake Dilolo

10th. Am now, thank God, much better, and will sleep tomorrow at Dilolo.

11th. Went half way, and a man falling sick we reached the lake on the 12th. The water we have been using of the Lotembua and lake is bad in taste and smell, and seems to contain much iron; colours beans &c black, and seems the cause of bloody urine &c. The latitude is 11° 32' south; and the piece of water seems to be 8 or 10 miles long & 5 or 6 broad,[3] of the shape of an obtuse-angled triangle, the Lotembua going out at the obtuse point and entering at the N. acute angle. The sight of the blue waters with waves lashing the shore has a soothing influence on the mind after so much of flat & forest. (The heart yearned after the vivid impressions created by the aspect of the broad expanse of grand old ocean. It has life, but in these flat uniformities one feels as if buried alive.)

Moene Dilolo (Lord of the Lake) is a fat jolly fellow, and lamented that when they had no strangers they had beer, and none when we came. He gave a handsome present of meal & putrid buffalo's flesh. It cannot be too far gone for them, for it is used only in small quantity at

---

[1] The twenty-seventh attack was that mentioned above on p. 254; cf. *Travels*, 472.

[2] Presumably millet, 'that article which is sold in England as the lesser bird seed' (12.x.55 Tidman: *Miss. Corr.*, 292, where DL enlarges upon the theme of this paragraph).

[3] '. . . six or eight miles long, and one or two broad' (*Travels*, 479).

a time as a sauce to their tasteless manioc. They are at present hunting the antelopes in order to send them as tribute to Matiamvo. Young water fowls are killed in abundance on the reeds & are extremely fat. Great numbers of fish are caught in it.

There are several remarkable traditions in this country respecting the origin of the human race. Bechuanas generally refer to a gregarious egression of a number from a cave called Loey (Noe), in company with animals of all sorts, whose footsteps were there imprinted in the soft rock. They were formed in that cave by one called Matsieñ, and thence departing they met women who built huts and taught them the value of artificial shelter.[1] They always point to the north-east as the place of their origin. They possess also the story of Solomon and the harlots nearly entire, and another which declares the future return of men though [they] have died.

The great Humbolt quotes the views of his illustrious brother in regard to such traditions, and more especially with regard to whether men were gregarious or single, and argues that the general prevalance of the tradition proves that it has arisen not by transmission but [by] an identity in the mode of intellectual conception, which has everywhere led man to adopt the same conclusion respecting identical phenomena.[2] It may be objected to this identity in human thought and imagination, when viewing the same phenomenon, that we do not find the natural man in any part of the world, when viewing the phenomenon of rain, concluding that it is caused and can be made by means of certain medicines, except in South Africa. Nor do we find lightning and its effects ascribed to a bird called tlari,[3] or that a comet announces the death of some chief or other & nothing else. If ballads & fables are known to have existed in a population for a thousand years, why not for 5 thousand?

[1] Lôwê, about 12 miles north of Mochudi (lat. 24.28 S, long. 26.05 E, in Bechuanaland), is said by many Tswana to be the place from which the first human beings and animals emerged on earth, out of a hole in the ground (the 'cave'). Matsieng is a deity featuring in the associated myth of origin. DL visited, and described, the site in 1848 (see *Fam. Letters*, i. 253-4).

[2] DL is apparently referring, but not very accurately, to the quotation by Alexander von Humboldt (1769-1859), naturalist and traveller, from the philologist Wilhelm von Humboldt (1767-1835), on 'the idea of our common humanity' (*Cosmos: Sketch of a Physical Description of the Universe*, 1849, i. 368-9). He had been given a copy of the book at Luanda by a naval officer (26.xii.54 Gabriel).

[3] Tswana *tladi*, 'lightning'; also the name of a bird (fish-eagle?) associated with that phenomenon and used in rainmaking ceremonies.

13th June '55. Lake Dilolo. Our rate of travelling I find to be at the rate of five hours per day for five successive days; on the sixth both men & oxen shew symptoms of knocking up. The distance travelled in an hour is three miles in a straight line, and four in the curves & windings of the path. This is the maximum speed, though all are anxious to get home. They carry about 70 lbs weight each, slung upon a pole and placed on the shoulder like coolies in India. They have abundance of the country food, but it does not give them much power of endurance. We lose one third of our time by resting or detentions by either friends or enemies. Including Sundays we rest 10 or 12 days per month. The slave merchant lost more than a half of his time, and the rate of travel was on the average 4 miles each travelling day, the value of each day being $10\frac{1}{2}$ or 11 miles in a straight line. Much time is also lost by them by sickness, for when one carrier is sick his companions refuse to part the load among them.

Katema

14th June '55. We came to Katema's town or collection of straggling villages this morning, and thank God again to see old faces. He is out hunting skins for his paramount lord Matiamvo, but his domestics sent five large baskets of manioc meal, a fowl, fifteen eggs, and some beer. We turn our attention anxiously to the south for news, but hear only that persons had been sent to enquire after us as far as Shinte's, and expressions of friendship made use of which have caused Katema to go to Shinte's in order to cement the proferred alliance. This will be some good done. Slave trading is going on between Lobale and Bié, and many flee from Kangenke in consequence of losing their children, Shinte refusing to give them up.

15th. Katema came home today, having heard of our arrival. He desires me to rest myself today, as, being a great man, I must be tired. This is in order that he himself may have a rest & prepare for our reception in style. His wife sent three baskets more of meal, some fish, and a fowl, with earth nuts and compliments. The Balonda of these parts are very kind. May God look on them in mercy.

A flock of real jackdaws floats about and alights near us. They seem busy with the grubs in the valley, which are eaten by the people as well.

17th. We were called to visit Katema yesterday morning, and when we went the great man had not fully ornamented himself. We went into the court, it being windy & cold outside, but were desired to retire. I did so, home, and he sent an apology for not having been ready to recieve us. After the usual talk about our objects, and many assurances of his goodwill and anxiety to afford assistance, he presented 6 baskets of meal, a basket of putrid buffalo meat, 3 fowls, & sweet potatoes, and promised to visit us in our encampment in the evening. I presented a red cloak ornamented with lace which cost 30/- at Loanda, a large piece of broad striped calico for a mantle, beads large & small, ¼ lb of gunpowder, and an iron spoon. He begged a drinking vessel in addition, and I gave a tin pannikin. He seemed greatly pleased with the liberality shewn; assured me the way was mine, and no one would molest me in it if he could help it, &c &c; asked if I could not part with a dress like my own; and one of the councillors beginning to talk in the usual country way for more goods, he checked him by saying, 'Whatever strangers gave, be it little or much, he would always recieve it with thankfulness and never trouble them for more.' He mounted on the shoulders of an attendant and marched home in what is considered the most dignified manner.

Today he presented an ox that I might eat the meal pleasantly, for the buffalo's flesh was putrid. This is a great present for a Molunda to give in this country. He goes back to his hunting, but assured me the town and everything in it was mine, and his factotum[1] would remain and attend to every want, then guide us to the ford of the Leeba and there leave us. We are very well pleased with Katema.

24th. We found Katema's cattle nearly as wild as buffaloes, and our present had to be shot like one, for as soon as they suspected us they fled many miles into the forest and were with great difficulty brought back, the herd even keeping at a great distance.[2]

We left on the 19th and going about 4 miles eastwards crossed the southern arm of Lake Dilolo, about a mile & a quarter broad and waist deep, very difficult from the masses of arum and rushes through which we waded. Going east of that about 3 miles farther we came to the Lotembua, running in a valley 2 miles broad, which in the rainy season is flooded. It contains numerous islands covered with dense sylvan vegetation, and its breadth is about 80 or 90 yards. It recieves the superfluous water of Dilolo, and on the plains beyond, as we found in crossing, it is about a mile and a half wide, and the water seems stationary

---

[1] '. . . his factotum, Shakatwala' (*Travels*, 481; see above, p. 91).

[2] 'On attempting to slaughter the cow Katema had given, we found the herd as wild as buffaloes; and one of my men having only wounded it, they fled many miles into the forest, and were with great difficulty brought back. Even the herdsman was afraid to go near them' (*Travels*, 481).

among water plants and coarse grass. Still farther north it flows towards the Casai and is a sort of drain for those plains. The Lotembua
thus presents the curious phenomenon of flowing in two directions.[1]
That portion of its waters which are discharged into the Casai northwards finds its way into the sea by the Congo in the west coast, while
that which flows south goes into the sea at Quilimane.

Having crossed it on the same day I observed an occultation of η
Leonis on its eastern bank. Next day we reached the Lovoa.[2] All the
waters are now drying up and great numbers of fish caught in the
diminished ponds and brakes. A nasty sort of slime of decayed vegetable
matter is left behind. The people when asked the news say, 'The
people are well, or are recovering (ba hola)', which seems to indicate
much insalubrity of climate.

On 21st we reached Soanamolopo's town, or village rather, and on
22d went down the Lokaloeje and forded it breast deep. In the evening
we slept at the village where our pontoon was left behind.[3] It was safe.
Although I rewarded the man who kept it well, he would not trust me
accross the plain in front as carrier, saying I would cheat him out of
his wages if I did not pay him at once. As I have been repeatedly done
by pre-payment I declined. They have not yet acquired any confidence
in a white man's word.

Sakatwala and another man came as guides accross the plain, and
brought us to a ford farther west than that at the Piri hills. All the
people have fled to the opposite bank except Kanyonke, a son-in-law
of Shinte, in consequence of having been attacked by a man called
Liato, by Shinte's orders. We rode $8\frac{1}{4}$ hours accross the plain. It was
drying. 3 or 4 miles only were covered with water, but the surface
was still wet over a great portion of it. Beautiful blue flowers of every
shade of that colour occurred in masses, and were succeeded for miles
by yellow ones of the same kind. A few eilands appeared, but there was
little to relieve the weary eye, except judging of distances by bushes &c.

In the evening we reached Kanyonke's village, in dense forest, and
now spend the 24th here. We cross the Leeba tomorrow, 25th June '55.

---

[1] DL did not observe this himself, but obtained the information from Shakatwala
and others (*Travels*, 473). The Lutembo in fact flows only into the Quifumage
(and thence into the Zambesi); the mistake may be due to its receiving a small
northerly feeder a few miles NW of Lake Dilolo (GSGS 2465, SC 34).

[2] Luvua-Tchiambo; joins the Luambo in lat. 11.57 S, long. 22.30 E (GSGS 2465,
SC 34). DL struck it in lat. 11.41 S (*Travels*, 685).

[3] See above, p. 71.

Cross the Leeba

30th. We crossed the Leeba on the 25th, and found it about 150 yards wide. They point to its source in the east-nor-east, and say it emerges from an earthen hill called Kaombo,[1] but is there small and narrow. They don't know the Zambesi up here. It must therefore be very far east, for they cross the Leeba alone in going to Cazembe. A hill to the eastward called Mbonda[2] yields copper, and the Saloisho hills give iron.

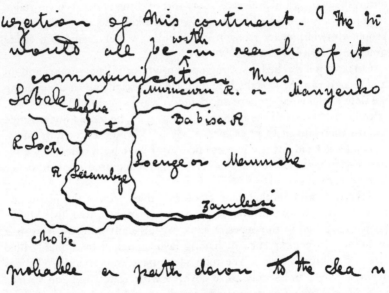

We crossed the Leeba about 20 miles west of the Peery hills, our former ford, and after a short stage slept on the banks of the Loambo,[3] which, however, was not flowing. The village happened to be that of Chebende's chief wife, and as he is a great man, nephew of Shinte, she treated us well. Next day we met Chebende himself, returning from the funeral of Samuñana,[4] his father. He was lean and haggard-looking, the probable effect of the orgies in which he had been engaged.

[1] The Zambesi rises near Kalene, lat. 11.10 S, long. 24.12 E. Arnot's map (*Garenganze*, facing p. 276) shows 'Border Craig (Kaomba Mt.)' in the vicinity.

[2] Not identified.

[3] Luambo; joins the Quifumage from the north in lat. 12.11 S, long. 22.28 E (GSGS 2465, SD 34). Cf. p. 78.

[4] Samoana (*Travels*, 482), for whom see above, p. 37.

Spoke to him about having a village of Makololo in the country by way of coming nearer to the white man's market,[1] but he cautiously did not express an opinion.

A commercial and missionary station anywhere in the vicinity of the bifurcation of the great rivers Leeambye, Leeba, Kabompo, Murucuru,[2] River of Babisa, & Loenge or Maninche, would in all probability rise to great importance as an emporium for the civilization and evangelization of this continent. The intertropical parts would all be within reach of it by easy water communication thus [*see facsimile*].

It is probable a path down to the sea may be in the Loenge. May God prosper the idea.

There is undoubtedly a very considerable amount of fever, and if I may judge of the mortality by what has taken place amongst our friends and acquaintance since we passed, the disease is very fatal even among the natives. They were performing the funeral ceremonies in the village of Muanzanza when we arrived there, and so at Kawawa's and another village. Zamozingua, a man whose neat court formed of banian, and flourishing young family, I admired on the banks of the 'Child of Kaloeye',[3] had lost his wife, and as is usual left the spot for another, unable to bear the recollection of the happy periods he had spent there, and probably afraid of remaining where death had once visited his establishment; and now we find a child of Shinte dead, and another of our acquaintance has gone too. I never met so many instances in the south during the course of one year.

The negroes are very prolific and keep up the population. They are an imperishable race. But it ought to be borne in mind that though fever prevails there are few other diseases. There is no consumption or scrofula, no hydrocephalus or mental diseases, though, considering they have no games, it is wonderful they don't go mad from ennui. The young make little huts as a play, plait the grass, or catch fish & grub up mice and moles. The prevalent complaints besides fever are inflammations of different parts and Maculo, and it is surprising they are not more afflicted, seeing that now is the winter in which the thermometer sinks in the mornings to 42° Fahr. and rises by day to

[1] In *Travels*, 482, DL says the project was 'concocted' and discussed with Chebende by Pitsane and Mohorisi.

[2] Shown on DL's map (see facsimile) as 'Murucuru R. or Manyenko'; not identified.

[3] See above, pp. 76, 78.

upwards of 84°. And with these vicissitudes of temperature there is also considerable dew, and they have no protection by night except the fire. The sensation of cold is very keen even to us, and on the plains of Lotembua and many other parts the cold has been severe enough to wither the manioc leaves and those on the more tender shoots of evergreens.

Welcome from Shinte

We passed through many large villages of Balobale, the inhabitants of which have fled from the chief Kangenke, who is favoured with the visits of Mambari from Bie, and as he sells his people to them a great part of the population escapes to Shinte and Katema. They come here also.

We reached this on the morning of the 28th, and hope to leave on the 1st July.

1st. We recieved a handsome present of meal, beer, earth nuts, manioc roots, a goat & fowl, from old Shinte, and he accepted our present thankfully. As he had never seen such a large piece of cloth, 2 yards square, he said, 'These Mambari cheat us with little pieces; I shall send people with you next time you pass, to trade for me in Loanda'. When we explained the use made of the slaves he sold, that he was destroying his tribe and building up that of the Mambari for a few small pieces of cloth, he seemed rather disgusted with the idea.

We had a long detail of his troubles, for having sent people down with a present to Sekeletu, on their return they were assaulted by the people of Masiko and the wife of one of them taken prisoner. He complained that though he wished to follow my advice and cultivate an alliance with the Makololo, his neighbour Masiko would not allow him, on account of an old feud his family had with that tribe. The brother of Masiko, Limboa,[1] had come to the same country, because while living at Nyenko, whither we had sent some of the rescued prisoners, he could procure no hoes nor honey, and when he sent to Masiko, his younger brother, for those articles his messengers were killed. He therefore removed to this side the Leeba, and the two brothers are now living on opposite sides of a valley 'at daggers drawn'. Shinte said he had agreed to my advice in passing and therefore had done no-

[1] Imbua, son of Mulambwa Santulu, and therefore Imasiku's paternal uncle, not brother (see above, p. 9). Like Imasiku, he had fled from the Kololo, establishing a chiefdom of his own in the country of the Nyengo (DL's 'Nyenko'), west of the Luanginga River (Jalla, *Litaba za Ma-Lozi*, 29).

thing to Masiko, though he had possession of one of the women of his tribe, untill I had returned and given my opinion on the case. I advised him to sit still, and I would go and speak to Masiko on the subject. In the meantime messengers came from Limboa to Shinte, requesting his assistance to attack Masiko. They report that Masiko killed one of his principal men and has since been nearly mad from remorse. It is difficult to get away quickly from these people. They want me to arbitrate between the brothers, and any business of this sort requires a world of time, for the negroes are the greatest talkers one can concieve of.

30th. I leave here the young orange trees, some fruta da conde, and one fig tree, and sow besides a number of fruit tree seeds, as the mango &c, in a bed enclosed in a court of one of Shinte's chiefs. I promised to give the old man some of them when I should remove them to another spot. As the courts are all planted with tobacco, sugar cane, &c, I think they will take good care of mine. My men have many seeds with them, and are much enamoured with the large breed of fowls of Londa. We have more than eighty in our encampment, and pigeons besides. If I had time to shew them how to cultivate trees, many fruits would be introduced into the Zambesi country. At present it is an experimental farm in a state of embryo.

Since the 28th of April, when the rains suddenly ceased, we have scarcely seen a cloud. But on the 20th June I observed some small masses gathering near the horizon, which presents a yellowish-red appearance in the evenings. We have now (1st July) an immense train of fleecy clouds every evening following the sun as if drawn by that luminary, for they are thinnest the nearer they are to him and thickest in the east. At night they cover the whole heavens, the stars appearing only among the chinks. The thermometer stands at from 42° to 52° in the mornings at sunrise, and from 84° to 96° at midday. In the evening it is about 70°, but falls rapidly. The instrument is in the shade of my tent, and that is usually in the shade of a tree. The sensation of cold after the heat of the day is very severe. The Balunda don't leave their fires till near midday. They don't clothe better, from absolute want of the materials.

The project in which I am at present engaged has at least novelty to recommend it. Instead of trying to carry civilization to the Interior, and thereby opening up Africa to the sympathies and succour of Christians (who will not fail to try and impart Christian knowledge as soon as it is practicable to do so), I am attempting to establish the system of the Africans proceeding on commercial speculations to the coast. There they learn in a short time to appreciate the power of Europeans, and the inference naturally flows: if those who have so much power and wisdom believe and value the truths of religion, how much more we. My men learned more in one day when introduced on board the Pluto and Philomel, commanded by Commanders Skene and Bedingfield, than I could have taught during years. They had the idea that they would be kidnapped, but when I said to them, 'There, these are all my countrymen and your friends', and the jolly tars who happened to be at dinner freely gave them beef and biscuit, a world of prejudice vanished at once. I felt a foot higher myself.

I found it impossible to convey to the Bakwains and other tribes with whom I spent many years any idea of our power or numbers. They would ask if Queen Victoria had many cattle, if we equalled them in numbers (about 4,000), and of riches in money they could form no idea. But my present companions very speedily set up a trade in wood-gathering for themselves at Loanda, and worked most vigourously at discharging a coal ship for 6d. per day. The goods they purchased are unfortunately nearly all expended by the sicknesses & delays of the way, but they are not a whit discouraged; and their accounts of the profits of a journey to the coast incite others, as old Shinte, to resolve to accompany them next time. This is much better than the visiting of the Mambari, for they circulate false statements about the sea, &c, which they never saw. From them my people imbibed the fear of being kidnapped. And they besides purchase slaves, who though not exported are used for building up little villages for their owners, who practice the most absurd and wicked superstitions.

The expenses of my expedition of 21 months are not large, and I have been well served. We had a common object in view, and they did not expect more than I gave. Wages of two shillings per month would amount to upwards of £50. Food and other expenses have caused me to expend more than that, but it has been a very cheap expedition after all.[1]

1st July. I have planted in the yard of one of Shinte's principal men

[1] 'My companions ... were given by Sekeletu for my assistance without any idea of remuneration. As wages are a most effectual means of breaking up the feudal system and that form of domestic slavery which prevails throughout Africa, I resolved to give them each a small payment in goods. For this purpose I drew on you for £50 by a bill in favour of Mr Gabriel. ... Finding subsequently the balance of that sum insufficient ... I afterwards drew £25 in the same way' (14.i.55 Tidman: Miss. Corr., 270-1).

two dozen orange trees, three or four cheremoya trees, and one fig tree, besides a number of fruit tree seeds, as mango, cheeremoya, coffee, araças,[1] papaw, &c &c. All are healthy, though having been carried on a pole over the shoulder through dense forests they have often been roughly handled. They will serve as a nursery for future planting.

3d July. Still at Shinte's, he being unwilling to allow us to depart without hearing formally the message of Limboa in presence of Chebende, his greatest councillor. The tsetse exists on the eastern side of the Saloisho hills, which here appear of considerable height and ten miles distant. Their direction is N.N.W. and S.S.E. They contain good iron, which is made much use of. The latitude of this town is 12° 37' 14" south, long. 22° 54' 40" east,[2] my former observation being erroneous in consequence of the extreme cloudiness of the weather preventing me from seeing when the star selected had actually culminated. But it is not of much importance, for in the event of the death of old Shinte the town would not only be shifted, but such an alteration of power take place as would leave no other town of equal importance in the country.

5th July 1855. We are now detained by the sickness of two men at Shinte's, but hope to get away tomorrow. They, however, take great care of themselves, the smallest pains inducing them to lay by till perfectly recovered. They are not ashamed to eat heartily in the meantime.

Masiko is said to have sold the wife of Shinte's man to a slave dealer. Would it be [right] if, in meeting this reciever of stolen goods, I should force him to deliver her up to me? There is no law of nations here. The weakest goes to the wall. Though I am favourably disposed towards peace principles, I believe it extremely questionable whether any Peace Society man[3] could travel among even the Balonda unarmed. No conduct could be more pacific than mine to the Chiboque, and yet it was only the presence of five guns, brought to kill game, that saved us from being plundered of everything. They sent a messenger to count them before commencing their outrageous attack. 'They have only five', said he as he ran off. I believe Kawawa, for instance, would

---

[1] Species of guava (Taylor, *Portuguese Dictionary*, 64).

[2] But see above, p. 59.

[3] The Peace Society, founded 1816, advocated 'the promotion of permanent and universal peace', and held that war 'is inconsistent with the spirit of Christianity and the true interests of mankind' (Norman Angell, quoted in *Fam. Letters*, ii. 143 n., q.v. for further details).

strip a harmless Peace man as naked as the women in his country, [which] would be equivalent to killing him. I say so though conscious of no mental bias against any of the Africans.

All my men can with ease discern the small star Alcor situated near Misar in the Bear's tail, which was called 'Sardak' (The Test) of old and employed as a test of good sight. I can readily distinguish it.

Kolimbota's wound

11th July 1855. Banks of the Leeba. We were informed that Kolimbota, who remained at Shinte's against orders, had as soon as we left mixed himself up with the quarrels of the Balonda. A refugee of Lobale, presuming on the friendship of one to whom he had formerly given some goats, took down the hive of his countryman and used the honey. This Londa friend, however, was not disposed to allow the liberty, and took a child from him and sold it to the Mambari. The Balobale, who swarm in the country, took the child out of the hands of the traders, and they complaining to Shinte of their loss of goods [he] ordered Sambanza to catch the primary offender. Kolimbota, glad of an opportunity of a little plunder, went unasked with Sambanza, entered the man's house, and took a cloak; then, running after the fugitives, came opposite to where the man was lying in wait for him, and recieved a bullet in his thigh, which put a stop to his marauding. Shinte supplied him during convalescence with four boys to buy oxen as provisions, & when he went to his own country gave him a wife. He took my canoe with him, which puts me to inconvenience, but Shinte sent orders to his sister Nyamoana to supply another. She is now a widow and lives at the Lofuje.[1] This is deserted. She said, 'We removed to where you found us, and had no idea that was the place where he was to die.'

After viewing the Coanza I find this river look at least a third broader than that at Massangano. The Leeba seemed formerly small, my eye having been accustomed to the broad Leeambye. It must have a width of at least 200 yards, if not more. Its rise during the rainy season after we passed [was] about 40 feet perpendicularly.

About 6 miles on this side the Lofuje we came to a patch of tsetse, and remaining at the border till dark rode 4 hours through dense forest, which, considering the danger to the eyes, head, and legs, is as disagreable a ride as can well be. On the morning of the 10th we observed flocks of the great Senegal swallow sunning themselves on the tops of

[1] Lufige (see p. 47).

trees and uttering the twitter employed in England when about to migrate. Here it is very cold during the nights and mornings. Everything except evergreens is withered, but there are insects, butterflies &c, and flies, by day. Are they going to a warmer region? The white-bellied swallow with forked tail is seen all about the Leeba. Saw a beautiful banana-eater this morning, it has crimson wings and the rest of the body black.

Africa has everywhere a peculiar air of repose. The mornings and evenings are lovely from their peaceful coolness, there being little or no wind during a great part of the year, and even then it is during midday. When the sun is high the peaceful sultry aspect of the landscape invites to sleep. It seems heavy on the eyelids. At night, too, we have not the same activity and sparkle as in the north. The stars scintillate but little except near the horizon. The wind changes almost always round from east to north, then round by west & south, very seldom in a contrary direction. At Kuruman a strong cold south wind occasionally blows for two days and a half. At Kolobeng and even as far as the Lake[1] it blows during the same time, but its direction is then south-east. The same bitter cold two & half days wind blows as far north as Cabango, but it is easterly then, probably influenced by the earth's rotation on its axis. Rains at Kolobeng & southwards often shew the same disposition to $2\frac{1}{2}$ days.

17th July 1855. Near confluence of the Leeba. Having recieved a canoe by orders of Nyamoana,[2] we descended this river to a small river called Lonkone, and were handsomely treated by the headman of a neighbouring village. Before reaching the Makondo, lat. 13° 23', we came into a patch of tsetse, and the insect was so numerous many bites were inflicted on the oxen, in spite of a man with a branch warding them off; and the very next morning the spots were shewn on my ox by about inch broad patches of the hair wetted as if blisters had been broken.

We remained on the afternoon of the 14th at the village of Soana-molopo, an old man, who complained that the buffaloes (ngombe) grazed in his gardens every night and destroyed the manioc. As we had no success in shooting the few game we saw on our route, we went to try and get a buffalo. Their footprints shewed them to be very large old bulls, and we found them very cunning. They selected the densest parts of a very closely planted forest to stand or recline in during the

[1] Lake Ngami, in N.W. Bechuanaland.
[2] 'We received the loan of five small canoes from her, and also one of those we had left here before' (*Travels*, 486).

day, and we were with[in] six yards of one before we knew of his presence. We heard him rush away but did not get a glimpse, though so near. It was very exciting to feel, as we trod on the dried leaves with stealthy cat steps, that for anything we knew we might next moment get a charge from one of the most dangerous beasts of the forest. We threaded out their doublings for hours, but, as I have often experienced in these forests before, without getting a single chance of a shot. We have been entirely without salt for a long time, and this begets a remarkably strong desire for animal food.

I tried often since to get a shot at other animals, but though they abound in the country the grass is now long, and they are additionally timid in proportion to the height of the covering afforded to their enemies. Oxen partake of the same timidity when among long grass. When a patch is burned off the game will stand fearlessly at about 300 yards distance untill they see guns with a longer range. In parts where bows & arrows alone are used, they keep out of the range of that instrument only, and are easily shot till they learn the longer range of firearms. The Balobale, having many guns, enjoy the privelege of hunting on both sides of the river. The Balonda are able to do little in comparison, except when the river fills. When this takes place the Leeba is about 2 miles broad, with numerous islands, on which the game having taken refuge is hunted in canoes, & immense slaughter results.

There are great numbers of small lakes in the valley in which the Leeba flows, some of which are 2 or 3 miles long & 200 or 300 [yards] broad. The water rises at least 60 feet in perpendicular height. I measured the breadth of it now that the water is low, and found by a line 28 yds long that 9 times between two canoes spanned the stream. This gives 250 yards, but allowing twenty for shifting of the canoes, and their not being always in a line, the Leeba may be stated as 220 yards in width. It is very deep at the part I measured, consequently it is a narrow spot. It flows peacefully, very few birds near it, and it does not abound in fish.

Having dispatched a messenger to Manenko we waited a day for her opposite her village, which is about 15 miles from the river. Her husband was dispatched instantly to meet us, she being unable in consequence of having got her feet burned.[1] She regretted not meeting with us, and promised to remove back again to the river in order to be in our way.

Sambanza gave us a detailed account of Kolimbota's evil doings, as

[1] '. . . in consequence of a burn on the foot' (*Travels*, 488).

well as of the politics of the country, and next morning performed the ceremony of Casendi,[1] which consists in making small incisions on the joined hands of the parties and on the pits of the stomach, right cheeks, and foreheads. The blood is taken off by a bit of grass. That of one party is put into one cup of beer, and that of the other into another. Each drinks the other's blood, and then they are bound to disclose to each other any evil which may be coming against them. If Sekeletu should resolve to attack the Balonda, Pitsane would be obliged to tell Sambanza (Manenko's husband) of the evil. They then gave each other valuable presents, and are supposed to be eternal friends.

Having met a man from Nyenko who had brought Limboa his son, whom he had left as vice-regent in his absence (the people of Nyenko however elected Nanañiko,[2] another son of Santuru, in his place, and the gaurdian (the man we met) was glad to get the lad away to his father), I sent a message to Limboa by some of his men, protesting against war with his brother, and giving him formal notice that the path up the Leeba had been given to us by the owners of the country, the Balonda, and must not be shut up as Masiko had attempted to do. I regret not being able on account of the state of my oxen to visit him.

Today Mboenga, a Kimbonda man of our company, absconded. He met his father, who was living with Seenkele (a subject of Masiko),[3] when we were going north, and probably arranged matters with him then. It was natural for him to wish to join his father again. He went off honestly, having left a parcel of flints which he carried for me. I regret parting with him thus, for after two years' absence I indulged the hope of placing the whole party safe and sound before Sekeletu. (Limboa sent messengers to me, but [they] were turned back by Mboenga saying I was angry with their master.)

Mambowe hunters

22d July 1855. Nothing worth the ink occurred in our passage down the Leeba. The Kabompo seemed about the same breadth as it, but deeper and confined between high banks and more rapid, the water of a lighter colour. The difference of animal life between the two rivers was at once apparent in the number of birds flying about, and

[1] Luvale *kasendo*, 'blood-friendship' (Horton, *Dictionary*, 296).

[2] Called Mebelo Nanañga by Jalla, who says (*Litaba*, 46) that soon afterwards he fled to the Kololo at Linyanti, where he was killed in 1859 by order of Sekeletu.

[3] 'His father was living with Masiko' (*Travels*, 489). 'Seenkele' was probably the Mbunda ('Kimbonda') chief Mwene-Chiengele (N. Rhodesia, *General List of Chiefs*, 1954, p. 1).

the animals on its left bank. The right is much hunted by the Balobale who have guns.

We came to a party of Mambowe[1] on an island near the junction of Leeba and Leeambye. They had been sent by Masiko to observe when the Makololo should come to his assistance against Limboa, and had been afraid to approach Libonta. They were employing their time hunting; had dried flesh of alligators and buffaloes in their canoes, and used the strategem of an imitation crane and lechwe's head & horns on their own heads when stalking the game. They used bows and arrows with poison only. Were much afraid of us, untill they were informed who I was. They presented me with three fine water turtles. One, which I had cooked for myself, had upwards of forty eggs in it. These, like the alligator's, have a flexible white shell, are of the same size at each end, and the white does not coagulate by heat. The flesh, especially the liver, is excellent.

The Mambowe came along with us, and yesterday discovered one of the hippopotami they had wounded.[2] I hunted most industriously all down the left bank of the Leeba, but though the country is full of game I got nothing. It is extremely wild, and often I did not even get a glance at animals which we approached. The work is very fatiguing, but desire to supply my men with that which we all needed much spurred me on to great exertions. I saw their strength failing fast, and now that we have got flesh am glad to see them gorging. They believe if they eat abundance of animal food roasted on the coals, and drink water only, a difference will be percieved in their condition in three days.

The game is wonderfully abundant all along the banks and inland too, for the ponds are all full and it is not yet necessary to come to the river to drink. The number of pokus is immense. This is nothing else but a smaller variety of lechwee.[3] There are many of this animal too, buffaloes, zebras, bastard gemsbuck, and eilands. I saw the largest black antelope I ever beheld on the left bank of Leeba, about ten miles from the confluence. The river swarms with hippopotami, and in spots where a herd is located one, two, or three, heads appear blowing away every 5 or 6 seconds. In parts where they are much hunted

[1] Mbowe, a tribe living chiefly round the confluence of the Kabompo and Lungwebungu with the Zambesi. They belong to the same ethnic group as the Lozi (Gluckman, 'The Lozi', 87).

[2] '... discovered a hippopotamus dead, which they had previously wounded. This was the first feast of flesh my men had enjoyed' (*Travels*, 491).

[3] See above, p. 24. The puku (*Kobus vardoni*) and lechwe (*Kobus leche*) together constitute the subgenus *Adenota* (Ellerman, *S. African Mammals*, 194–5).

one is never seen to blow: they become more cunning and lie among the reed near the bank, making no noise when breathing. Here they often utter a loud grunting sound as they hold their pug-dog shaped heads above the water. They graze by night on the meadows, and cut the grass short like a horse.

Among birds the scizzor bill is conspicuous in breeding, for it makes only a little hollow in the bare sandbanks in the river, and its eggs are exposed to the scorching heat of the sun. It flies round and round any one who approaches & thus gives an intimation of the vicinity of its nest. I observed one feign lameness in the wings when I came near her eggs. The ostrich feigns a broken leg when one comes near the young. He (I observed it in a male) cannot make a feint with his wing, it is so short and he does not fly. A kind of partridge which abounds on the Leeambye screams out and tries to decieve with her wings as well as legs. If intention to decieve constitutes a lie, birds are not unaccustomed to fibbing. The casuists have not taken bird morality into consideration yet. The scizzor bill eggs are about the size of a pigeon's, of a greenish ash colour spotted dark chocolate externally, & shew similar spots shining through the shell.

Our Mambowe friends rob all the nests as we go along. The Barotse do that in their parts too, but geese and all the river birds have been famed for their abundance on the Leeambye from time immemorial. I got a fine Egyptian goose's egg which had been dropped on the bare sand.

When coming down the Leeba we were frequently invited by the honey guide to go to the hives. When fairly past the inhabited parts I one day followed this wonderful bird, and about a quarter of a mile distant she shewed a hive in the hollow of a motsouri tree. She sat on a branch about 20 yards distant, preening herself with satisfaction when she saw we had observed the bees, and as we sat waiting for an axe from the canoe came to with[in] three yards of the hive and seem[ed] conscious of having performed her duty. I did not see her attempting to eat any of the bees. She calls chichi-chat-chirr, has a light-coloured conical bill, under the bill black, a light-coloured spot on the ear, breast ash colour, back brownish grey, size about that of a sparrow. This is the lesser honey guide. There is a larger one in the south, but both have the same note of invitation.[1] I wished to shoot it to ascertain

[1] Roberts (*S. African Birds*, 236-7) distinguishes three species of true honey-guide: Greater (*Indicator indicator*), Scaly-throated (*I. variegatus*), and Lesser (*I. minor*).

whether it eats bees, but could not murder a friend. Hottentots give it a piece of the comb, but the Blacks or Bechuanas say it is a villain and often leads a person to a lion, buffalo, black rhinoceros, or serpent, instead of honey. This is in accordance with their way of talking of all good as if it were evil. Pain, guilt, hunger, &c, are called God. I believe the honey guide leads to honey only but the above-named dangerous animals are accidentally in the way to it. I was once led to a black rhinoceros, and having killed him it was too late to follow our little friend beyond.

We saw two very large lions when coming down the Leeba. Wherever these are seen game is to be found. There are few or none in Lunda.

Yesterday (21st) I went to a lot of zebras, but they did not allow me to approach near enough. I broke a hind leg by a long shot. This does not immediately disable an animal, for it gallops with three legs. The foreleg is more fatal. My men ran far, but he escaped. When waiting for their return, on a wide grassy plain, I observed a buffalo, disturbed by those of our party who go on foot, galloping directly towards me. There was no possibility of escape by running. The grass, being higher than the knee and being about six feet long, was *laid* by its own weight. He came on at the gallop. I placed myself so as to give a steady shot in his forehead when he should be within 3 or 4 yards distant. When at 15 yards he swerved a little to avoid a bunch of grass, & exposed his shoulder. The ball gave him such a rap just beyond it, in a slaunting direction, he renounced his intentions and made off at a quicker rate than usual. My men followed the blood trail till they came to grass so tall & dense they were afraid to go farther. I thank God for my deliverance. (Found afterwards in the water.)

As soon as we saw the Kabompo, I observed the reddish-headed oblong spotted-bellied swallows of Kuruman. This was on the 19th July. They appear at Kuruman between the 12th & 19th of September. There were also white-bellied forktails, black swifts, & sand martins. On the Leeambye I saw a swift with a white rump emerge from a bank as if breeding. Bee-eaters swarmed out of their holes in the banks. There are goatsuckers and bats in the evenings, though this is midwinter. Clumps of thorn trees (mimosae) appear about a mile above the confluence, camelthorns below it. Lunda is a land of evergreens and no thorns, except those of nux vomica tree & one plant.

The Mambowe say that the river Kabompo as far as they ever heard of it goes by that name. They never heard the names Murucuru and Raposa.[1] The confluence of the Loeti is marked by great numbers of the fan palm, as if it had brought the seeds from the N.W. when flooded. The Langebongo is said to flow into the Loeti,[2] and it comes from near Bihé.

The Mambowe say that when my message inculcating peace among the tribes came to Masiko, the people living under him were so glad of the prospect of 'binding up the spears' they ran to the river and bathed & played with joy. They lament the coming of Limboa among them as the cause of unbinding the spears again. The person who took the wife of one of Shinte's people was not one of Masiko's men, but a Mambowe, who did so from a private grudge against the individual whom Shinte sent. He said, 'Tell Shinte I take this woman and child,

because this man of yours stole my children of old.' Shinte represents Masiko as hostile to the Makololo and wishing to stop this way. Had our oxen not been bitten I would have gone and tried to get these chieftains together. Bloodshed would have been prevented by explanations.

The dense forests of Londa in which are scattered the little villages seem to give a sombre direction & aspect to the feelings of the people. Near every village may be observed oblong spaces carefully kept free of weeds. They are about four feet broad and 30 long, and occasionally have a fence on each side. At the end next the path a branch is inserted in the ground and split, each half reaching to the side thus [see facsimile]. There are little divisions accross it, and at the end a tree. Here they go, when anxious for anything, to pray to the gods, and this they do singly and at night. If what they desired comes to pass, the worshipper takes some food and presents it to the tree or gods. Sometimes it is (as meal) sprinkled all along to the tree. At other times a little bow and arrow are suspended there. Some of these spaces are frequently used, and shew the devotional feelings to be strong. There seems to be a reverence for anthills too. The graves are neatly made, and shew a

[1] Not identified.

[2] As already mentioned (p. 1), Loeti (Luete) is in fact another name for the Lungwebungu.

belief in the continued existence of the departed. Pieces of manioc, maize, &c, are often seen placed at the entrances to forests, and cuts are made on trees, sometimes the rude outline of the human face with a long beard, as deprecatory of the anger of the souls of the departed in passing through the still sombre thicket. They don't appear to dread the anger of sylvan deities like the Greeks & Romans.

Reception at Libonta

Loena,[1] near Libonta, 25th July 1855. We have at last reached the country of the Barotse, and thank God for his great goodness to us all in all our wanderings beyond. My men, though they have parted with everything they acquired by labour in Loanda, and are now nearly naked, are in good spirits, and begin to collect hippopotamus tusks in hopes of returning. They do not look upon our time as having been misspent; to use their own expression, 'though we return as poor as we went we have not gone in vain.' I have lost none of my influence with them. They see all my goods are spent too, and that I have been exerting myself for their benefit alone.

We hear the bad news of Sekeletu having gone on a marauding expedition against the people of Sebolamakoa. By the advice of an uncle he goes, expecting them to flee at once, as they did when Rya Syde came there. This opens a bad prospect for me, for this foray is in the direction I expected to take, but it is just what I expected from his character and the advice he recieved. His wish is to be great, and he knows greatness only as reflected in his father's deeds. My people pronounce the whole affair as 'bad, bad'.

Mahomo used liberties with Sekeletu's wives (?; once those of his father), and was peevishly ordered by the chief to depart to the Barotse & live there. Some one informed him that it was intended to send men after him & murder him while still in the way. He set off to the Matibele with one wife and three attendants, and when pretty far off sent back two of them to inform Sekeletu that he would come again & take his oxen. 'Let them feed', said he, 'I shall return'.[2] This opens up the prospect for Sekeletu of punishment for the slaughter of Sebolam-

---

[1] Luena, lat. 14.46 S, long. 23.22 E (*Barotseland Gazetteer*, 53).

[2] Sekeletu had 'inherited' some of his father's widows (*Private J.*, 131-2; cf. *Travels*, 185). I have found no other reference to Mahomo by name (he is not mentioned in *Travels*), but Sekeletu in 1858 told Silva Pôrto about 'his brother (seu irmão), now in the land of the Batevere [MaTebele]', whom Mpololo and others were plotting to make chief in place of himself (*Viagens e Apontamentos*, 154).

akoa. One tribe is employed by Divine Government to punish another.

27th July. Libonta. On arriving today we were recieved by demonstrations of joy such as I never witnessed before. The women came to meet us with their curious dancing gestures and lullelooing. Some carried a mat and stick in imitation of spear and shield, others rushed forward and kissed the hands & cheeks of different persons of their acquaintance, and the whole commotion of the moving cavalcade raised such a dust it was a relief to gain the men assembled and sitting in the kotla.

After many expressions of joy at meeting, I rose and thanked them for their good wishes, and after stating the causes of our long delay told them I left further information to be communicated by their own countrymen, who would tell them what they saw. Pitsane delivered a speech of upwards of an hour in length, and gave a highly flattering picture of the whole journey, of the goodness of the white men in general, and in particular of Mr Gabriel, the English officers, and myself; I had done more than they expected, had opened up a path for them, and conciliated all the chiefs. The oldest man present answered this speech, and among other things alluded to my disgust at the marauding of the Makololo against Lechulathebe[1] & Sebolamakoa, and entreated me not to lose heart but to reprove Sekeletu as my child. Another followed with the same entreaties. We were then abundantly supplied with what food could be got at the moment.

Recieved information that the soldiers of Mosilikatse had brought provisions to the south bank of the Leeambye and laid them down for me and left. I conjecture they are sent by Mr Moffat when on a visit to Mosilikatse.[2] The Makololo think it a snare. Mr Oswel too came in as far as Chobe,[3] and when told I had gone north said, 'No, you have eaten him'.

[1] Letsholathebe, chief 1848(?)–74 of the Tawana in Ngamiland. Sekeletu's raid on that tribe is described more fully below, p. 290.

[2] Robert Moffat (DL's father-in-law, and senior missionary at Kuruman) had visited Moselekatse, chief of the MaTebele in S. Rhodesia, during July–October 1854. He brought letters and supplies for DL, hoping to take them himself to Linyanti. When that proved impossible, Moselekatse sent them on by a party of some twenty men (*Matabele Journals*, ed. Wallis, i, esp. 254–5, 294–8, 316–17). The Kololo refused to take delivery, and the packages were left on an island near the Victoria Falls (cf. *Travels*, 499–500, and below, p. 293).

[3] William Cotton Oswell (1818–93), an English sportsman, had accompanied DL both to Lake Ngami (1849) and on the first expedition to the Kololo (1851). He did not again visit S. Africa; the rumour of his having been to the Chobe possibly referred to Edwards (see below, p. 288).

D

28th July '55. We had a day of thanksgiving to God for his goodness in enabling us all to return in safety and see our friends again. The men decked themselves out in their best, and all had managed to secure suits of European clothing, which with their white and red caps gave them a rather dashing appearance. They tried to walk like soldiers, and called themselves my braves. Having been again saluted with salvoes from the women, we met the whole population, and having given an address on divine things I told them we had come that day to thank God before them all for his mercy in preserving us in dangers by strange tribes and sicknesses. We had another service in the afternoon.[1]

They gave us two fine oxen to slaughter, and the women have supplied us abundantly with milk and meal. This is all gratuitous, and though I feel ashamed that I can make no return my men explain the total expenditure of means in the way hither, and they remark gracefully, 'It does not matter, you have open[ed] a path for us and we shall have sleep.' Strangers from a distance come flocking to see me, and seldom come empty-handed. I distribute all presents among my men.

The Leeambye rose higher than usual this year, approaching quite close to Libonta fences and doing great damage among the cattle. The Leeba seemed by the wreck left behind to have attained a height of about one hundred feet perpendicularly from low water mark.

29th July '55. A cold east wind prevails constantly for some months or untill the rains commence. It blows in the same way at Kolobeng and through all the intervening country. It begins with sunrise & calms down before sunset. Long ere the rains begin in October or November it is very hot and dry. The north wind occasionally blows for two and a half days and is very hot & dry, carrying occasionally fine reddish dust with it. During this period a bunch of ostrich feathers held against it becomes charged with electricity, and when the hand is applied to it all the piles rush to the fingers with a crackling sound and adhere thereunto. The skin cloaks of the natives, called karosses, shew at these times so much electricity when moving about at night bright sparks are emitted, and a slight rubbing evolves the sparks in great numbers with cracking. When I first noticed it, the native whose cloak was the subject of remark said, 'That is not an effect observed since white men came amongst us, we saw it of old, we and our fore-

[1] If, as the context suggests, this was a Sunday, the date beginning the paragraph should read '29th July'.

fathers'. Otto von Guerrike was the first who saw this effect in Europe.[1] The black race were familiar with it from time immemorial, but they looked upon it with the eyes of oxen. Nothing was ever developed. The human mind under black skins has remained stagnant in reference to the physical operations of the Universe. The earth was and is believed to be illimitable, and one part has the clouds fixed upon it. My men say with pride, 'The elders believed that the earth had no boundary, but we reached it. The earth was finished. Where we turned there was no more land.'

[1] DL's source for this statement (cf. *Travels*, 123, and below, p. 414) was Humboldt, who says (*Cosmos*, ii. 727) that 'von Guerike', experimenting 'with a rubbed piece of sulphur', first 'recognised the phenomena of repulsion, which subsequently led to the establishment of the laws of the sphere of action and of the distribution of electricity'. Otto von Guericke (1602–86) was a distinguished natural philosopher.

XIII

WITH THE MAKOLOLO

Naliele

31st July 1855. We parted with our very kind Libonta friends yesterday morning, after planting in Seruane's & Morisi's courts[1] some of the seeds of the demdem palm, which yields the palm oil of commerce. We placed them in the courts because there they will be well taken care of & watered. If they succeed, then they may easily be propagated farther.

We reached another village, that of Moroa Chutlane,[2] who gave us an ox in going north. An old man, Tebeleñ, gave another now, and we were most liberally supplied by the women with milk, butter, corn, and maize. A harvesting of the young of a large black bird called liñkololo[3] took place as an offering, and 175 nearly fledged birds were presented to me. They were rather late in harvesting, otherwise double the number would have been yielded. They are very fat, though the old ones, which feed chiefly on shellfish, look lean & scraggy enough. The Leeambye is remarkable for the numbers of its birds, and they are generally in good condition, which shews that their proper food abounds. I shot yesterday 14 duck (histrionica) with one discharge; four or five more struggled into the water and thence into the reed, and escaped.

This village is situated, as all others in the Barotse valley are, on an eminence over which the water in the annual floods does not rise. There is a true banian tree, with roots growing from its branches, growing on it.

Both Libonta and this village contain very many patients complaining of bowel complaints, probably because they have plenty of food and no salt or other condiments. (The first case of fistula I have seen was met here.) The Balonda use different herbs as condiments to their tasteless food, and complain less of pains in the alimentary canal. But they have no clothing, and the vicissitudes of temperature produce lung diseases and fevers which are very fatal. A kind of solaneum is

---

[1] See above, pp. 16 (Seruane), 19 (Morisi).
[2] 'Son of Chutlane' (in *Travels*, 494, called simply 'Chitlane'); possibly the same as Mathukwe (see above, pp. 16, 19).
[3] Openbill stork (see p. 15).

used as a condiment. It is bitter, but the leaves and fruit are both eaten with relish by those who are accustomed to it.

The vicissitudes of temperature in winter may be known by the thermometer standing in the morning at sunrise between 42°–46°, and 86°–96°–100° & upwards at midday. It falls to 70°–68° about sunset. The above observations were taken from the thermometer in the coolest parts of my tent at midday and afternoon when covered with a thick horse rug. A variation of from 40° to 60° in so short periods must prove trying to the constitutions of the inhabitants. I have generally one or two of my people on the sick list.

31st July. Today one of the cold south winds direct from the pole is blowing. It is S.S.East here, and will blow tomorrow and on the morning of next day. The sky, in the south especially, has a peculiarly white milk & water tinge.

(2d Augst. Blew 4 days, & was succeeded by a hot easterly breeze.)

Those who are accustomed to obtain a livelihood by hunting or gathering the fruits & other kinds of food in the forest (as honey), or by rivers, never submit willingly to servitude. Even herding cattle, in which occupation they can partially indulge their favorite habits and have abundance of milk besides, does not secure their permanent residence. They are constantly escaping from the Makololo and resorting to their old haunts. This is an excuse with the Makololo for marauding.

Remember to examine whether the period of the rise of the Nile corresponds to the period of low water in the Leeambye. The Ibis religiosa appears in vast flocks at the time when the Leeambye is rising. At present, during the dry season, I see groups of 8 or 10 only.

Pulane's vil[lage], 2d August 1855. Libonta contains about 100 huts, Moroa Chutlane's vil. 30, Pulane's 45, Tseola and Mokhosi 40, Moboeana 20, two cattle stations 19, Naliele 200.[1]

1st August '55. A dog killed Pitsane's female pigeon after it had been brought all the way from Golungo Alto. A wolf or hyaena came into our midst at Shinte's and carried off, from amidst 80 fowls, one of a large breed we brought from Cassange. A valuable article is sure to be the first spoiled or lost.

Yesterday and today I have written 20 pages of geology from memory, beginning at page [286.][2]

[1] Pulane, a kinsman of Sekeletu, is mentioned in *Private J.*, 212, as having a large village. The other men named (Tseola, etc.) I have not identified.

[2] MS '448'; the present entry is on p. 439. '20' should read '30'.

4th August 1855. At Naliele, which we reached on the 2d.[1] Got 14 ducks (histrionica) by one shot; 4 more, disabled, got into the water and reed & escaped. A large pelican was shot, measuring 6 feet from tip of bill to toes stretched out behind. The bill was $17\frac{1}{2}$ inches in length, and has a hook at the end of the upper mandible. A large cap was made of its pouch, and a *Glanis siluris* was found in its stomach undigested. They are sometimes very fat, and eaten by the Barotse, but the taste is fishy and disagreable. The Barotse name is 'liya'.

We found Mpololo exercising the office of Lord of Borotse. When we passed he was overruled by Lisebane, who is believed to be a wizard. We did not consult him, and he prevented Mpololo from giving us food. He has been expelled [from] Naliele by Ma-Sekeletu. He seems to have an unhappy disposition, and tries to frighten others by sprinkling blood &c on their thresholds, corn safes, &c, wandering about at night. It will end in his being murdered by some one. His own son disowns him, and that son's mother denounces him as the wizard who bewitched Sebituane.[2]

Mpololo is low spirited at present, in consequence of his daughter having been murdered by a man called Santuru. She had been confined and was doing well. Her father naturally remembered her when an ox was slaughtered or other food came in his way, he sent presents of it to her. This displeased Santuru, and he told his wife that he would kill Mpololo's child in revenge because he got no food from her father. He entered her hut by night and strangled her,[3] and when endeavouring to fire the hut, in order to make it appear she had been burned to death, he was discovered. His wife was killed as well as himself, because, said Mpololo, 'She knew of her husband's intentions and did not reveal them'. I tried to ascertain if selling of children of the Borotse had anything to do with the deed, but it does not appear to have had any influence.

The Mambari came while we were absent, and again carried off a great number of children. I denounced the sale of children in general. Mpololo says the only children sold in Borotse were two by order of Sekeletu. Most of them came from the small villages east of this, which though owned by Makololo are nearly independant and sell

[1] '... on the 1st of August' (*Travels*, 495).

[2] None of this appears in *Travels*, where Lisebane (see above, p. 11) is not even mentioned.

[3] '... strangled both her and her child' (*Travels*, 495, where he is described, anonymously, as 'one of the Makololo'). Among the descendants of Kololo refugees in the Tawana tribe (Ngamiland) is a family bearing his name (Schapera, *Ethnic Composition of Tswana Tribes*, 1952, p. 101).

children for a mere trifle. A sixpence exceeds the prime cost of articles required to purchase a boy.

Lerimo, the man who conducted the foray against the Balonda previous to our going north, was soon after our departure seized by a species of leprosy called 'mbingua',[1] which soon produces anchylosis of the joints. When he had given up hopes of cure by medicines, he, in rage, tried to commit suicide by thrusting a spear into the hollow above the collar bone and side of neck, but his stiffened joints did not admit of the elevation of the arm necessary. He will remain a monument of the terrible ravages of this disease. And but for our incapacity to determine what are divine judgements, and what not, we might say he is suffering the effects of the divine displeasure.

Nokuane has gone, carried off by his strange disease, which I have no doubt was caused by terror and remorse after enacting the chief part in the murders of Mpepe, Mpepe's father, and another.[2] ('Blood had left upon his soul its everlasting stain'.)

Ramasantané went with the party against Lechulathebe, and the exertions necessary to shew himself brave and nimble before the young in his state of obesity proved fatal by vomiting of blood, discharge from nostrils, &c.[3]

In order to give a clear idea of the actual state of these heathen, I must multiply facts and actual everyday occurrences. Rya Syde ben Habib, whom we met here in our progress north, was most kindly recieved by Sebolamakoa, but his party having discharged their guns on first entering the village the people unfortunately fled, and confessed afterwards that it was from the belief that the party were Makololo. Rya Syde was well treated, and large presents of very large tusks were made to him. He told the people at Sesheke how afraid Sebolamakoea was (an old woman is the chief), and Moriantsane,[4] uncle by marriage to Sekeletu, went to inform him immediately of the chance of a haul of

[1] '. . . a leprosy peculiar to the Barotse valley' (*Travels*, 503); Lozi *mbingwa*, 'leprosy' (Jalla, *Dictionary*, 152). Ledimo's attempt at suicide is not mentioned in *Travels*.

[2] Nokwane was a leading Kololo headman; his role in Mphephe's 'murder' (see p. 15) is described in *Travels*, 182, and his 'strange disease' in *Private J.*, 236, 237, 239.

[3] He is mentioned in *Travels*, 503, as one of 'the influential Makololo' who had died during DL's absence.

[4] Morantsiane (Lozi 'Mulanziane'), official name of the headman of Sesheke. The man referred to here was the husband of Sebetwane's sister, and is often mentione in *Private J.* He was executed, c. 1860, for 'bewitching the chief [Sekeletu]

cattle without difficulty. Rya Syde is the guide to the expedition and will recieve his reward in prisoners, as on a former occasion. A more heartless expedition I have not known in Africa.

Several of my men have on our return found that their wives had married other men during our absence. (Others have borne children by other men, but this creates no discontent.) This is a great annoyance, chiefly on account of the reflection that while they were toiling another was devouring their corn &c. Mashauana's wife had borne him two children, yet proved faithless. They generally have more than one, but do not agree with me when I tell them they have enough still.

All the people we have yet met have been most liberal in supplying us with food. Besides large supplies of milk and meal at Libonta we recieved two oxen, one at Moroachutlane's, two at Tseola's, one at Mobeana's, 3 at Naliele, one at Puleane's, ten in all, & 3 more from Mpololo (thirteen). We have thus more food than we can consume. But Mpololo exerts himself in every way to supply our wants. We leave Shinte's canoes with him.

The Mambowe were well recieved, and left this morning to return to Masiko. They are certainly brave and expert hunters of the hippopotami, attacking and spearing them in the water, the element in which they can exert such fearful power in destroying canoes.

Planted a potato, demdem palms, pepper, and tamarinds, in Mpololo's court, 4th August 1855.

5th Aug. A large audience listened attentively to my address this morning, but it is impossible to indulge any hopes of such feeble efforts. God is merciful, and will deal with them in justice & kindness. This constitutes a ground of hope. Poor degraded Africans! A permanent station among them might effect something in time, but a considerable time is necessary. Surely some will pray to our merciful father in their extremity, who never would have thought of him but for our visit.

It seems pretty evident from the course of the rivers that the country of the Cheeboque and Ganguellas[1] is the highest part & watershed of the region. On the north the Quango recieves its supplies. On the N.-West the Coanza flowing N.W., on the S.W. the Chobe, and on

with leprosy' (*Narrative*, 270; cf. *Expedition*, 257). Eldridge ('Short History of the Sesheke District', 1956, p. 174) says he was a Lozi tribesman with the personal name of Kalimukwa.

[1] A name 'used by the Portuguese to refer, because of their linguistic and cultural affinity, to a variable number of tribes in south-east Angola', such as 'Luchazi, Luimbe, Mbunda, and sometimes Luena' (McCulloch, *Southern Lunda*, 52).

the east the Casai, S.-East Lotembua and [Leeba][1] likewise drain that same elevation. The season in which we proceeded N. was an unusually rainy one, but I have no reason to believe that the abundant supplies of the aforementioned rivers are derived from anything but rain percolating through the soil. The Leeambye rose so high the mounds of Naliele and Libonta were nearly submerged. This was never known to occur before. The river too broke into numerous new channels, so that a future traveller may view it differently from what I copied. It contains a wonderful supply of insects and fish, hence the marvellous numbers of birds on its banks. I counted a string of 150 pelicans going to roost yesterday evening.

The watershed above named forms part of the rim of the continent. The interior is evidently lower than it, and if I find the same everted edge on the Eastern Coast then the form may be described as a sort of trough, the rims being a little though not much higher than the hollow along the middle. This is different from the prevailing opinion and from my own while going north.

Left pontoon at Mpololo's, a hole having been made in it by mice in its long stay in Londa.

I have observed flocks of birds rising off the cattle and game, and know the bird well from frequently noticing it in other situations. I am assured by the natives this is the 'likala', or bird which gaurds the rhinoceros and buffalo & other game. We observed it in immense swarms at Icollo i Bengo, where there are no cattle. I think there are three kinds of them.[2] The hasty glances I have had of them when seen riding on buffalo or rhinoceros backs at full gallop made me believe it to be of a dark colour, but this is drab and ash-coloured. A pure white ardea[3] frequents the buffaloes too in large flocks. When the animals are driven away, both betake themselves to the insects in shallow reedy marshes. That shot at Barro do Bengo lake[4] had a curiously-

[1] My conjecture; MS (p. 445) has 'leave'.

[2] 'Likala' = oxpeckers (see p. 50). Roberts (*South African Birds*, 402) recognizes only two kinds: yellow-billed (*Buphagus africanus*) and red-billed (*B. erythrorhynchus*). In *Travels* DL identifies 'kala' (sing.) as both *Textor erythrorhynchus* (p. 252) and *Buphaga africana* (p. 546); the former is a synonym of *Bubalornis albirostris*, buffalo-weaver, a bird of very different habits from those described above (cf. Roberts, op. cit., 1st ed., 1940, pp. 331–2).

[3] The bird DL means is presumably the cattle egret or 'tickbird', *Bubulcus ibis*, family *Ardeidae* (Roberts, 24).

[4] Presumably L. Panguila, near the mouth of the Bengo (GSGS 4646, SC 33; see above, p. 160).

formed bill and bright yellow near it. Had the insects which infect[1] cattle and a few hairs alone in its crop. It was shot in the morning, and did not fear the presence of man.

Lehututu or wild turkey[2] kills serpents very expertly with the bill, striking just behind the head.

People of Naliele complain much of diseases of the joints, rheumatism, and coughs. Town surrounded by a foul hollow containing mud & much vegetable matter.

7th August '55. At Naliele, waiting for canoes which have been sent for. Masiko sent a party after me with a tusk, 2 calabashes of honey, 2 baskets of maize, & one of earth nuts. They report that Mboa attacked his fort, capturing the women who were going to their gardens &c, but Masiko's men repulsed them with great loss, and Limboa has given three men as a fine for attacking Masiko. This will cause peace for a time. Succeeded in getting the Makololo to recieve them well, though it is against the grain even to speak civily to them. 10 were killed and 10 wounded in the engagement between the brothers.

It is remarkable that there is no tradition of an earthquake ever having occurred in this region. Their quickness of perception of any event which may be recognized by the senses, and retentiveness of memory, renders it probable that no perceptible movement of the earth has taken place from lat. 27° south to lat. 14° S. in the centre of the continent, during this century at least. No appearances of recent fracture or disturbance of rocks are seen in the country. The drying up of the rivers which flowed westward may be indicative of a gentle elevation there. . . .[3]

8th August 1855. Naliele. Waiting for canoes. I am informed by the people of Masiko that the Kabompo contains a very formidable waterfall at some distance beyond them. The rocks through which the river has forced a passage nearly meet in the middle over the stream. It then assumes a northerly course & comes from the country of Matiamvo. West of the waterfall a branch is given off, called 'Ndongo',[4]

[1] infest (?).

[2] *Bucorvus leadbeateri*, ground hornbill (Roberts, 228-9).

[3] I have here omitted MS 448-79, containing a lengthy dissertation entitled 'Notes on the geology of a portion of Africa'; see above, p. 281.

[4] Dongwe; joins the Kabompo from the east in lat. 13.59 S, long. 23.52 E (GSGS 4648, sheet 3152). The 'waterfall' may be either the Pokolo Falls or the Shikota Rapids, both of which appear on Gibbons's map (1904) in the vicinity of lat. 13.30 S, long. 24.30 E.

which flows so near the Bashukulompo they with ease transport their canoes from one river into the other. According to them the Bashukulompo or Loenge has another source than the Kabompo, and flows parallel with the Ndongo for some distance only. They are not, however, certain about it.

A tribe comes from the eastward of them bringing large quantities of copper for sale, and they refuse to exchange it for ivory. Cloth is in great request. They sleep exactly ten days in the way, and cross the Kabompo. They are called 'Balokolue'.[1] South of them the country is densely populated by an agricultural race who raise vast quantities of corn &c. They kill elephants by means of bows and arrows, and get beads from the south. Their name as known to the Barotse is the Bamasasa,[2] their country flat and wooded like Londa.

A large party of Moors came last year to Masiko, and from him went westward to Bihe. They have returned to their own land again. Were all well clothed with cotton clothing, had English guns, and swam rivers readily. They did not wish to have guides with them. Their object was the purchase of slaves. The Barotse call them the 'Manjonjo', but from the description of them, & their talking about ships, I have no doubt but they were Moors of Muscat.[3]

9th. I am sorry to hear of that frightful waterfall which exists in the Kabompo beyond Masiko, and that the Bashukulompo river too is spoiled by cataracts. The sea after all is the great civilizer of nations. If Africa, instead of simple littoral outline, had been broken up by deep indentations of glorious old ocean, how different would have been the fate of its inhabitants. The waterfalls of Mosioatunya, Kabompo, & others, explain why commercial enterprise never entered the interior of the continent except by foot travellers. I am sorry for it. My dreams of establishing a commerce by means of the rivers vanish as I become better acquainted with them. But who can contend against nature? Can these cataracts not be passed by placing boats on frames with wheels? Difficulties are not always insurmountable.

There is a wonderful uniformity in the direction of the mountain

[1] Lukolwe, living south of the Dongwe in Mankoya District, Barotseland.

[2] Mashasha, inhabiting the south-eastern portions of Mankoya District. Both they and the Lukolwe belong to the 'Nkoya group', who are akin to the Lozi, 'though they speak different languages' (Gluckman, 'The Lozi', 87).

[3] 'Manjonjo' does not appear in Jalla's *Lozi Dictionary*. Elsewhere DL gives 'Mojojos' as 'a name by which travelling Moors or Arabs are known' (23.v.56 Murchison, from Quelimane; cf. *Expedition*, 49), and the *Manual of Portuguese East Africa* (1920, p. 89) states that there coastal Arabs are called 'Mujojos'.

chains of this country. They lie in conformity with the major axis of the continent, viz. N.N.W. & N.W., South-South-East and S.E. There are of course numerous exceptions, and chiefly where cross bars have been thrown up by an eruptive rock, whose force has been exerted mainly in elevating the N.N.W. & N.W. & S.S.E. & S.E. ranges. Does this not explain why Africa has no deep indentations of sea as other continents have? It appears as if it had been pressed up from the sides, and in successive portions or additions to the southern end(?). The active erupted rocks generally lie flat, the rocks elevated by them constitute the ranges.

9th. Masiko's people departed this morning, highly pleased with the present which fortunately I had goods enough left to make. They have great numbers of expert hippopotami hunters with them, and as the river swarms in some parts they will not want for provisions. Mpololo gave them an ox, a great stretch of charity on his part.

10th. The Senegal Long Claw here has a yellowish-white breast and reddish-brown wings. Near Loanda the breast is grey. Swallows in abundance: white breast, brownish red head, with black band accross throat, another under forked tail. If they don't migrate now they never do.

11th August 1855. News have come from the Chobe that a large party of white men have come to the village of Moremi and have been making enquiries after me.[1] It is remarkable they have not heard of my arrival at Loanda from the 'Times'. They may be Griquas only, for 'Makoa'[2] is often applied to them.

The canoes have come, and we expect to leave on the 13th (Monday). Did not observe a single aerolite last night, though I looked out often for them. We sent off the donkies this morning to go by the overland course down to Sesheke. Mpololo has been extremely obliging; supplied us with everything we needed, and has sent orders to others along the banks to 'see that we do not become hungry'.

12th. A very good and attentive audience. Surely all will not be forgotten. How small their opportunity compared to ours, who have been carefully instructed in the knowledge of divine truth from our

[1] The 'large party' included only one European, the well-known trader Samuel Howard Edwards (1827–1922), who visited Sekeletu early in 1855 (Chapman, *Travels in South Africa*, 1868, i. 279, 286–9). Moremi's village, lat. 17.58 S, long. 24.06 E, was on an island in the Linyanti River (*Travels*, 177; cf. *Private J.*, 122 n.).

[2] Tswana *makgowa*, 'Europeans, chiefly English' (Brown, *Dictionary*, 177). DL's arrival at Luanda had been reported in *The Times*, 25.ix.54 (copy of a letter from Gabriel to the President of the R.G.S., 22.vi.54).

earliest infancy. The Judge is just and merciful. He will deal fairly and kindly with all.

Note. In reference to what I mention in another volume, concerning the 'mantle of happy existence which encircles the land',[1] I would add what naturalists tell us of the universality of animal life in the ocean. 'Each stratum of sea-water is animated with polygastric sea worms, cyclidiae and ophrydinae. The waters swarm with countless hosts of small luminiferous animalcules, mammaria (of the order acephalae), crustaceae, periodinea, and circling nereides, which when attracted to the surface by peculiar meteorological conditions convert every wave into a band of flashing light.' (Humbolt's *Cosmos*, Vol. I, p. 315.)[2]

Gonye

Litofe, 16th August '55. Left Naliele on 13th, and when proceeding along the shore at midday a hippopotamus struck the canoe with his forehead and nearly overturned it. The force of the butt knocked Mashuana out of the canoe. I sprang to the shore, and saw him come up about 10 yards off, evidently to see if he had done much mischief. It is believed that a female at that part got her young speared lately. This may have excited the ire of the male.[3] No damage was done except a wetting of person and goods.

We hear that the people of Joñkue[4] have been removed from the vicinity of Mosioatunya by the Matibele, in [order] to clear the way to the Makololo. The Bajoñkue fled to Sekeletu, and the elders proposed that they should be dispersed among them as slaves! They appear to be thoroughly degraded & vile. Sekeletu refused to comply with their counsel to pounce upon the refugees and enslave them. The natural man resembles the brute creation in abuse of those overtaken by misfortune. Buffaloes and other animals butt and gore the wounded or sick out of the herd.

[1] 'God has clothed this fair world with a vast mantle of happy existence' (*Private J.*, 289).

[2] DL's quotation is not wholly accurate; the original reads '. . . mammaria (of the order of acalephae), crustacea, peridinea. . . .' (His page reference shows his edition of *Cosmos* was that published in *Bohn's Scientific Library*, not the rival translation issued in the same year by Longmans.)

[3] In *Travels*, 498, DL says the canoe was struck by 'a female, whose young one had been speared the day before'.

[4] Hwange, commonly termed 'Wankie', chief of the Najwa (Nanzwa), a western Shona (Kalaka) tribe living SE of the Victoria Falls ('Mosioatunya').

Lechulathebe when driven over to an island called out in his affliction, 'I am a child of Monare'—a cry for mercy. But he brought it all on himself. When he got guns nothing could exceed his arrogance. Sekeletu, having a wish to purchase sheep, sent ten cows, with a most friendly message, but ten sheep alone were returned. The proper price would have been 100. And when subsequently attempts were made to purchase with hoes, insulting messages were sent and one man forced to sit for hours in the sun and on the bare sand, which torture nearly killed him. A man who deserted from Sekeletu went to all the Makololo balala on the Teoge and collected the ivory for Lechulathebe.[1] Indeed, the arrogance and impudence were quite sufficient to rouse the vengeance of the Makololo, though disposed for peace. Lechulathebe shewed his valour by long shots and cursing till fairly pent up, then his poor squeak for mercy. It is a pity the Makololo were excited to begin their old course again.[2]

17th. At Mboela.[3] About 300 pelicans sit on the sands opposite our sleeping place. When killed they generally have numbers of large fish in their crops. Such an army must diminish the fish of the Leeambye. (The ñuanye or fish hawk[4] makes a dash at the pelican when there is a fish in his pouch. The latter of course roars out, 'murder'. The mouth being open allows the whisking out of the fish, which was all ñuanye intended by his descent.)

Observed a young sand martin fed by its dam. It was sitting on a reed. Other martins and swallows are breeding now. The martins and bee-eaters come out of their holes and the swifts and swallows leave their new nests as we sail by them. The storks too are breeding in their enormous nests, which appear at least three feet square.

20th. Gonye Falls. Mokuala, the headman,[5] presented a tusk, and I gave it to Pitsane, who is busy in collecting for another trip to Loanda. Mokuala's wife died after we passed, and like the Balonda he abandoned the old village because some one must have bewitched him there. He has just returned from killing the people of Sebolamakoea,

[1] *Balala* is the Tswana term for 'inferior' peoples exploited as serfs; the Teoge (Taoge) is the main channel on the western side of the Okovango delta. For the Kololo 'deserter', accused of the same offence in 1853, see *Private J.*, 151.

[2] The Kololo raid on Letsholathebe's tribe was made early in 1854 (cf. Moffat, *Matabele Journals*, i. 167; Chapman, op. cit., i. 297; *Fam. Letters*, ii. 264).

[3] Lat. 15.53 S, long. 23.08 E (*Barotseland Gazetteer*, 70).

[4] Lozi *ñwanyi*, fish eagle or African sea eagle, *Cuncuma vocifer* (Jalla, *Dictionary*, 393).

[5] Of a village just north of the falls (*Private J.*, 196).

but though he fears death so much he laughed when I spoke of his murdering others while so afraid of death himself. He looked serious enough when I said, 'You and I will meet before God, now don't say I never warned you.' The apparent callousness of these people is really remarkable, but I think it is more apparent than real. He presented a tusk, & I gave it to Pitsane.

23d Aug. '55. Island above Katima Molelo.[1] Furnished with men and canoes by Mokuala, we continued our descent of the Leeambye,

which has evidently burst a passage through the rocks for itself. The banks are covered with large masses of a reddish grey sandstone, which when seen in situ is in horizontal layers or slightly tilted up from the south. In many parts it is perforated by madrepores, and masses of lighter colour appear, while elsewhere the rock has been impregnated with iron ochre, & that hardened and glazed on the surface. The madrepore holes are often exposed thus [*see facsimile*], shewing a section of the course of the insect and its descent farther into the stone. This rock prevails to Nambue, where a porphyry and porphoritic basalt form the river's bed. Agates lie on the surface among fragments of clay schist.

22d. This is the end of winter. The trees begin to bud and blossom, and some shew the influence of the new sap which will soon push off the old foliage by assuming a very bright orange colour. I mistook this colour of the leaves at first for blooming. Others have various shades of yellow and purple, and one shews its leaves purple, another inky black. The scenery is lovely, though still murky in consequence of the atmosphere having the smoky tinge of winter. This is certainly deepened by the extensive burnings of grass which take place annually over

[1] Katima Mulilo, lat. 17.28 S, long. 24.14 E (*Barotseland Gazetteer*, 32).

hundreds of miles of country, but whether this accounts for the whole phenomenon of the wintry atmosphere I am unable to say. I imagined at one time that the appearance of smoke in the air was the effect of the cold of winter upon the warm current of air from the tropics, but the dryness of the air at Kolobeng, no dew being precipitated in winter, makes me doubt the correctness of the idea.

The Kuruman swallows were flying in flocks at Gonye, and so were the white-bellied fork tails, but these are breeding too.

The tsetse abounds all the way down from Nameta, but game is abundant on the banks. I observed, in confirmation of a former remark, that the insect does not bite one while turned aside for 'ease of nature'. I remember a medicine used to prevent the bite of tsetse, by a tribe which came to Kolobeng from the far east, was composed of 'woman's milk, a root, and *the dung of the animal smeared over it*'. It was asserted the animals might be driven through an infested spot unharmed if this measure were employed. When a village is placed in any spot the insect decamps to some distance, expelled, as the people believe, by the smoke. May it not rather be by the stench arising from ordure around the place?[1] When game is scarce the insect must diminish. Guns effect this with certainty.

The insect inserts his proboscis in different directions, always withdrawing it a little untill a plentiful supply of blood comes. It is a sharp sting-like tube, flexible, and having a conical bulb at the root. A pair of forceps stand out horizontally from the front part of the head; these are not employed in the operation of sucking. To oxen this operation is death, to man it is only blood-letting. He is the most expert fly alive except the dragon-fly. One can scarcely get the hand on him, unless it is cold. He darts off & returns to the identical spot as soon as the hand is gone, and he shews signs of bad temper if driven away.

We slept last night (22d) at the confluence of the Njoko, which is about 25 yds wide.[2] There are villages of Banyeti all along the banks, who are good carpenters and supply the Makololo with canoes, oars, basins, and stools, very well made. They do duty along the river, assisting passengers with canoes and carrying their goods at the dif-

---

[1] 'The well-known disgust which the tsetse shows to animal excreta, as exhibited when a village is placed in its habitat, has been observed and turned to account by some of the doctors. They mix droppings of animals, human milk, and some medicines together, and smear the animals that are about to pass through a tsetse district' (*Travels*, 83).

[2] The Njoko joins the Zambesi from the NE in lat. 17.08 S, long. 24.04 E (WAC 3177).

ferent cataracts. Christianity diffused would touch the very centre of African wants, by making men more manly and just to the poor and degraded. The black is as hard a taskmaster as any white can be.

Here (23d Aug.) we sleep on an island with the river nearly a mile wide. There are baobabs on it, and many aloes. These we saw last in the lowlands of Angola. Tomorrow (24th) we expect to sleep at Katonga of Sekhosi,[1] & next day at Sesheké.

Sesheke

Sesheke, 25th. Found that Sekeletu had left this yesterday with his ill-gotten goods; but he will be lauded by all, so that if I were not here to lift a warning voice he would have no chance of knowing the true nature of his deeds. He is very much in the position of princes at home who are surrounded by courtly flatterers.

Having sent persons before us to desire the headman Moriantsane to send down the river for the parcel left by the Matibele, he at first refused, because the persons who have charge of it have gone to Linyanti, and there is no person of authority there (near Mosioatunya) to whom he could deliver the message. I managed to persuade him that there was no danger to be incurred, and men were sent off at once. Great circumspection was used after the Matibele had left the spot, a rock in the Leeambye. They went round and round it in canoes, and some thought they saw movements as if, like [the] Trojan horse, it contained an enemy. At last, after recieving the orders of Sekeletu,[2] they approached with as much care and more fear than the officers of Sir C. Napier's fleet did the infernal machines off Cronstad,[3] and erected a hut over it to protect it from the weather till my return. It is wonderful they fear death so much, and yet the wrath of God for shedding human blood so little.

My men are recieved everywhere with demonstrations of hearty

---

[1] Sekhosi (Sikosi) was a Subiya headman living at 'Katonga ... latitude 17° 29' 13", longitude 24° 33' ... about 25 miles W. of Sesheke' (Travels, 208, 684). There is a village of his name in lat. 17.26 S, long. 24.27 E, in the immediate vicinity of Katongo (Bld Gazetteer, 32, 136).

[2] Chapman (op.cit., i. 288) says those orders were given only after Sekeletu had learned from Edwards (see above, p. 288.1) 'that the goods had actually been sent by Dr. Livingstone's father-in-law'.

[3] Admiral Sir Charles Napier (1786–1860) was in command of the Baltic fleet, some ships of which had been sent in June 1854 towards the Russian port of Cronstad 'to take soundings, and make a closer inspection, but with orders to keep out of cannon range' (Annual Register, 1854, p. [400]).

welcome. The Bashubea recieved their friends of our party with as much lullelooing as we had at Libonta. It is pleasant to see their affection. Some, however, as Mashauana, Mobita, &c, find their wives have married other men.

Yesterday we came to a herd of elephants on an island, and having landed at 60 yards distance I shot one in the ear. The others fled, but he came to a stand at a short distance and shewed by a horizontal movement of the proboscis on the ground that he was writhing with pain. Another shot which happened to pierce the proboscis near the root made him advance again with a gruff snorting. This is the first elephant I have killed. I mean the tusks for my companions should they return to Loanda. The numbers of elephants and other game, especially buffaloes, near Katimamolelo, are astonishing.

A strong east wind prevails at this season of the year in these parts, and will continue till the rains begin.

Sunday, 26th August 1855. A very large number of people attend the services and listen attentively. Surely not in vain. But the religion of Christ makes but slow progress in the world. Even Paul lamented over the sad spectacle presented in his day: 'All seek their own, not the things of Jesus Christ'. It is distressing and disheartening in the extreme to hear of the woes & miseries inflicted by man on his fellow-man. 'Man's inhumanity to man makes countless thousands mourn.'[1] Poor human nature! Where are the noble qualities with which, in the dreams of fat philosophers, thou in thy unsophisticated state art endowed?

Rya Syde went with the marauders and gathered great spoil of ivory and slaves. The people of Kaintu attacked his party for bringing the Makololo into the country, but with firearms he repelled them successfully, and captured their chief. They paid 3 (three) tusks for his ransom, and he replied, 'Take him and go; the guilt lies with the Makololo, not with me, who am a trader only'.[2]

31st August 1855. Sesheke. We have been waiting here for some days, in expectation of the appearance of the persons who have been sent down the river for the parcels left by Mr Moffat. The horses have come from Linyanti, and we shall leave as soon as the goods come, which will probably be tomorrow.

[1] From the dirge 'Man was made to Mourn', by Robert Burns (*Poems and Songs*, ed. J. Barke, 1955, p. 123).

[2] Kaindu was a Kaonde chief living north of the Kafue (in Mumbwa District, N. Rhodesia). Smith and Dale briefly describe the campaign mentioned, but say nothing of his capture (*Ila-Speaking Peoples of N. Rhodesia*, 1920, i. 40).

We have had much wind from the east and occasionally from the north. The sky is of a very deep blue by day, and nearly quite black by night. It is difficult to discern the Milky Way, and the planets have frequently 9 or 10 tails. My little glass enables me to see the sattelites of Jupiter, but the tremor of the earth near the river & near towns prevents observations accurate enough for longitude. I find the occultations good only for verifying the results yielded by the sextant.

2d September 1855. People more attentive and decorous at the services. They are remarkably fond of the pictures of the magic lantern, and explanations founded thereon. Part of the decorum by day may be owing to the activity of Moriantsane, who acts as a sort of church-warden, and got up silently last Sunday and hurled a club at the heads of some who were behaving improperly.

I find the longitude of Sesheke to be 25° 2′ 15″ east, latitude 17° 31′ 34″ south.[1] The river, measured by a line, has 230 yards of deep water, all of which appears in motion at the rate of 1⅔ miles per hour. From bank to bank it is a little over 300 yards. (This year (1855) the Leeambye rose high enough to allow passage in nearly a straight line between parts above & below Sesheke and Linyanti of the Chobe. It was a remarkably rainy year all north of the Chobe to Angola.)

Planted potatoes, pimento, and palm oil palms, in the court of Moriantsane, in order that they may be well taken care of and watered.

Rya Syde remains at Linyanti till I come, in order to hear our report, and will then return to the Eastern Coast, probably near Zanzibar. I declared my intention of going in his company if the Makololo did not desire another path to the coast than that we have already opened. All expressed a desire that I should try to open the Zambesi to Quilimane, and so we could choose which was best. In the event of going with Rya Syde, I would have it in my power to dis-cover Tanganyeta or Lake Nyassa, but down the Zambesi seems more in accordance with what I set before my mind as the path of duty, viz. 'open up paths to the East or Western Coasts from the Interior'. I wrote 'that having set this duty before me, I should either succeed or perish'.[2] I have steadily kept my resolution, and now after much

---

[1] For the amended version, see above, p. 4.4.

[2] Elsewhere DL says he wrote those words to 'my brother' (*Miss. Corr.*, 318; cf. *Travels*, 229, and *Fam. Letters*, ii. 265 n. 12). I have not seen the letter in which they occur.

thought consider it will not be right to go with Rya Syde for the sake of the fame of discovering another lake, if the Makololo prefer my making the attempt to open a path by water to the East Coast.

The path we have now traversed will never admit of waggons by a private individual, the rivers are so numerous and the forests so dense. The people now so hostile could all be conciliated, but the path would admit of carriers only, and their expenses are too onerous to allow of profitable commerce.

Rya Syde, or Tsaeré as he is called,[1] accedes to the proposition of Sekeletu to take a party of Makololo with ivory to the coast and purchase horses. It is difficult not to entertain doubts of his sincerity. However, some bitter things must be learned by experience alone.

3d Septr '55. Sekeletu is learning that his plunder and murder do not secure peace of mind. When he came here, he was informed [that] a man called Mococho,[2] who lives near Sesheke, intended to poison his food. Though this is probably untrue, the belief in its verity will spoil the poor fellow's enjoyment. The people evidently dislike him. The flight of Mahomo was in order to escape assassination after it was known that some preferred him to the chief. Sekeletu has to bear comparison with his father Sebituane, who had among chiefs no equal.

Certain alligators frequent the landing place here and destroy a large number of the young who go to draw water or bathe after dancing. The reptiles are absent at present, as the winter months are not quite spent. They destroy cattle too, and are probably so ferocious here as they are never hurt by the inhabitants. I cannot find a single bird in alliance with them. The Ibis religiosa, spoonbill, marabout, &c &c, roost at midday near the alligators, and when passing in a canoe they appear on a higher part of the bank as if sitting on their backs; and this must have given rise to the fables of certain birds picking his teeth, &c. They dread their devourer, and none of the river people I have questioned ever saw any familiarity between bird and reptile. Ichneumens are met with along the banks, but the Barotse know nothing of its eating the eggs of alligators. The alligator lies on the spot and gaurds them with considerable care. The testimony about the ichneumen is only negative; that of the ancient Egyptians may be positive.

[1] Evidently a corruption of 'Syde' (Said). Smith and Dale (i. 33) say he was known to the Ila as 'Saidi'.
[2] Not identified.

Linyanti

Linyanti, 13 September 1855. The goods sent by Mr Moffat from the country of Mosilikatse came to hand on the 6th in pretty fair condition, seeing they had remained on an island near Mosioatunya a whole year. The meal was damaged by the weevil, unpalateable and purgative. This kind of weevil was never seen in this country before. A whirl of thoughts rushed through my mind as I opened my letters, but thank God I had no cause of sorrow. Mr Maclear says,[1] 'I have no hesitation in asserting that no traveller on record has determined his path with the precision you have accomplished.' Letters and newspapers have been a great treat, as may easily be imagined by any one remembering that three years have elapsed since I heard from my family.

We reached this two days ago. Yesterday I delivered the presents of the Government of Loanda, viz. a general's dress coat, trowsers, sash, sword, and cocked hat. The tail of the horse was shewn by my companions as proof of its death. Also the presents of the merchants, viz. 2 bales of different kinds of cloth, beads, an umbrella, bells, powder, and two guns. The 2 donkies sent were left at Naliele. The abundance of water would have killed them if we had brought them farther, though tsetse does not. Great satisfaction was expressed, and yesterday we had a pico[2] in order to discuss the question of removal to Borotse in order to be nearer the market. Some of the older men objected to abandoning the line of defence afforded by the Chobe against their southern enemies, the Matibele. Sekeletu at last said, 'I am perfectly satisfied of the superiority of the path for trade which you have opened, and when you return with Ma-Robert[3] you will find me there'. A party has been sent with Tsaere with ivory for Loanda. My companions are allowed to rest meanwhile, and it is probable when the others return they will be ready to start. The trade is fairly set agoing.

Mr Moffat in visiting the Matibele saw English guns which had been brought by English or white men up the Zambesi. I hope to meet them in my way down that river. Ben Habib informs me that the path he follows to Zanzibar goes to Cazembe, where there is a person

---

[1] In a letter dated 27.iii.54, now in the Rhodesian National Archives. The original reads: 'I do not hesitate to assert, that no explorer on record. . . .'

[2] Tribal assembly (see p. 10).

[3] 'Mother of Robert', i.e. Mrs Livingstone, who in accordance with widespread native custom was thus named after her firstborn child.

from Pernambuco who drills his soldiers. The river Loapola flows past Cazembe, coming from the east or country of the Nyassa to fall into the eastern branch of the Kabompo.[1] 10 days beyond Cazembe, N.E., the path winds round the end of the Lake 'Tanganyenka', and if it is crossed, as necessary if they go a little farther west, it takes them three days with the canoe. The Tanganyenka is continued into the 'Calague', another lake of equal extent,[2] and that flows into Habesh or Abyssinia. There are three considerable chieftains in the route beyond Cazembe, viz. the Oututa (chief of the Batuta), Moarori (chief of Barori), and Mogogo (chief of Bagogo).[3] But the country is covered with small chiefs and their villages, and no difficulty is experienced in travelling among them. Ben Habib calls the Red Sea 'Shutla-sham'.[4]

There are many streams in the path, and three large rivers. From all I can hear, the Zanzibar route would be only a repetition of that to Loanda. It does not admit of land carriage by means of waggons. As there is a prospect at least of water carriage all the way to Quilimane, except at Mosioatunya, it is clearly then my duty to try the latter road, and leave the eclat of discovering another lake to him for whom God has reserved the honour. The lake called Nyassa is probably so named by the inhabitants on the coast from the fact that the Nyassa trade there.[5] Ben Habib met some of them.

We left Sesheke on the 7th. Saw flocks of drongo shrikes, probably going south. The water on the plains was not yet dried up, and on many parts in which efflorescence of nitrate of soda appeared, on ground containing much lime, strong effluvia of sulphuretted hydrogen were evolved. Though the Niger expedition could not detect its

[1] The 'Cazembe' referred to here is obviously the chief of the eastern Lunda (see p. 67), but the Luapula flows into L. Mweru, and does not join the Kabompo. Pernambuco is in Brazil; I have found no other reference to a (presumably Portuguese) military instructor from there.

[2] Possibly L. Victoria, on whose south-west (in northern Tanganyika) was the great Bantu kingdom of Karagwe.

[3] The Tuta, named after their original leader Ntuta, were a group of Ngoni who had migrated northward from Zululand early in the 19th century. Like the Rori (Sangu) and Gogo, they lived on the trade route from Zanzibar to L. Tanganyika.

[4] Shaṭṭ al-Sham; shaṭṭ = shore, Sham = Syria (information from Mr E. Kedourie). In Swahili the Red Sea is *Bahari ya Sham*; *bahari* = 'sea, ocean' (Johnson, *Standard Swahili-English Dictionary*, 24, 416).

[5] The usual explanation is that 'Nyasa' (Nyanja) means 'lake, lagoon, wide water', whence the name WaNyassa (ANyanja), 'lake people' (cf. Tew, *Peoples of the Lake Nyasa Region*, 1950, p. 30).

presence by the most delicate tests, it must not be believed that there is none. It may be a different gas having the same smell. It is very disagreable, and many cases of fever are met with at present. Some peculiar combination may convert it into the malaria of fever, which appears to be unappreciable by our most delicate chemical tests. I wish I had an opportunity of trying those for the sulphuretted hydrogen.

The rivers rose unusually high this year. Persons travelled for a long time in canoes in nearly a straight line from this to Sesheke, and even higher up. It seems to have been an unusually wet year in the north.

Mashobotuane,[1] a Motonga chief who lives at the falls of Mosioatunya, came to Sesheke while I was there. He says it is quite possible to drag the canoes past that part, and he is not aware of any falls beyond. The first chief met with beyond is Moemba of the Balenyare, the second Mpande, the third Makonde, the fourth Chiboa, and beyond him are the Bambala or whites who trade in ivory and beads.[2]

Sat., Septr. 22d 1855. When the Makololo are in my presence they refrain from beating their servants, and often threaten, 'if it were not for his presence I would cut you up'. My waggon stands in the court of Sekeletu's houses, and I sometimes see when not observed by the actors. Yesterday morning a man was deliberately beating a poor captive from the east for having endeavoured to escape. She was quite naked, and holding up her poor dress on both hands as a sort of shield against the frequent blows of a strip of hippopotamus hide. The sight made my heart both sick and sore. 'Man's inhumanity to man makes countless thousands mourn.' It is distressing, besides, to see poor boys going about picking up grains of corn which have fallen in the kotla— almost skeletons. Their masters, being niggardly, yet retain them in starvation, though their parents would gladly feed them if only allowed. Slavery is bad, unutterably bad, all the world over.

23d Septr '55. We have large meetings here, the town being much enlarged. I hope the story of the love of Christ, in coming down to die for us all, has some effect on some minds. Many of the elders pay

[1] 'Moshobotwane' (Narrative, 233, 248, etc.); possibly a variant form (or the personal name?) of Musokotwane, 'hereditary title' of the Tonga chief at the Falls (cf. Clark, The Victoria Falls, 1952, pp. 70, 71).

[2] Chiboa I have not identified. The other 'chiefs', whom DL met on returning from his visit to the Kololo in 1860, were heads of Tonga communities in the Gwembe valley, Middle Zambesi (Narrative, 318, 319, 321). Moemba (Mwemba) is included in the official N. Rhodesian List of Chiefs (1954, p. 14), Mpande and Makonde are not. For Bambala, see below, p. 336.

marked attention to the addresses, the great difficulty in preparing which is to make the truth plain enough. Surely the tale of love will sink into some hearts and yet bring forth fruit, though I may not live to see it. God grant that such may be the case, and my efforts not be in vain. One's own heart is warmed by the touching and wondrous tale of Jesus giving himself for us.

The chief and principal men sit guzzling the nasty drink called boyaloa[1] during the whole day. The attendants keep [up] a continuous roar of chaffing, railery, badinage, and laughing. Cases come on for judgement, but scarcely [any] attention is given them, though it often happens, as yesterday, cases of theft of goats & sheep are brought forward. All are speaking at once, each regardless of the other. Then dances are got up, which consist of stamping one foot after another, lifting one arm after the other, and rolling the head round about and roaring. The women stand clapping their hands continuously, and the admiring old men sit looking & say, 'It is really very fine'.

Habib asked Manchunyane, the daughter of Sebituane, in marriage. I have a vote in the matter, as having been Sebituane's bosom friend she is called my daughter. She is about 12 years old. Ben Habib will probably get her after my departure. It is one means they employ of gaining influence in a tribe.

I have no reason to fear such influence so long as fair means are resorted to. A missionary following conscientiously the principles we hold is soon seen to be of a superior race to that of the wonderfully selfish Arabs. Our acts are keenly scrutinized by all, both young and old, and on no occasion have I ever found an unfair or uncharitable judgement pronounced by the heathen. As much cannot be said of those we call bretheren in Christ.

If I am permitted to enter on this large and interesting field I shall get copies of the Arabic Testament, of the edition furnished to Mungo Park, and distribute them among the Arabs, and copies of the New Testament in Portuguese for the bastards of that nation who come into the Interior. Perhaps the truth may find its way into Angola, but great caution must be used in order not to rouse the emissaries of Rome.

What a fine soul-expanding religion that of Jesus is! The heart embraces in generous affection all the tribes of men, and longs that all may be made partakers of the same blessed hope of eternal life through the blood of Christ. The poor Boers who plundered my house and

---

[1] Tswana *bojalwa*, beer made of sorghum or millet.

wished to take my life knew nothing of my feelings towards them. I never spoke to or thought of them but with feelings of deep commiseration. What would Potgeiter and Pretorious give now to reverse the sentence they passed in forbidding us to preach unto the Gentiles that they might be saved. Yet Pretorious is almost canonized in the public prints of the Colony. 'Blessed are the dead who die in the Lord', is the concluding sentence of the paragraph in which his end is mentioned, 'for they rest from their labours, and their works do follow them'. The murderous attack on the Bakwains was by his orders. The children were sold under his surveilance. They were registered by his clerk as a feint by which they might be able to swear they were not slaves. These will follow him, no doubt. Who will fancy the meeting?[1]

25 September 1855. It is now excessively hot. Clouds shew rains will soon come. Hope some showers will fall before I set off for Quilimane. At present travelling is exceedingly distressing.

I wrote letters by Ben Habib for the Bishop and merchants of Loanda, dated 12th September, also a note for Mrs L., Mr Moffat, Mr Maclear, and Thompson, dated 13th. They go back to Angola to my friend Mr Gabriel.[2] There is not the smallest prospect of any communication with Kuruman. The policy of Government in stopping ammunition from Griquas and Bechuanas[3] will effectually drive commerce into other channels.

[1] Andries Hendrik Potgieter (1792–1852) and Andries Willem Jacobus Pretorius (1798–1853) were the main leaders of the Transvaal Boers during DL's residence in Bechuanaland. The former had opposed his attempts to extend missionary work eastward (1848); the latter was responsible for the commando that attacked the Kwena in 1852, sacked DL's premises at Kolobeng, and carried off several hundred native children into captivity. There is much detail about both in *Fam. Letters*, *Private J.*, and *Miss. Corr.*

[2] The letters to the Bishop and the 'merchants' (viz. Schut, see p. 156) were published, in Portuguese, in *Boletim official d'Angola*, nos. 575 (4.x.56) and 580 (8.xi.56) respectively; those to Moffat and Mrs Livingstone appear in *Fam. Letters*, ii. 260–7, 267–9, and that to William Thompson (1811–89, agent of the LMS at Cape Town) in *Miss. Corr.*, 278–83. There were two letters for Maclear (12.ix.55 and 13.ix.55, received together at Cape Town on 26.xii.56); both are now in the Rhodesian National Archives.

[3] One clause of the Sand River Convention (January 1852), by which the British had recognized the independence of the Transvaal Boers, stipulated that 'all trade in ammunition with the native tribes is prohibited, both by the British Government and Emigrant Farmers [Boers] on both sides of the Vaal River' (*PP England*, 1854, XLIII, 527).

'My soul is wearied because [of] murderers'[1] shews a state of morality similar to that which exists in this country, for I have often a similar feeling in hearing the tales of blood which constantly arise from deeds of Boers & others. Kaiñko was murdered in cold blood by Sekeletu because Moriantsane said he refused tribute. He and two of his principal men were strangled, and in the morning they pointed out the bodies of Kaiñko &c to the person who was acting as guide to Sebolamakoea. He laughed only, and as they went along one was ordered to kill him too. This was his recompense. (Kaiñko sent for Sekeletu to take the cattle of a man who was living near him. When they arrived no cattle were found. He had wished the removal of the other only.) Two chiefs on mountains defied them. One was driven off, and the other was unmolested. Sebolamakoea fled, but many cattle fell into the hands of the Makololo, and one of Sebolamakoea's children. Many of Kaiñko's children were also taken.[2] O, who can stop this bitter fountain but thou, my gracious Lord, by the influence of thy love and Holy Spirit. Fiat voluntas tua.

27th September 1855. A note from Sr. Porto of Bihe informs Sekeletu that he will endeavour to come this way, and not allow so good a trade to slip out of his hands without an effort. Habib is detained at Sesheke.

It is excessively hot at present and clouds threaten rain. I hope some may fall and cool the ground before I start. Slight sprinklings fall occasionally, accompanied with thunder and lightning, but no good shower.

Fruits of missions

29th Septr. The expelled missionaries write that they saw no fruit of all their labours—the Bakwains, Bakhatla, and Bahurutse, are all worse.[3] As I acted on the rule invariably of making no enquiries

---

[1] Jeremiah 4: 31.

[2] Kainko (Kaingu) is the official name of an Ila chief living on the Kafue River at Itumbi, Namwala District. Smith and Dale's description of the Kololo raid (*Ila-Speaking Peoples*, i. 40) does not mention the 'murder' described by DL. According to them (i. 33), Kaingu was killed in an earlier raid led by Mphephe (for whom see above, p. 15).

[3] Rogers Edwards (1795–1876) and Walter Inglis (1815–84), LMS missionaries among the Kgatla and Hurutshe respectively, had both been expelled from the Transvaal by the Boers in November 1852, for protesting against the enslavement of native children captured in war; I have not traced the statement DL says they made. The Hurutshe, considered senior in status to all other Tswana tribes, live mainly in Zeerust District, W. Transvaal.

respecting other missionaries among natives, I can say nothing about the Bakhatla or Bahurutse. But I think the assertion as regards the Bakwains is totally unfounded. During the whole period of our sojourn among them we strove that no occasion of offence should be found in us except concerning the law of our God, and I feel most grateful to Our Heavenly Father for enabling us to do this. We left without a single enemy. Even when the waggon was inspanned on our departure for the country of Sebituane, Sechele and his principal men pressed us to go with them to Limaoe, where the Boers afterwards massacred his children & people, offering to build a house and church free of expence.[1] But the rejection of the gospel by the people generally, and other causes, made me decide against it. We, however, parted with perfect good will. This is an important element in estimating success or non-success.

Well, this hostility to the gospel, and to that alone, I consider to have been a most important step in advance, and no one who knows the callous indifference of the heathen when missionaries come first among them will entertain a doubt on the point. It is a terrible advance for them if they continue finally impenitent, but it is God's will that men get the offer, though they often do despise it. But the effect of the truth on their minds & hearts without doubt has a favourable influence on their morals, and without any bias against the Boers I can aver that the general morality of the Bakwains excel them in truthfulness, honesty, and honour. They cannot be compared with the Makololo, and the general influence of the gospel is much more than missionaries are aware of.

I am most thankful that I was permitted to sow the good seed among them, and I believe that seed is not dead. It is the living word of the living God. There are few souls which can withstand its force, and no hatred however deep can quench its power. I have strong faith in that vitality which God's word possesses, and now record my conviction that the seed will yet grow among the Bakwains, though I may not see it.

1st October 1855. Ben Habib returned in order to communicate some information respecting a squabble of Porto and an agent. The

[1] The Kwena, of whom Sechele was chief 1831(?)–92, moved from Kolobeng to Dimawe, eight miles away, in August 1851. DL had left Kolobeng, on his first journey to the Kololo, in April 1851; the Boer attack was in August 1852. See *Private J.*, 1, 3; and, for the Boer attack, ibid. 85–91; *Fam. Letters*, ii. 184–6; *Miss. Corr.*, 219–37 *passim*.

real object Porto had in view was to get a trusty word as to his safety from Sekeletu himself. He will come again.[1] Commerce is spreading its ramifications in all directions, and friendly intercourse will be sure to follow in its wake. This commerce effects readily, but sullen isolation gives way to good will and the feeling of mutual dependance by the influence of the gospel alone. As far as I have observed the Africans, they are not by any means unreasonable. I think unreasonableness is more a hereditary disease in Europe than in this land. I would trust rather to the blacks with whom I have come in contact for a good character than to the whites, who either know or don't know me, but who have quite a remarkable set in the opposite direction to charity & candour.

Wrote a note to Thompson, Fridoux, & Gabriel, and sent a model of Great Exhibition to Mr Pires per Ben Habib.[2] 27th Septr.

6th October 1855. Mem. Found invoice of books [and] thermometer in box, dated 22 July 1852, from Mr Snow, amount £6. 18. 6. Among my letters brought by the Matibele a letter from Mr Snow, dated 23 August 1853, containing an account as follows:

1851	1 Moffat's Africa	£0	14	0	Jany 21	
	Sundries	£8	10	7	Feb 14	
	Do.		8	4	June 24	
	Do.	£6	18	6	July 22, 1853	
		£16	11	5		
July 1 '51, By cash		10			L.M.S.	
		6	11	5		

Mr Snow says this balance he will obtain at the Mission House according to my request.[3]

---

[1] Silva Pôrto revisited the Kololo in the middle of 1858, when he claims to have been well received by Sekeletu (*Viagens e Apontamentos*, 143–57).

[2] The letter to Thompson, 27.ix.55, is published in *Miss. Corr.*, 284–7; the others mentioned I have not traced. Jean Frédoux (1823–66) was a French evangelical missionary at Motito (Bothithong) in Bechuanaland, and husband of Mrs Livingstone's younger sister Ann. The 'model of Great Exhibition' was one of the Chrystal Palace in London, sent to DL from Scotland by his sister Agnes (see *Fam. Letters*, ii. 288).

[3] John Snow, of Paternoster Row, London, was a bookseller and publisher, whose list included Moffat's *Missionary Labour and Scenes in Southern Africa*, 1842. The 'Mission House' was the London headquarters of the LMS, in Blomfield Street, Finsbury.

It is excessively hot at present. The thermometer stands at 100°
in my waggon, though in a box exposed to the cool current which, when
both ends of the vehicle are open, flows throughout. After sunset and
before it is dark it shews 89°, at 10 o'clock 80°, and at sunrise in the
mornings 70°. At 9 a.m. it has reached 88°, though feeling cool and
pleasant. The natives keep themselves pleasant by a continuous
guzzling of beer or rather boyaloa. The perspiration produced seems
to give enjoyment.

They were well pleased to see the pictures in the Naturalist's
Library,[1] but the lion, which is made to look excessively fierce, recieved the remark, 'That we should not have known to be a lion
had you not told us.' The worthy painter would scarcely thank
them for the criticism. Some animals of the feline class put down as
natives of India are recognized by them. I must examine this point.
The royal tiger seems never to have come so far along the continent as
this.

7th. News came, just as we were about to commence the services,
that the people of the Lake[2] had come among the people of Sekeletu
and taken away a large number of tusks and people. The chief men
of the village were killed. This is a fresh cause of irritation. Sekeletu
said that I appeared to think he had no reason of attack in his last
year's foray against Lechulathebe, and that it appeared as if I thought
he alone had guilt. I replied that he saw now that the old method of
settling disputes did not secure peace, perpetual irritation always followed the old ways; that I did not excuse either the one or the other,
both had guilt. He admitted the truth of some of my remarks, and
shewed he had followed my advice respecting giving presents to his
poor people for bringing ivory;[3] but I could see from the temper of
the people that these small forays of the Lake people will lead to an-

[1] Among works ordered by DL from Snow, 12.i.53, were: 'The following
volumes of Sir W. Jardine's Naturalist's Library: Birds of Western Africa, 2 vols.;
Ruminating Animals; Lions and Tigers; Elephants and Rhinoceros; Sun Birds;
Fly Catchers; Entomology.' Vol. III (*Mammalia: Lions, Tigers, &c, &c*, Edinburgh
1843) contains four plates illustrating lions, which are not as unrecognizable as DL
suggests.

[2] The Tawana ('Batauana'), Letsholathebe's tribe, who lived in the vicinity of
Lake Ngami. They were southern neighbours of the Kololo, though separated
from them by intervening communities of servile peoples.

[3] In 1853 DL had tried 'to introduce a system of kindness into the dealings of the
Makololo and conquered tribes', by suggesting to Sekeletu that those bringing
ivory as tribute should be given beads in return (*Private J.*, 142, 259).

other expedition and probable extermination of the Batauana. Sekeletu professed to wish to have arbitration between the parties and himself, without my suggesting any such course.

The people listen very attentively and behave more decorously than formerly at the services. Some children on the outskirts of the crowd sometimes raise a laugh at the conclusion of the prayer. An address to an unseen God seems to them ludicrous, but we shall get over that. It is really a very inviting field of labour. There are so many people, and many would learn. Boys bring little presents of milk to me, and I have no doubt feel interested [in] some of what they hear. May God grant his blessing to the poor efforts made to shew forth his goodness & love in giving up his own son to death for sinners. I wish I had more love to Him in my own heart, so that my words might enter still warm into theirs. Holy Spirit, work thou thine own work.

Dr Duff has taken up the theme, from Baptist Noel,[1] that by concentration of missionaries much more good may be done than by the same number placed in isolated positions. The proposition is plausible, and well calculated to attract the fancy of a commercial people, the more especially as it tacitly takes responsibility from mission constituents and places it on Directors and missionaries. This is not the object present to their minds. They undoubtedly are influenced by the simple desire to promote the interests of Christ's cause, and they, I have not the least doubt, desire by what they recommend to gather in the greatest possible number into the fold of Christ. But an intelligent appreciation of the actual working of missions, and the previous state of the people, capacity to read, &c, are as important elements in forming a judgement as to concentration as zeal. And there are so many modifying circumstances in the actual experience of different missions that, even with all the knowledge which can be obtained, it is very doubtful if a positive verdict can be given either for or against centralization.

Let us look at South Africa by itself, and we shall fail to see the centralization theory so beautiful as it may appear on the platform:

---

[1] Alexander Duff (1806–78), missionary in India and subsequently 'first missionary professor' at New College, Edinburgh; Baptist Wriothesley Noel (1798–1873), 'divine; ... minister of John Street Baptist Chapel, London, 1849–68; published controversial pamphlets and devotional works' (*DNB*.).

	Mission-aries	Members		Ratio	
United Bretheren have	28	1882	or	68	for 1 of
French S.	16	1265		80	the force
London M.S. Colonial	22	2800		133	employed
L.M.S. Caffraria	3	240		80	
L.M.S. Bechuanas & Griquas	9	1488		180	
Wesleyan M.S. Colonial & Namaqua	22	2765		122	
Wesleyan Caffraria	16	900		57	
Basuta W.	5	561		112	
	121	8)13901		8)832	
		1737		104	Mean

All M.S. in India, by statistics furnished by Revd. Joseph Mullens (Report, 1852, p. 25):[1] number of missionaries 403, but not more than $\frac{2}{3}$ of that number have been employed during the last 25 years. Let us reduce the number $\frac{1}{3}$ (say 134)

members
= 269)17300(64   ratio per each one of force employed
  1614

  1160
  1076

  84

Take even the whole number, 403, we have a ratio of 42 for each one of the force employed. We have thus in India very nearly the same ratio as among the Moravians in South Africa.[2]

[1] Joseph Mullens (1820–79), LMS missionary at Calcutta, 1844–65, had written a pamphlet from which the Indian figures quoted by DL were reproduced in the LMS annual *Report* for 1852. In the S. African figures DL has made several arithmetical mistakes: in the second column the total should read 11,901 (not 13,901), and in the third the only correct 'ratios' are those for 'L.M.S. Caffraria' and 'Basuta W[esleyan]'.

[2] The Moravians are the 'United Bretheren' heading DL's list of missionary societies; 'very nearly the same ratio' is explicable only if we assume that he meant that of the 'reduced number' for India, viz. 64.

Preparation for eastern journey

9th October 1855. Lebeole[1] having made enquiry respecting my intentions in proceeding down the Leeambye, I explained my wish to have water carriage if possible to the coast, and the superiority of such a mode of conveyance over that by carriers, whose expenses eat out all the profits of a journey to the coast. He asked if I should purchase any ammunition for them, or rather if such were possible. I replied that I had now nothing to purchase with, having expended all my money at Loanda. He replied that the ivory being all mine, it would be my own fault if I left any here; I could take four or five canoes to carry it, they had implicit trust in my fidelity, &c &c.

Sekeletu repeated the same kind expressions next day, Lebeole having informed him of my intentions. I stated distinctly my purpose of appropriating some of the ivory to my own use, as also for the purpose of buying some presents for him in England, particularly a kind of ball used for killing whales by the Americans, which as it explodes in the animal will be an excellent means of killing elephants. He expressed entire satisfaction with the plan: all the ivory was mine, and whatever I did with it would be proper, the more especially as much of what I had left here was now useless, and Ma-Robert needed other & new articles of cookery. This arrangement will enable me to serve them and make good presents without encroaching on my resources for my family, and as all is fair and above board, with full understanding that their own ivory furnishes the means of purchasing, there will be no reflections when they come to purchase in the same market themselves. All know I am doing a real service in leading them to better markets and teaching them to trade with advantage.

I look on this willingness to assist and forward my plans as tokens of God's approbation on my efforts for this miserable country & people, and I thank him most sincerely for his favour, so entirely undeserved. It is singular that the very same text which recurred to my mind at every turn of my course in life in this country, and even in England, should be the same as Captain Maclure, the discoverer of the North-West Passage, mentions in a letter to his sister as familiar in his experience: 'Trust in the Lord with all thine heart and lean not to

---

[1] 'A Makololo gentleman' (*Travels*, 210). Some of his descendants are now living among the Tawana, to whom he fled in 1860 through fear of being executed by Sekeletu (*Expedition*, 260; Jalla, *Litaba*, 43); they are the group known by the name of his son Shwanka (Schapera, *Ethnic Composition of Tswana Tribes*, 97).

thine own understanding. In all thy ways acknowledge him, and he shall direct thy steps. Commit thy way unto the Lord. Trust also in him, and he shall bring it to pass.'[1] Many more, I have no doubt, of our gallant seamen feel that it is graceful to acknowledge the gracious Lord in whom we live and move and have our being. It is an advance surely in humanity from that devilry which gloried in fearing neither God nor men nor devil, and made our wooden walls floating hells.

Travelling from day to day among barbarians exerts a most be-numbing effect on the religious feelings of the soul. One is refreshed in spirit by a few weeks' rest and reflection, and more compassion is excited for the lost and perishing around us. In looking at the progress of literature, arts, & sciences, as exhibited in the pages of reviews & papers, the utter impossibility experienced of following out a sys-tematic course of study fills my heart with regret. Building and other mechanical labour, with journeyings oft to prepare the way of the Lord, have fallen abundantly to my lot. I do not grudge them to my good and loving Lord, and hope he may accept the little I can do for him yet.

A servant of Sekeletu, said to be good-looking, was sought in marriage by five young men. He very cooly ordered them all to stand in a row before her, and let her choose whom she liked. Two refused to stand, not relishing the idea of a repulse, although willing enough to take her if Sekeletu had acceded to their petitions without her consent. Three dandified fellows stood forth, and she quickly decided on the best-looking. It was amusing to look at the mortification expressed on the black faces of the unsuccessful candidates. This was all the marriage, and it is seldom any more fuss is made about that affair than described. Arrangements are generally made by the parents of the girl, and she is almost always pliable enough in acceding to their wishes, whether the husband is old or young, handsome or ugly. The readiness with which Rebecca said, 'I will go',[2] is quite African. Yet there are many instances of true and strong affection by 'falling in love', I suppose, after marriage.

10th. I find from intelligent persons who went in the late expedition

---

[1] Captain Robert John Le Mesurier M'Clure (1807–73) had discovered in 1850 'the Arctic Channel between the Atlantic and Pacific, commonly called the North-West Passage'; for this he was awarded the Patron's Medal of the RGS, 1853 (*JRGS*, 1854, pp. xli, 240–5). I have not located the letter in which he quotes the 'text' mentioned (Proverbs 3: 5, 6; Psalms 37: 5).

[2] Genesis 24: 58.

against Sebolamakoea that the country is intersected in every direction by rivers, which generally [flow] into the Loenge or Bashukulompo River. Close to the chief town of Sebolamakoea there is a lake, which may be that called Maravi. Several rivers flow from it into the Loenge, and a large river named Lokanga (or Lokanka) flows into it from the east. This seems to be the river of the Babisa, perhaps Loapola. The lake is named 'Shuia'. Another says the river of the Babisa is called Lohubu. [*See facsimile*] Lokonkue and Molonka likewise flow into

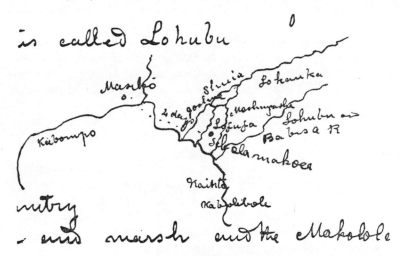

the Loenge, but these are small compared to the Lokanka.[1] The country contains much reed and marsh, and the Makololo could not secure all the cattle. The swamps proved a great impediment. There are high mountains to the east of the point where they turned.

Kainko and two of his chief men were strangled because he sent men to call the Makololo to come and capture cattle, and when they arrived he shewed them a stockade, made by one of his enemies who had lately come into his vicinity, and only wished to get rid of his neighbour and live in the stockade himself. When his real design was manifest they strangled him. This was the real reason of his murder, and not, as I was previously informed, on account of the ill will of Moriantsane.

[1] Maravi is the lake nowadays known as Nyasa, far to the east of 'Shuia' (L. Suye, lat. 14.27 S, long. 27.30 E). The Lukanga, which flows through L. Suye, is a tributary of the Kafue (Lwenge), and the 'Lohubu' (Lufubu) is a tributary of the Luonga, which in turn joins the Luapula. 'Lokonkue' and 'Molonka' I cannot identify.

They came upon a female chief of whom they never heard before. She had much cloth, which her people purchase with ivory from white men. She offered her children to Sekeletu, but he took 3 only. She asked him afterwards to give them back. This he did, and she then returned one, promising to come and visit it.[1]

11th Octr. Lebeole complained today that the Makololo bring forth so few children. The Bechuanas generally are not prolific like the Barotse & Negroes. But [in addition] to sorrow on account of barrenesss I have often heard lamentations among this people of the fatality which has happened to their offspring. Sebituane complained of many of his children having died; indeed, his tribe with which he subdued the country reduced to a mere shadow. The women complain of profuse and long-continued menstruation, such as they never experienced in the south.[2] This may account for their numbers being so little reduced by disease. Most of those who have perished fell by the spears of their enemies.

In answer to Lebeole I mentioned polygamy as a probable cause of sterility, but I now remember in the statistics of the Bakwains that the fact was brought out that the polygamists had the greatest number of children.[3] This class had the pre-eminence in comfort, which may have had some influence in determining the result. In Europe, however, the poorer classes are the most prolific. The harrassing forays of the Matibele may have been an impediment to fertility among the same class among the Bakwains. It ought also to be borne in mind that poor persons suckle their children longer than those in better circumstances. They have often nothing else to give the poor things, except roots and very undigestible fruits &c, and having strong affection for the little ones are glad to give them the 'bottle'. The richer have milk for the children, and when supplied with that [they] make fewer calls on the parent, which tends to cause a diminished flow and earlier drying up.

Women, however, in general prolong the period of suckling till the

---

[1] This may refer to the Sala of Mumbwa District, N. Rhodesia, who have a tradition that during the reign of their chieftainess Longo they were defeated by the Kololo; but the story, as told by Brelsford ('History and Customs of the Basala', *J.R. Anthrop. Inst.*, lv, 1935, p. 208) differs considerably from that given by DL.

[2] Cf. *Private J.*, 24, 47, where DL associates this phenomenon with the malarial climate.

[3] DL had taken a census among the Kwena in 1848, which showed that '157 monogamists have 193 children; and 121 polygamists 259 children' (quoted by Freeman, *A Tour in South Africa*, 1851, p. 280).

child is 3 or four years old, or untill symptoms of pregnancy appear. From the first appearance of this, & untill the child is 2 or 3 years of age, there is a separation between husband and wife among those who have more wives than one. Intercourse before the child is thus grown is considered prejudicial to the child. Occasionally the first child continues to suck a portion of his brother's milk, but grandmothers desirous of full growth to both volunteer a supply to the elder. I witnessed a case at Kuruman, in which a middle-aged woman, who had not suckled since the weaning of a daughter who bore twins (15 or 16 years), took one of them to her bosom, and yielded it a supply of milk in appearance the same as that of her daughter. The child afterwards died, being 2 years old, not in as far as I could discover from defective nutrition. I saw another case at Taung, in which the elder child, strong and hearty, was suckled by his grandmother.[1]

Indeed, it seems as if the application of the child to the breast, and desire (the mental influence being directed to the organ), will generally produce a flow of milk, at least in Africans; and I don't see why it should not in whites as well, or even in men, the structure being identical in both sexes. The fact of a man suckling a child is given as a miracle in the 'Cloud of Witnesses', the mother having been killed in the time of the persecution in Scotland.[2] Here girls desirous of having large breasts get them sucked, and milk appears in a short time, with the desired increase of size; and I have witnessed a very large developement of the mammae in men as the result of severe illness.

Machonise, one of the people of the famous chieftain Changamera, informs me that there exists a very high mountain in his country (now that of the Mashona and Matibele) called 'Limilo' (=a nose). Another, named 'Chica', is situated about north of it and 200 miles distant[3] The latter I may see in going down the Leeambye. 'Manoa'

---

[1] These cases are described more circumstantially in *Travels*, 126. Taung, visited by DL in 1842, was an LMS station among the Tlhaping, in lat. 27.34 S, long. 24.45 E (*Miss. Corr.*, 3, 42).

[2] *A Cloud of Witnesses for the royal prerogatives of Jesus Christ; or, the last speeches and testimonies of those who have suffered for the truth in Scotland since the year 1680* (1st ed., 1714; often reprinted), describes the persecution of the Covenanters during the reign of James II. I have not found in it the story of the 'miracle' mentioned by DL.

[3] Changamire, who flourished at the end of the 17th century, was a warrior chief of the Rozvi group of Shona; 'he successfully attacked the Portuguese, drove them away and destroyed some of their settlements; at the same time he conquered a number of tribes and became the paramount ruler' of the region between the

is the country where he was brought up, and he says that there are lofty mountains there, having walls built on them, *by the antients,* *of* *hewn stone.* Those who reared these edifices are said to have attempted to raise a scaffolding up to Heaven, but the wood gave way and precipitated them to the earth again. Is this a version of the tower of

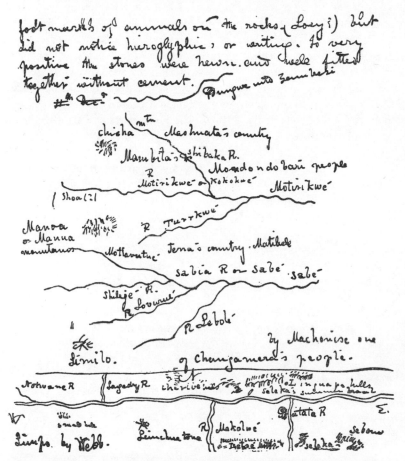

Babel, and are these walls the work of those who came to Ophir to search for gold? He, however, knows nothing of gold digging or washing. He has an idea of footmarks of animals on the rocks (Loey?),

Zambesi and Sabi rivers (Posselt, *Fact and Fiction*, 1935, pp. 137–9; Axelson, *Portuguese in S.E. Africa*, 1960, pp. 178–85, 194). Limilo and Chica I have not identified; the latter may perhaps be Chicoa (see below, p. 394).

but did not notice hieroglyphics or writing. Is very positive the stones were hewn and well fitted together without cement.[1] [*See facsimile map.*]

12th October 1855. It is extremely difficult to study in the position I now occupy, for there are perpetual calls on my attention, and every one thinks he may come and at least look at me. If I could devote my time to instruction it is probable many would learn. A most desirable missionary field is open here, and I hope God may yet send his gracious message of mercy to the desperately wicked inhabitants. A medical man has a better opportunity of ascertaining the state of people than a mere missionary. As soon as they appreciate his real object they hide their failings as much as possibly *more* good people at home, who by mere chance, of course, allow the minister always to find the Big Bible lying open on the table at that edifying chapter containing the Lion and Unicorn.[2]

The excessive heat alone prevents my departure at present. The thermometer stands at sunrise at 70°, noon 100°, sunset 92°–94°. Clouds rise in the south every afternoon, very thundery looking, and occasionally we have slight sprinkling showers. None have yet wetted the soil.

12th. In reading the speech of Sir R. Murchison today, I was 'struck all of a heap' in finding the very same views of the structure of this continent mentioned as those of Mr Bain and others.[3] After most patiently working out the idea from my observations, I felt considerable chagrin in finding others were before me; and yet I do not well know why I should feel so. I have been reasoning with myself ever since, and while inclined to believe it is the effect of too much pride, I can

[1] 'Manoa' is said in *Travels*, 662, to be another name for 'Manica', the region round Umtali and Inyanga (see below, p. 426). Debenham (*The Way to Ilala*, 108) comments: 'This would appear to be the first information about the stone walls and terraces of the Inyanga mountains of Southern Rhodesia'. Posselt (p. 140) relates briefly a Rozvi legend, similar to that given by DL, about 'the building of a wooden tower to reach to the heavens'; he says it occurs 'in different parts of Southern Rhodesia'.

[2] Cf. Psalms 22: 21 ('Save me from the lion's mouth: for thou hast heard me from the horns of the unicorns').

[3] In his presidential address to the RGS in May 1852, Murchison suggested (see *JRGS*, 1852, pp. cxxii–cxxiv) 'an original basin-like arrangement of all Africa' just as DL himself had done (see above, p. 285). Andrew Geddes Bain (1797–1864) was a S. African geologist and road engineer, whose 'explanation of the geological phenomena of the Cape Colony' formed the basis of Murchison's theory (op. cit., p. cxxii).

sympathize sincerely with my black bretheren who the other day were disregarded when placed before the lady for choice.

15th October 1855. We had good and very attentive audiences yesterday, and I expatiated with great freedom on the love of Christ in dying, from his parting address in John XVI. It cannot be these precious truths will fall to the ground. But it is perplexing to observe no effects. They assent to the truth, but 'We don't know', or 'You speak truly', is all the response. In reading accounts of South Sea missions it is hard to believe the quickness of the vegetation of the good seed, but I know several of the men, and am sure they are of unimpeachable veracity.

In trying to convey knowledge I use the magic lantern, which is everywhere extremely popular. Though they listen with apparent delight to what is said, questioning on the following night reveals almost entire ignorance of the previous lesson. O! that the Holy Spirit would enlighten them. To His soul-renewing influence my longing heart is directed. It is His word, and cannot die.

17th October 1855. The chief is gone hunting. I must be off as soon as he arrives, though the attention the people pay to God's word of truth might tempt me to stay longer. Wrote a sort of report for Dr Tidman. . . .[1]

Civilization beneficial

20th October 1855. Civilization as it increases the beauty of the human form augments the personal courage. I have been led to this opinion by many years' observation of the success attending hunting among parties of natives, Boers, and English gentlemen. The natives and Boers certainly excel Englishmen in long shots, a certain peculiarity in the atmosphere making objects appear much nearer than they actually are, and which difficulty can only be obviated by a long residence in the country. The possession, however, of personal courage by the more civilized makes full amends for his deficiency otherwise. It is not pretended that all Englishmen are so endowed; but taking the different parties of natives, Boers, and English, who go elephant shooting, as each influenced by the belief that they are equal to the task —not to mention the boasting of natives, Griquas, and Boers, as to their

---

[1] I have here omitted some detailed lists of temperatures, etc. (MS 530–2). The 'report for Dr Tidman', a lengthy discussion (dated 12.x.55) of missionary prospects in west-central Africa, is published in *Miss. Corr.*, 287–302.

own vast superiority over the whites in knowledge of the animals, correct shooting, and bravery—it has invariably turned out that the Englishman *bags* the greatest number of game.

In fact, during a residence of 15 years the highest number of elephants killed by any Boer, Griqua, or native, even when assisted by crowds of people and dogs, to the former [of] whom cows were promised for their aid, never amounted to ten. Large parties have often returned with a smaller number even as the bag of the whole, several not having killed a single elephant, while parties of Englishmen, who numerically would bear no comparison with the others, returned having killed upwards of 20 each, sometimes more than thirty, and that too without aid of dogs or natives, a single servant only excepted. The reason frankly assigned by the natives is that Englishmen alone go close up to the animal. Boers, Griquas, and natives, keep at least 100 yards off, while Englishmen go as near as 25 or 30 yards. Much of the force of the bullets of the former is spent in the air, while those of the latter, entering in full force, pierce farther, and fewer are needed. Hence elephants have been found with many wounds which, from not entering into the vitals, may be called superficial, those who had attacked them having evidently been afraid to go near enough.

The observations were made in order to form an idea of the probable number of elephants destroyed in the country, and as that animal is undoubtedly a much better test of courage than lions, it was not out of the way to draw the inference that civilization does not necessarily involve a diminution of manly courage. The same inference may be drawn from the slaughter of other animals. Although it may be admitted that individual Boers and natives have occasionally displayed great coolness in the slaughter of lions, &c, it is an undoubted fact that the English alone may be depended on not to run away and leave a companion in a difficulty.

Many marvellous stories are retailed by Boers of their encounters with lions, and travellers have sometimes eked out their narratives with what requires a large amount of credulity not to regard as apocryphal. Lichistein, for instance, tells a tale, given by the Boer himself, who executed a shot compared to which that of William Tell will bear no comparison. The wonder is great when we find a wife and two children sitting facing an enormous lion, but with heroic fortitude allowing, allowing I say, the husband and father to fire over them.[1] It

[1] The story, told by a Boer named van Wyk, appears in M. H. C. Lichtenstein, *Travels in Southern Africa* (English trans., 2 vols., 1812–15), ii. 179.

is very wonderful that these people were never afterwards heard of in the world where moral courage is so much needed.

20th October 1855. Sekeletu sent an ox for my use today. He has been hunting for some days past, and kills eilands and giraffes with the horses. The latter animals seem to thrive here, the terrible horse sickness which deprives Kuruman of that useful animal being here as yet unknown, & the tsetse seems unable to destroy the donkeys. The chief came home in the evening, and protested against my going off in such a hot sun. 'Only wait for the first shower.' This is quite reasonable, for the sun causes the thermometer to rise to 138° on a deal box, and is 108° in the waggon at midday, 96° at sunset in [the] same place. The bulb held under the tongue shows 100° or within a fraction of that number.

21st. People most attentive to the instruction offered, especially when telling of the need all have for the favour and forgiveness of the only saviour. Are very eager for the pictures of the magic lantern on week evenings, and they are a good means of conveying instruction. Feel more alive to their utterly hopeless condition so long as they continue without Christ. In travelling the heart became so benumbed I feared much I was becoming a heathen myself, but a little rest has, thank God, quickened my spiritual feelings.

22d. Excessively hot east winds have a depressing effect on the spirits. The Makololo obviate their effects by guzzling of boyaloa and singing, or rather roaring, all day long. There is a considerable amount of illness in the town, bowel complaints and rheumatism being the chief diseases.

Ntlaria[1] and some others sat some time with me tonight, and the conversation having been drawn quite naturally from enquiries respecting certain eclipses of the sun & moon to the other world where Jesus reigns supreme, they let me see my attempts to enlighten them were not without effect. Many of the children talked about the strange things brought to their ears, and the old men, when asked about them, shew a little of that opposition which generally precedes success by saying, 'Do we know what he is talking about?', &c. Ntlaria and others complain of treacherous memories, but surely all is not lost; the Holy Spirit will not let his faithful fall to the ground, though I may not see the fruits. Here they still possess the tradition of the builders of Babel, but end it without the confusion of tongues by the catastrophe of the fall of the building & loss of many lives. Is this, and the tale of Solo-

[1] One of 'the principal men of the Makololo' (*Travels*, 515).

mon's judgement on the harlots, not preserved in tradition because it is part & parcel of the word which liveth and abideth for ever?

Moral Status

23d October 1855. It would not be fair, in estimating the moral status of this people, to enumerate their bad actions only. If the same were done in England, the lower classes of that country would appear worse than they are here. It seems better to compare the actual amount of goodness in each class, the badness in both being rather exceptional than otherwise. From intimate knowledge of the poorer classes in England and Scotland, I have no hesitation in ascribing to them a very admirable amount of kindly feeling towards each other, which is manifested on all occasions of real necessity. There is a constant stream of benevolence flowing from the rich to the poor, but this, large as it is, cannot be compared with the unostentatious attentions of the poor to each other. Of this disinterested kindness of the native poor to each other there exists only a vestige here. If one gives food or anything else to a poor person, it is always with the hope of being repaid with interest, & should no hope of payment appear in the borrower (we may call him) falling sick, the lender would without blushing take back what he could.

The poor of this country might be fairly compared with the Jewish money-lenders of England, and by no means with the common run of the poorer classes. A poor person who has no relatives will seldom be supplied with water in illness, and when death ensues will certainly be dragged out to be devoured by the hyaenas, instead of being buried. Only relatives of the deceased will condescend to touch the dead body. Food is given to servants in consideration only of services expected. Boys and girls may be seen undergoing absolute starvation when their masters or rather owners are scarce of food. No one else will give a morsel to the poor wretched skeletons, public opinion being that such generosity without hope of an equivalent is stark folly.

An interesting-looking girl came to my waggon in a state of entire nudity, and almost a skeleton. Giving her a little clothing and food I enquired after her owner, and offered to provide for her if he would allow her to come and live near us. He would 'allow me to feed her and make her fat, and then take her away'. I protested against his heartlessness in expecting service from one whom he refused to feed. She did not again appear clothed, and in a day or two was lost sight of.

She had gone out a little way from the town and, too weak to return, had been cruelly left to perish.[1]

In another case a poor boy appeared going to the water for a drink. On enquiry I found the master belonged to a party notorious for starving their dependants. He proposed that I should fatten this one too for his private benefit. I expatiated in public on the meanness of wishing me to do what he would not from humanity or self-interest do for himself, and said that though I was willing to assist the poor skeleton with the little I could spare, I could not submit to do it only to prolong his misery, as on his return he would certainly be starved again. If he wished to kill the boy, let it be known as his act. Sekeletu decided that the owner should give up his alleged right rather than destroy the child. He was so far gone as to be in the cold stage of starvation, but soon came round on a little milk three or four times a day, and other food when I have it; and I shall be able to hand him over to Sekeletu when I depart, certain he will recieve at least enough of food.

This act, little as it may seem, would assuredly not be performed by a single individual in the tribe, and the majority look upon it as proof of a soft corner in my cranium. I might keep him as my own servant, or slave rather, but I have invariably declined such, even when offered as presents from chiefs, believing it better to give a negative and state my objections to the entire system than to take a protégé by giving the slave liberty afterwards. To the donor one appears as if acquiescing in the slave system, and the protégé almost always turns out ill, for being much carressed by kind friends afterwards the poor head becomes turned and top-heavy—an effect rather too common among stronger races when subjected to sudden or great elevation.

The poor manufacturing classes are also remarkable for great independance of feeling. There are of course many exceptions to this, but these are decidedly not so numerous among them as among the classes immediately above them, & among whom bribery and other forms of venality flourishes. The astonishing efforts they make for the support of relatives, or before misfortune can bring them down from their own status of respectability, I have often witnessed in Scotland with patriotic pride. I have never seen anything like [it] among the heathen. Very few are above begging in the most abject manner,

---

[1] 'She was a captive from another tribe, and had been neglected by the man who claimed her' (Travels, 511). The incident, or at least one very like it, had occurred in October 1853 (see Private J., 258).

though they may have no need of any assistance. All are disposed to take advantage of any one's necessities in the most unmerciful manner. There is little manliness, and no gallantry. The women are made prematurely old by toil and exposure to the sun. Miss Martineau would among them have been a withered old hag many years ago.[1] It is scarcely possible there can be love where there are perpetual changes from one husband to another and every woman is married. In their public dancing songs a man will say all the impudent things he can about his own wife. Even Sebituane did so. I listened last night to a dancing rhyme. It was nearly in the words of this doggerel ditty,

> Where's the woman dare jilt me,
> However sharp her tongue may be.
> Where did she throw away her shield?
> She can do nothing now but yield,

and they roar away at this for hours together.

Nor have they any of that respect for law and order which are found among our own poorer classes. They are kept in order by fear alone, and when they are taken on forays against their neighbours every one, from the highest to the lowest, is for the time an undisguised thief. Life is destroyed with a callousness which I cannot understand.

In confounding proximity to these vices, which are really not too darkly drawn, a little child just able to walk never goes near a company of men eating without getting a handful, and, in eating meat, pieces are handed generally to all the company, as if they were of a most generous disposition.

There is a wonderful mixture of good and evil. They have been remarkably kind to me. The conclusion I have come to is that they are a strange mixture of good and evil, as everywhere else, the evil predominating. Shew great forbearance and justice sometimes, yet sometimes also will kill the parents of children, in order that the latter may not desert service and flee to the former. But this happens only among Makololo.

The servitude rendered from time immemorial by the poorer to the richer classes cannot be called slavery, though akin to it. The poor man is called a child of the rich man, and their intercourse is on a sort

---

[1] Harriet Martineau (1802–76) was a well-known writer on political economy, population problems, etc. She is also mentioned in *Miss. Corr.*, 194, where DL refers to his wife's 'frequent confinements' (17.iii.52 Tidman).

of equality. At this Mr Burchel wondered, from the impression that they were slaves.[1] The rich man lends the inferior his cattle, and gives or lends him and his wife clothes, but the poor man can leave the master and transfer his services to another, and all that can be done is to resume possession of the cattle and clothes. The poor man has his own garden, hut, &c, and eats his own produce, having the advantage [of] recourse to his master in case of need. The services rendered are assistance in sewing & preparing skins, in erecting cattle pens, in service in case of going to visit other towns, or in war as squires. The wife assists the mistress in the same way. The arrangement is absolutely necessary for the poor who cannot conveniently be independant. It is like slavery only in no specified wages being paid, but the obligations are well understood.

25th. Observed a Great Senegal swallow this morning, flying swiftly and alone in a straight line away to the east or F.N.E. Great numbers of two species of drongo shrikes not paired walk about everywhere. The young pallahs are now seen in abundance. September is called Pallane.[2] Lions when old and toothless condescend to eat mice even, and so do alligators. The charadrius sometimes alights on the latter reptile, I know not for what purpose. Abundance of black head fork-tailed swallow appear.

26th October 1855. The leaves of the boabob pounded and mixed with a little water form an excellent poultice for indolent ulcers.

People of Sebolamakoea attacked village of Kainko in revenge for the late expedition. Those of Lechulathebe killed several people of a village of Bapalleñ,[3] Sekeletu's subjects, on a similar principle.

27th Octr '55. A continued rain commenced during the night, and though not heavy holds on through the day. The wind is from the N.E., as it always was on like occasions at Kolobeng. The rainy season may therefore be said to have fairly begun, and I must get ready to go.

Sekeletu called Ponuane, to enquire about Mosioatunya, which I

[1] William John Burchell (1781–1863, explorer and naturalist) was describing conditions among the Tlhaping, whom he had visited in 1812. He comments on the obvious distinction between rich and poor, but does not speak of slavery except in regard to prisoners-of-war, and then merely to dismiss the term as inappropriate, considering the way in which they were treated (*Travels in the Interior of Southern Africa*, 1822–4, ii. 347–8, 535–6).

[2] Phalane (dimin. of *phala*, impala) is the Tswana name for October (Brown, *Dictionary*, 486).

[3] Phaleng, a servile people of Kgalagadi stock living in the northern parts of Ngamiland.

proposed to pass, carrying the canoes on land till past the falls.[1] He says the distance which must be traversed before we should reach smooth water would be as far as from this to the falls of Gonye, or one hundred miles. The river seems to enter a narrow fissure in a broad chain of mountains, and most of the sides of this fissure are perpendicular, the raging rushing stream below appearing like a white cable ten or fifteen yards broad. The natives who have ventured to look down into the frightful chasm say they descended from the mountain sides towards the stream on their hams, afraid of sliding down the precipice, and when they came to the edge of the gulph their eyes became dim when they attempted to look down, and they fled for fear the commencing giddiness should make them roll down into the chafing dashing waters. It must be very deep in order to carry the large body of water of the Leeambye. It seemed, they say, a white cord very far down, which could be crossed by those accustomed to it; others would perish. It seems as if I must go to the Loenge and descend it to the Zambesi. The carriage of canoes for 100 miles could with difficulty be accomplished among people who hate the Makololo.

In the afternoon Sekeletu brought Sequebu (a Letibele) and Konyata to me, as the persons who were to accompany me down the river. Sekuebu knows the country well,[2] and thinks we had better go near to Mosioatunya, and instead of carrying canoes trust to Senamane's generosity to give one.[3] If he will not, we can buy one from the many tribes who use them on the Zambesi. When the chief found we must travel overland some distance, he sent and bought two tame riding oxen for me.

Sunday, 28th October 1855. Feeling it might be my last opportunity with this people, I felt very anxious to convey to them a clear view of Christ's holy gospel and their need of his mercy and love in

[1] Ponwane (see p. 13) 'had lately headed a foray' in that direction (*Travesl*, 507).

[2] 'Sekwebu had been captured by the Matebele when a little boy, and the tribe in which he was a captive, had migrated to the country near Tete: he had travelled along both banks of the Zambesi several times, and was intimately acquainted with the dialects spoken there' (*Travels*, 513). He accompanied DL from Quelimane to Mauritius, where, unnerved by his experiences of sea travel, he committed suicide by drowning (*Fam. Letters*, ii. 290-1; *Travels*, 682-3). Konyata (Kanyata) had stayed behind with the other Kololo at Tete, and returned to Barotseland with DL in 1860; he 'was the only real Makololo of the party; and he, in virtue of his birth, had succeeded to the chief place on the death of Sekwebu' (*Narrative*, 156, 158, 175, etc.).

[3] Sinamane was a Toka (Tonga) chief living on Chilombe island in the Zambesi, near the Sebungwe confluence. DL first met him in 1860 (*Narrative*, 315).

view of our future state (John iii: 16–19). This precious message cannot & will not, I firmly believe, fall to the ground. May Almighty God command a blessing.

30th October 1855. The black bird which drives away crows, and is a species of crow itself, has begun to build or rather repair the old nests on the macuiri tree[1] near the town. About a dozen fly out and in [of] five or six nests in great excitement; these seem a mere bundle of sticks, about a foot in diameter, loosely thrown together. They seem not to migrate at all.

Mamire came yesterday to laela.[2] He said, 'You go among people who cannot be trusted, as we have used them badly, but you go with a different message from any they ever heard before, and Jesus will be with you and help you, though among enemies. And if he carries you safely and brings you and Ma-Robert back again, I shall say he has bestowed a great favour on me. May we obtain a path whereby we may visit and be visited by other tribes and by white men.' On telling him my fears that he was still inclined to follow the old plan of marauding, which produced 'want of sleep only', and that he from his influential position was especially guilty, he acknowledged all, too freely for my taste, but seemed aware the old system was far from right, even when viewed apart from the future judgement. Mentioned my design to take some ivory, on account of all my money being expended and I should have nothing to give those who went with me to endeavour to open a path by means of canoes. He replied that the whole ivory in the country belonged to me, and if I left any it would be of my own accord. 'Truly a man wishes to appear among his friends, after long absence, with something of his own to shew, so you must take as much as you can, and Sekeletu must furnish men to carry it.' This, from one who has as much influence as any in the tribe, is a proof of confidence in my integrity very gratifying.

I intend to appropriate most of what I may take to return presents, and some to purchase others in England, among which I must not forget the newly invented bullet used by the Yankees for killing whales, as it will enable the Makololo to secure great numbers of elephants. It is formed of gutta percha, with an explosive mixture enclosed.

[1] Tswana *motswiri*, leadwood, *Combretum imberbe* (Miller, *Woody Plants*, 61).

[2] 'To say farewell'. Mamire (Mamidi) was Sekeletu's maternal uncle, and also his step-father. After Sekeletu's death he tried to usurp the chieftainship, but was defeated by Mpololo and fled to Letsholathebe, who put him to death (see *Private J.*, 236 n.1, for fuller details and sources).

XIV

DEPARTURE FOR QUELIMANE

Descent of the Leeambye

Sesheke, 9th November 1855. Left Linyanti on the 3d current, accompanied by Sekeletu and 200 followers, who are of course all fed at his expense.[1] The principal men (Lebeole, Ntlarie, Nkuatlele, &c) are in the party. Had a long discussion with Mothibe, S.'s father-in-law, on the new system. He parried the imputation of guilt by every possible subterfuge. He threw it towards the Boers, the Matibele, every other tribe except their own. 'Teach them to lay down their arms first, then we shall live in peace. Have all the white men recieved the gospel?', &c &c.[2] He heard some wholesome truths, however, and we parted good friends.

We passed through the patch of tsetse by night, and had some of the most vivid lightning I ever saw. When absent it was so pitchy dark the horses and men were completely blind, and a new flash would reveal all taking different directions. The horses trembled and cried out, the men laughed and stumbled against each other. The pelting rain came on and completed the confusion. Having passed several fires we were at last compelled to go to one. It felt miserably cold after the intense heat of the day. Wet to the skin, we lay down under a bush, and Sekeletu kindly covered me with his own blanket, lying during the remainder of the night uncovered himself.[3] All shew great kindness. It is a pity that such men must perish by the advance of civilization. God grant that ere the ruthless Colonists advance so far the saving gospel be recieved as a solace for the soul in death. If they must perish, as certain races of animals, before others, by the decree of Heaven, we would seem to be under the same 'terrible necessity' in our Caffre wars as the American Proffessor of Chemistry said *he* was to dismember the man he murdered.[4]

[1] '. . . and he took cattle for this purpose from every station we came to' (*Travels*, 515).

[2] Mothibe, as a youth, was once thrashed by some Boers who had 'attacked' his family, presumably while the Kololo were still in the south (*Travels*, 514). He is often mentioned in *Private J*. Nkuatlele I cannot identify.

[3] This blanket was subsequently lost (or stolen) on the ship taking DL from Quelimane to Mauritius (*Miss. Corr.*, 325).

[4] In 1849 John White Webster (1795–1850), Professor of Chemistry and Mineralogy in Harvard University since 1827, had murdered and then completely

Swallows in flocks roost in the reeds every night. They are both dock and fork tails, and certainly emigrants. Saw some this morning collecting on trees as if preparing for flight. It must be southwards, but perhaps not. The white-backed Senegal crow extends as far as Kuruman and perhaps the Orange River, yet does not breed in the south, nor even here. This seems proof that it is migratory from the north. The vulture is not known to breed here. The brown falcon or kite never. Its wing feathers are often much worn, as if it had come off a long journey. I once saw a nearly full grown one at Mabotsa.[1]

21st November 1855. Having left Sesheké on Monday the 13th[2] currt., we sailed down to the confluence of the Chobe, to the town & island of the Makololo called of Mparia, from which Licuane was expelled. It is on a low hill composed of an igneous rock having chrystals of serpentine(?)[3] diffused through it, each coated with a pellicle of green copper ore. Proceeding down the river next day, we were detained some hours by a strong east wind raising waves which threatened to swamp the canoes. In the evening we reached the village of Molele (at Nampene isld.),[4] at the beginning of the rapids, and there were obliged to leave the canoes and proceed along the bank on foot. The rapids extend all the way down to Mosioatunya, a distance of at least 30 miles. In the evening we remained at the village of Nambowe, opposite an island called Chondo.[5]

dissected an importunate creditor. Convicted and sentenced to death, he stated in a written confession: 'I saw nothing but the alternative of a successful removal and concealment of the body, on the one hand, and of infamy and destruction on the other' (Bemis, *Report of the Case of John W. Webster*, Boston 1850, p. 566).

[1] Where he had lived as a missionary in 1844–5 (see above, p. 232).

[2] *Sic*; correctly, '12th'. (The paragraphs beginning here, and ending 'now lives with Moselekatse', p. 329, have been published, though with occasional errors of transcription, in *The Victoria Falls*, ed. Clark, 1952, pp. 24–5.)

[3] Query in MS; 'crystals of quartz' (*Travels*, 516). Mparia (Mpalela) is the large island opposite Kazungula, at the Zambesi-Chobe confluence; DL describes it as 'four miles long and about one mile broad' (*Narrative*, 306). Licuane (Leswane) was a Subiya chief, who after having been put to flight by Sebetwane was invited back and then treacherously murdered (Sillery, *The Bechuanaland Protectorate*, 1952, p. 191).

[4] Molele was 'a tall old Batoka, who was proud of having formerly been a great favourite with Sebituane' (*Narrative*, 264); Nampene island is 'about ten miles' below Mpalela (*Travels*, 517).

[5] Chundu, lat. 17.48 S, long. 25.41 E (Livingstone SE–35 NW). Nambowe was 'one of the Matebele or Zulus' who had fled to seek refuge with the Kololo 'from the anger of Moselekatse' (*Narrative*, 262).

Victoria Falls

Next day we reached the village of Moroa-Mosia at the island of Sekote, which is called Kalai,[1] and on the day following we went down to see the falls of Mosioatunya or, as it was called antiently, Shungue.[2] After 20 minutes sail we viewed for the first time the vapour or, as it is appropriately called, 'smoke', arising exactly as when large tracts of grass are burned off. Five columns rose and bended in the direction of the wind against a low ridge covered with trees, and seemed at this distance (about 6 miles) to mingle with the clouds. They were coloured white below and higher up became dark, probably as the vapour condensed and returned in showers.

Having got small and very light canoes farther down, we went in the care of persons well acquainted with the rapids, and sailed swiftly down to an island situated at the middle and on the northern verge of the precipice over which the water roars. At one time we seemed to be going right to the gulph, but though I felt a little tremour I said nothing, believing I could face a difficulty as well as my guides.

The falls are singularly formed. They are simply the whole mass of the Zambesi waters rushing into a fissure or rent made right accross the bed of the river. In other falls we have usually a great change of

[1] About eight miles above the Victoria Falls, 'near Palm Island and Kandahar Island' (Clark, *The Victoria Falls*, 24 n.), i.e. in lat. 17.52 S, long. 25.47 E; DL gives the same lat., but long. 25.41 E (*Travels*, 524, 686). Sekote (Sekute), 'a Batonga chief' (below, p. 328; cf. *Travels*, 517), is described by Jalla (*Litaba*, 32) as a Leya, and by Clark (p. 70) as of Subiya origin, though settled among the Leya (for whom see p. 328). Moroa-Mosia, 'son of Mosia', seems to have been merely a village headman.

[2] 'Shongwe' (*Travels*, 518). 'Mosi-oa-tunya is the Makololo name, and means smoke sounding; Seongo or Chongwe, meaning the Rainbow, or the place of the Rainbow, was the more ancient term they bore' (*Narrative*, 250). The earliest record I have found of DL's suggesting their present name is in a letter to Lord Clarendon, 19.iii.56: 'I would fain call them the "smoke-sounding falls of Victoria"; but it smacks of impudence, rather, in a private person to make free with Her Majesty's name' (*PP England*, 1857, Sess. 2, XLIV, 63; cf. also *JRGS*, 1857, p. 375: 23.v.56 Murchison). But on 13.ix.55 he had already written to Maclear: 'I would have named the Tanganyenka after our Queen had I gone. There is a bit of pure loyalty & respect, I being in a line to which royal favour can never come. . . . As for Dilolo, I cannot muster courage to name it Victoria, it is too little . . . I may yet have an opportunity of offering a tribute of respect to the Royal Lady. It will look better in a map of Africa than in frozen regions which henceforth nobody will ever go back to see.'

level both in the bed of the river and ajacent country, and after the leap the river is not much different from what it was above the falls; but here the river, flowing rapidly among numerous islands and from 800 to 1,000 yards wide, meets a rent in its bed at least 100 feet deep and at right angles with its course, or nearly due east and west, leaps into it, and becomes a boiling white mass at the bottom ten or twelve yards broad.[1] Its course is changed also. It runs, or rather rolls and wriggles, from east to west untill it reaches what above was its left bank, then turns a corner, and follows or rather is guided by the fissure away in its usual route of S.E. and by E.

The lips of the rent are in some parts not more than fifty or sixty feet apart. The southern lip is straight & except at the west corner, which seems inclined from a split in it to fall into the gulph, is straight and level with the general bed of the river above. Its wall is quite perpendicular. The northern lip is jagged, several pieces having fallen off, and five or six parts have the edge worn down a foot or two. In these, when the water is low, as it now is, the falls divide themselves, and from each ascends a column of vapour which rises from 200 to 250 ft. Three of these falls throw more water each now, at low water, than the falls of Stonebyres do when the Clyde is flooded.[2] At the parts where portions have fallen in the fissure it seemed 150 feet wide. The entire length is certainly not less than 600 yards, and there are at present at least 400 yards of water, which looks about 2 feet thick. The measurements are given as approximations only.

My companions amused themselves by throwing stones into the gulph, marvelling that a stone an inch or two in diameter should disappear before reaching the foaming waters. The depth below, which recieves the whole body of the water, must be very deep. The eastern half of the rent, which recieves most water, never exposes its bottom. In peering down over the edge we could see only a dense white cloud with two rainbows on it. A smart shower from the ascending columns falls when the wind shifted eastwards, and soon drenched us to the skin. This falls almost constantly on the southern lip, and a thick bank of evergreen trees enjoy perpetual showers. Several little streams

[1] '... fifteen or twenty yards' (*Travels*, 520). In 1860, after more careful measurement, DL gave the width of the Falls as 'a little over 1860 yards', and their height as 310 feet (*Expedition*, 396; *Narrative*, 253). These figures agree closely with those nowadays accepted (Clark, op. cit., 18, 20).

[2] Stonebyres is one of the four falls of the River Clyde in the vicinity of Lanark, about 30 miles SE of Glasgow (*Bartholomew's Survey Gazetteer of the British Isles*, 1932, pp. 160, 646).

are formed and run down that side, but never reach more than half way. The ascending vapour swills them up into the air with it. When the river is full, the noise is said to be terrific and the vapour seen ten miles off. The water is said to well up in surges to the opposite lip.

Returning with Sekeletu on the following day, I planted a lot of peach and apricot stones and coffee seeds on the island,[1] which being already covered with trees seemed well adapted to be a nursery. The spot selected for experiment was one which is visited with a fine sprinkling of the condensed vapour many times daily. The parts nearer the gulph are adapted for water plants only, and a curious sort of polypus flourishes. We gave directions for the construction of a fence to prevent the hippopotami from treading down our seedlings, and as this climate requires tender plants to be frequently moistened I have no doubt but Mosioatunya will prove a more careful nurseryman than any of the Makololo would be.

The chiefs Sekote, Mokuine,[2] and Licuane, appropriated the three larger falls as places at which they prayed to the gods or departed spirits. The roar of the waters were well fitted to inspire feelings of awe. Sekote was a Batonga chief, and he and Licuane enjoyed despotic sway over the fords of the river. On Kalai, as Sekote's island was called, we saw the grave of his father surrounded by 70 large elephants' tusks stuck in the ground, the points turned inwards. About 30 others were placed as sort of gravestones over the members of his family. They think, in cases of sickness, that the departed are angry with them for not offering food &c &c. There were fifteen skulls placed on poles, of persons who had been executed, and a pot which when opened they believed would inflict death on those they hated.[3]

As the island is surrounded by a strong current, these Batonga felt themselves quite secure, and excelled in pride and cruelty. A party of Bamangwato were, on pretence of ferrying over the river, ferried on to an island and cruelly left to perish. They took possession of their wives and children. Sebitane arranged better, having induced the chief to sit by him untill all were over on the other side. Sekote having ferried the

[1] Now known as Livingstone island; originally called Kazeruka, and named 'Garden Island' by the natives because of DL's plantation (*Narrative*, 258, 259). On revisiting it in 1860 he found his trees destroyed by hippopotami; the same fate befell others he then again planted (ibid., 259).

[2] Mukuni, chief of the Leya, a people closely akin to the Tonga. There is a village of his name in lat. 17.58 S, long. 25.56 E (Livingstone SE–35 NW).

[3] 'The Batoka believe that Sekote had a pot of medicine buried here, which, when opened, would cause an epidemic in the country' (*Travels*, 518).

Matibele over to attack Sebitane, the latter expelled him from his island, and he now lives with Mosilikatse.

(The system of government pursued by these negroes was wonderfully like that of despotic governments everywhere, viz. of extensive espionage. Every relative of the chief is a spy, and no one dare answer a question on any subject whatever. They often try to appear stupid, and afterwards indulge in loud laughter in giving a minute account of their success in deception. It is well this detestable system is done away with here. However bad the Makololo may be, they have generally a manly frankness in answering questions. Many other circumstances lead to the conclusion that God has been smoothing our way before us.)

The scenery on the river is very fine. There are numerous islands in its bed, and all covered with sylvan vegetation. There is a distinct physionomy in trees. How different the great burly boabab looks from the graceful feathery palm. Then the Mohonono, with its cedar of Lebanon or fir-like form, how pleasantly it contrasts with the cypress form, dark leaves and pink-coloured delicious fruit [of the motsouri].[1] The forms of the date palm, with its airy elegantly-curved fronds and vivid fresh green, contrast so beautifully with the rounded masses of many evergreens it is delightful to look upon them.

The people here leave the fruit trees in their gardens and do not level them indiscriminately as do the Bechuanas. Of these, the Mamosho is a very agreable fruit, having the edible portion as large as common apricots. The Motsouri has a delicious acid. The Mohorohoro or Setokamane, nux vomica, boito, has a grateful pulp between the seeds, which latter form the deadly poison; when swallowed whole they purge violently. The Manéko is a curious woody-rinded fruit split into five parts, and about the size of a walnut; the woody rind when chewed emits a large quantity of mucus of sugary taste, resembling the sap of the elm. The Motsintsela is a lofty large tree; when the fruit is pounded in a mortar and mixed with water it is nutritious and pleasant. Moshugo or Moshuka has yellow pulp among 4 seeds, which tastes exactly like ripe pears. Mohoho is like grapes, but not very pleasant. Nju, square pods, edible, an arborescent legume.[2]

The people of Mokuine actually plant many of the fruit trees in

[1] Words in brackets supplied from *Travels*, 519. Mohonono (mogonono)= *Terminalia sericea*, assegai wood (Miller, *Woody Plants*, 64); for motsouri, see above, p. 5. Both names are of Tswana origin.

[2] Of the plants mentioned, mamosho = moshomosho (*Travels*, 260; see above, p. 5); mohorohoro = *Strychnos spinosa*, Kaffir orange, also *S. cocculoides* and other

their gardens. I know not another instance in Africa. The soil is a rich reddish sand, from the detritous of a basaltic rock.

Monyelenyele, pretty black kidney-shaped berries which yield a strong smelling oil with which people anoint their bodies; the bean grows like as on the stigma of pink flower and is eaten in times of scarcity, but is unpleasant in taste. Moretologa, intensely sharp acid if unripe; very pretty scarlet with a dash of pink; seeds pounded yield a sort of oily pulp, like brain, which people put on their heads to protect them from the sun's rays. Mokucong or [moshoma][1] is different from that on the Zouga: unpleasantly astringent, though sweet in taste; canoe's wood. Molondo = a lesser kind of Masuka, and more delicate in taste and rind. Sombo, fruit of a large tree.[2]

Part with Sekeletu

Sekeletu, Lebeole, Moriantsane, Nkuatlele, &c &c, pressed me to take as many tusks as I chose. If any were left, the leaving would be my act, for all were mine. I therefore resolved, as a means of serving them, to take a list of those things they needed most, and purchase them with what ivory could be carried. It is intended by this means to promote legitimate commerce and work out the extinction of the trade in slaves carried on by the Mambari among the Batoka in the east.

The Makololo are not inept scholars in learning the value of ivory. They proposed preventing the Mambari from crossing the Leeambye for this quarter, but as the people to whom they come are much in need of hoes, I proposed that such should be purchased from the Batoka and Banyeti of Moriantsane, and that the Makololo by purchasing all the ivory would both supply the eastern Batoka with implements so much needed and render the Mambari visits unprofitable, for slaves alone will not pay. The people to whom we are going would not part with either children or ivory for cloth, but the Mambari, discovering their need of hoes, went north to the smiths above referred to, purchased

spp.; maneko = *Thespesia garckeana*; motsintsela = *Berchemia discolor*; moshuka = *Uapaca kirkiana*, wild loquat (Miller, 50, 56, 70; Wild, *Botanical Dictionary*, 132, 134). Nju is described in *Travels*, 535, as 'beans, which are contained in a large square pod'. Mohoho I have not identified.

[1] Blank space in MS; name supplied from *Expedition*, 172.

[2] Of the plants named in this paragraph, monyelenyele = *Ochna pulchra*; moretologa = *Ximenia caffra*, sour plum; mokucong = *Diospyros mespiliformis*, African ebony; (mu)sombo = *Syzigium guineense* (Miller, 12, 58, 67; Wild, 75, 107, 130, 139). Molondo I have not identified; it may be *Uapaca nitida* (cf. Wild, 134, though it is not listed there as a vernacular name).

hoes, and then got their will of both ivory and children. Having pointed out to the Makololo that it was their interest to put a stop to this branch of slavery by preoccupation of the market, they entered eagerly into the project, and instructions are sent to the smiths to furnish a large number of hoes. They do furnish many, indeed all now used by the Makololo, as tribute, and a little encouragement in the way of payment will induce them to exert themselves still more. If the Makololo can be furnished with European goods, I have not the smallest doubt but the visits of the Mambari will be prevented.

In order to lead to the formation of commercial habits, I now, contrary to my usual custom, have undertaken to act as agent in the selling of this ivory. There are fifteen large tusks, and 6 or 7 smaller. The large are intended to purchase the articles contained in the following list, the small to be expended defraying the outlay incurred by such a large body of followers as are necessary for carrying them. There are at present 115 men. The majority are employed in carrying provisions for those who bear the ivory and my little luggage. If loaded as the carriers of traders are, fewer would be needed, but heavy burdens produce much mortality, which to any one acquainted with the animal part of man is criminal. They are chiefly Batoka and a few Barotse. Sekuebu (a Letibele Mokololo) and Kanyata are the chief men, but there are several inferior officers.[1] I intend to make some payment to them all. The popularity of the first journey had a good effect on the volunteering for this. Of the two rifles mentioned in the list, one is to be mine in consideration of my services. I accept it on the principle that work paid for is invariably much more valued than when given gratis.

List of articles to be purchased with the proceeds of the sale of Sekeletu's ivory.[2] I beg, in case of anything having happened to me, him to whom this ivory and list may come to send as many as may be procurable.

1. Two superior double barrelled rifles, complete
2. The newly invented bullets for shooting whales (American), to be applied to shooting elephants
3. Small and buck shot

---

[1] DL, first given 114 men, was joined at the Falls by a Kololo headman, Monaheng, who was put in command of 'a large number' of Mukuni's Toka. His other attendants included some Najwa, under Mosisinyane, and 'a small party of Bashubia and Barotse under Tuba Mokoro' (*Travels*, 526, 533).

[2] The list that follows is not given in *Travels*. For what DL actually brought back, in 1860, see *Expedition*, 261.

4. Fine powder
5. Percussion caps
6. Powder horns, one for Lebeole
7. One large Colt's revolver
8. Common powder and lead
9. Black cloth with long wool, such as is used in making gun cover
10. White Spanish blankets, round figures in corners
11. 2 pairs moleskin trowsers, and
12. 2 shooting jackets (strong moleskin)
13. Blue check shirts (strong)
14. Blue naval caps & wide-awake hats
15. Coarse black cloth with white selvage
16. Dishes (tin), cups, and cooking pot
17. Dark blue gambroon jacket
18. A soldier's uniform coat or jacket
19. Shoes, black and brown, my size
20. Small sugar rollers, for expressing juice (of sugar cane)
21. Brass wire, thick & triangular
22. Beads, blue (as specimen), green, pink
23. Large white neck beads
24. At Quilimane: horses, pigs, all sorts of domestic animals as dogs, ducks, turkies, fowls, pigeons, &c; rabbits
25. Checked trowsers, cotton & woolen stockings
26. Folding knives
27. Gowns for wives
28. Knives with ivory handles marked S. & D.L.
29. One double-barrelled pistol for Lebeole
30. One long single-barrelled pistol for Moriantsane
31. Small brass chains & common tinder boxes
32. Iron rocking chair
33. Green spectacles
34. Fine copper wire

Measurement for clothes:

Inside the leg	33 inches
Entire length outside leg	$42\frac{1}{2}$–43
Round waist	30
Round chest	36
Centre of back to elbow	17
Do. to wrist	31
Round wrist	6

Sekeletu presented at Sesheke 10 slaughter oxen and 3 riding oxen for our use on the journey, and 3 subsequently,[1] besides large quantities of corn & earth nuts. At Sesheke, too, a kind of large coarse beads and some hoes were presented, as these are much valued among the tribes to whom we are going. Everything that they could give, as butter, milk, &c, was freely bestowed, untill I was quite ashamed to recieve more. I have reason to be thankful to Him who moved their hearts to liberality, and to them, to serve them in both temporal and spiritual things.

The Lekone

On 20th Novr. I parted with the Makololo and came to the Lekone,[2] where we are obliged to wait for some provisions which have been sent for. The Lekone is a fine little stream, equal to the Kuruman, and flows in a most lovely open valley, bounded on the S.E. & N.W. by a low range of hills covered with beautiful green fruit & other trees. The former are not cut down in the gardens as elsewhere, and give them a pretty orchard-like appearance. It is excellent for pasturage, and once contained a large population which, relying on numbers, ventured to attack Sebituane & were dispersed. There were so many cattle the Makololo would not take possession of the herds of goats and sheep. The tsetse has been brought into some deserted parts by buffaloes since, and the insect exists all around this. Ramoshobotuane[3] was here, but all were ordered to remove to the river to serve as gaurds against the Matibele. The island on which my goods were placed is about a mile from the falls of Mosioatunya.

23d Nov. Having remained a day at Lekone, we proceeded by night on account of the tsetse, and seemed to travel on the high bank of the ancient bed of the Zambesi. It and the opposite ridge or bank was about 400 feet high, and the bed rocky and rough, the bank worn into those peculiar ruts which the tide leaves in soft mud. The Lekone now winds in it in the opposite direction from the river, betokening a

[1] '. . . presented ten slaughter-cattle and three of the best riding oxen he could purchase among his people' (*JRGS*, 1857, p. 358); '. . . twelve oxen – three of which were accustomed to being ridden upon' (*Travels*, 516).

[2] DL 'bade adieu' to Sekeletu at Kalai 'and proceeded northwards to the Lekone' (*Travels*, 518, 526), which according to him joins the Zambesi about 6–8 miles above Kalai (cf. below, and *Narrative*, 262). The Lukuni, 'just behind Livingstone Airport', is in fact a feeder of the Sinde, which joins the Zambesi in lat. 17.50 S, long. 25.44 E (D.C., Livingstone, 15.i.1962; Livingstone SE–35 NW).

[3] 'Father of Moshobotwane' (see above, p. 299.1).

change of level at the time of the Mosioatunya rent. It falls into the Zambesi about 6 miles above Sekote island.

The level of the lower portion of the Lekone is about 200 feet above that of the Zambesi at Mosioatunya, and considerably more than that of Linyanti. Consequently, when the river flowed along this bed instead of through the rent, the whole country between the ridge north of Sesheke and Nchokotsa, and thence westward round and south of Lake Ngami and northwards to Libebe,[1] was one large fresh water lake. There is evidence that such was the case wherever ant-eaters make deep holes on the plains south of the Lake, for they turn out fresh water shells identical with those now existing in the Lake and Zambesi, and the whole of the surface indicated is paved with a bed of tufa more or less soft according as covered with soil or exposed to atmospheric influences. That the same influence opened out another immense lake in the Barotse valley, which was probably connected by the Nyenko side with the other lake, is apparent in the fizzure-like form of the falls of Gonye, and a tradition of the waters having burst out long ago and killed many of the inhabitants. There is no tradition, so far as I could discover, of any earthquake having happened. The event is probably too antient for that. Yet information of any remark-able event is often transmitted in names. There is, however, not a town Earthquake or Sam-shake-the-ground among them. Yet they retain a tradition which looks like the building of the tower of Babel; but it ends in the bold builders getting cracked crowns by the fall of the scaffolding.

Moyara's village

24th. We remained a day at the village of Moyara.[2] Here the bed in which the Lekone flows trends away to the east. Our course is more to the north-east. The country is rocky and rough; soil red sand, covered with beautiful green trees which at present yield abundance of fruit. The grass is excellent for cattle, and supported thousands before Sebituane captured them and carried off all the younger population. They attacked him first, believing their numbers would secure success,

[1] Nchokotsa (Chukutsa) Pan, lat. 27.17 S, long. 25.00 E (WAC 3274), is a well-known watering-place in the Kalahari Desert, on the route to L. Ngami. Libebe, lat. 18.01 S, long. 21.29 E, is on the Okovango River, in western Caprivi Strip.

[2] Mujala, a Leya headman subordinate to the Toka chief Musokotwane and living in Lukuni native district, Kalomo District (General List of Chiefs, 13; Clark, 73 n.).

but long-continued fighting rendered the Makololo superior to any numbers the Batoka could muster.

Moyara now, with four or five wives, sits in the midst of what must have been a very large town. By this hamlet a number of stakes are stuck in the ground, and between fifty and sixty human skulls[1] are hung on their points. These were Matibele who, having been unable to attack Sebituane on Loyela,[2] returned sick and famishing. The father of Moyara took advantage of their reduced condition, and exhibited the heads of his victims in the manner described. On looking at them I remarked to Moyara that many of them were mere boys. He assented readily, & pointed them out as such. 'This is the way we shew our fierceness.' 'By killing boys?' 'Yes, they had no business here.' 'But your fierceness will ensure your own death if Matibele come again.' 'But when I hear of their coming, I shall hide the bones.' His father lies in the middle of the son's huts with a lot of rotten ivory over him. One cannot help feeling thankful that the reign of such wretches is over.

The son knows a root which, when sprinkled over the oxen, disgusts the tsetse, so that it flies off without sucking. He promised to shew the plant or tree for an ox; but as we are travelling, and time is required to experiment, so as not to be cheated, as I have too often been by my medical friends, I deferred the investigation till my return.[3]

My men, who are not thoroughly drilled yet, forced Moyara to carry a tusk for them, but having put an instant stop to the imposition, and told the son of the head-curer to go back with his wives who had come to help him, he poured out a shower of thanks. They will go to a woman's house and deliberately strip it of thatch in order to make their beds. I must have them broken off from all their pilfering, otherwise we may have trouble.

25th Novr. 1855. Tsetse again forcing the men to drive the cattle by night, I came on again on foot to a fine well dug under a very large fig tree. Water delightfully cool. Therm. 104° at noon, 94° after sunset; very cloudy. Wind strong N.E. & E. The well, which our large party emptied, is called Namilanga, from the sound of musical instruments.[4] Here the parties returning from cattle-lifting and murder-

---

[1] 'I counted fifty-four human skulls' (*Travels*, 530).

[2] An island in the Upper Zambesi; see above, p. 9.7.

[3] He was in fact shown the 'medicine for tsetse' on revisiting Mujala in 1860 (*Expedition*, 258; *Narrative*, 233).

[4] It is a spring near Senkobo siding, lat. 17.38 S, long. 25.57 E (D.C., Livingstone, 15.i.1962; Livingstone SE–35 NW).

ing and plundering sat and were regaled with boyaloa, music, and the lullalooing of the women, as we, at the very apex of civilization and all good, do the same by 'See the conquering hero comes', waving of handkerchiefs, & public feeds.[1]

The old headman told us that his father once went to Bambala,[2] where white traders live, when he was a little boy, and returned when he had become a boy of about 10 years. He went again and returned when it was time to knock out his son's teeth (puberty), thus spending four or five years in each journey. He added, many never returned. They liked that country better than this, although their wives and children were here. The children of some were so enticed and flattered by the finery bestowed on them, they disowned their parents and adopted others.

Novr. 26th. Walked 4¾ hours north to Marimba, an old man having several villages under him. We crossed the Unguesi, a river which runs back like the Lekone and falls into the Leeambye a little above the commencement of the rapids. At midday we crossed that of Marimba, which falls into the former.[3] Bed of gneiss, stratified generally with so much elevation it is nearly on its edge. Its strike is N. & S. mostly, but when first seen it ran easterly & westerly. The dip [is] towards the centre of the continent, yet when first seen it shewed towards the north, as if the eruptive force which placed [it] in this position had been in the direction of the rent in the bed of the Zambesi. Passed a very old town in which the granite millstones were worn 2½ inches deep. Some of quartz & hard porphoritic trap were similarly worn. This is the only memorial these people leave behind them. The ivory gravestones(!) soon rots away. Moyara's father must have died not more than ten or twelve years ago, yet the ivory & skulls were falling to pieces.

It is remarkable that we now meet with the same trees we saw in Angola. A kind of sterculia, the most abundant tree near Loanda, and the boabab flourish here. We were presented with upwards of a bushel of the fruit of the Moshuka at Namalanga, and this tree now

[1] Conjectural reading; MS has 'foeds'.

[2] 'The place . . . which they named Bambala, was probably Dambarari, . . . close to Zumbo. This was the first intimation we had of intercourse with the whites' (*Travels*, 532). Cf. below, pp. 351 (Ambala), 432 (Dambarari).

[3] The Ngwezi joins the Zambesi in lat. 17.40 S, long. 25.07 E (GSGS 2465, SE 35); the Marimba, not named on maps consulted, 'passes near Mutoka village in the old Siakasipa's area' (D.C., Livingstone, 15.i.1962).

makes its appearance, just as it did on the slopes down from Tala-mongongo. The rhododendron, too, abounds. Young ones twist their leaves round during the heat of the day, so that just the edge is exposed to that luminary. Those which standing perpendicularly at the top of the branch don't require any twist of the petiole don't turn, the others have during most of the day a half twist on it. The   ,[1] a kind of acacia with bipinnated leaves, folds them together when the sun is fierce. They then present a thin edge to the sun. Others generally droop down mournfully at midday.

The soil is quite dry just now. The rains have fallen everywhere behind us just after we passed. Some spots are green, others parched up; much of the young corn is in this state. Though there is generally abundance of rain in these parts, it is often partial. After passing through a fine green district we often enter one thoroughly parched. The fruit trees are unaffected except by drought at the time of blossoming. At present they are laden with fruit, though not a drop has fallen on the young corn. My men go out to the woods and return laden with different kinds of fruit for their companions, their own stomachs exhibiting a beautiful state of rotundity. The people say no one ever dies of hunger here.

It looks as if the same trees adorned all the banks of the antient lake. The tree ferns shew a low elevation. The Marama or desert nut also appears here, and so does euphorbia trees & Mopane,[2] with the Acacia tortuosa or wait-a-bit thorn (also a curious kind of shrubby grass common at Kolobeng, having sweet-scented blue flowers).

[1] Blank space for name; 'the acacias' (*Travels*, 535).

[2] Marama (morama) = *Bauhinia esculenta*, 'Kalahari plant yielding a rich bean'; mopane = *Cochlospermum mopane* (Miller, *Woody Plants*, 30, 94).

XV

THE BATOKA PLATEAU

Soldier ants

Novr. 27th 1855. At Marimba's. The country over which we have travelled is very pleasant to the eye. Though parched it looks not so. The brillant green of many trees contrasts agreably with the dark rufous green of the Mola,[1] whose lovely shade & spreading oak form graces the scenery. Palms abound, and there are numbers of flowers and bulbs just shooting out from the soil. The surface is rough & broken into gullies. In the distance there are low ranges of hills 300 or 400 ft. high. To the north stands one called Kanjele. In the east, to which we proceed tomorrow, stands the range of Kaonka.[2]

We have made this detour to the north on account of tsetse, and to see people. Those of Kaonka are the last in friendship with the Makololo. But God will be our protector and guide. 'In all thy ways acknowledge him, and He shall direct thy steps.' This is the statement of the Strength of Israel, who is not a man. If we would credit the promise of Queen Victoria, much more should we that of the King of Kings. 'Great Britain', said Lord John Russel,[3] 'will fulfill her engagements', even to an enemy. Will the Great Creator, the fountain of all honour in the Universe, fail in his? I think, nay verily, and thence will go on with confidence. May He grant me wisdom.

In walking down to the forest this morning after service,[4] or rather telling these poor people for the first time in their lives that the Son of God loved them so that he came down from Heaven to save them, I observed many bands or regiements of the black soldier ant returning from their marauding expeditions. All I saw yesterday evening were returning laden with one or two white ants as their booty. They march in a line three or four abreast, and follow certain leaders who carry nothing. They seem to be guided by a scent left by the leaders in the path, for when I took a handful of ground and threw it over the

[1] Mmola (mobola), cork-tree (see p. 5).
[2] Kanjele hill is not named on maps consulted; Kaonka (see below) was a Toka headman.
[3] Lord John Russell (1792–1878), British foreign secretary 1852–3, president of the council 1854–5 (*DNB.*).
[4] If, as this suggests, it was a Sunday, the date should read '25th'.

path in the middle of the regiment they were completely at a loss, running backwards and forwards in the greatest confusion. They usually ran back untill they found the leaders' scent leading them towards the earthen barrier, turned towards it, and when they arrived wheeled round as at first, but never attempted to pass over, though not a quarter of an inch high. After a quarter of an hour's running backwards and forwards, and chirping, one happened to make a circuit of about a foot round and came to the scented path, and soon all went that way home. Though perplexed, they never parted from their burdens, all of which were in a half comatose state, being able to move the two front legs only, the rest being quite motionless. I thought this was effected by the soldier having squeezed his victim too tightly with his mandibles round the throat, for that is the way they carry them.

This morning I had the pleasure of seeing them going forth to their slave catching. Having come to a stick enclosed in a white ant gallery, I was surprised to see them passing it, though I knew it contained abundance. I lifted it up, and breaking the portion at the end laid it[1] smartly across the path in the middle of the regiment. They paid but little attention to the white ants which scampered about and under the leaves with great celerity, untill I noticed one, with a rather larger belly than the others, catch them and applying his sting to them for an instant throw them on one side in the state of half coma I had observed the evening before. The operation was performed in the same off-hand style farmers' boys cut off the tops & toss on one side turnips in a field. The others immediately took them up. It is as if they were placed under the influence of chloroform instantaneously. I have often observed this stupefaction before, but never till now saw the fluid injected. I believe the dauber or plasterer[2] employs the same injection in his captures of caterpillars and spiders. They were as much puzzled now as the evening before, the leaders having gone past the stick to secure some younger ants. The confusion and running backwards and forwards was remarkable, inasmuch as they now had the untouched path behind them. Are the leaders capable of shewing by the scent which way the others must follow? They surely cannot see foot prints, they seem to have little power of vision.

I fear it spoils the poetry of the blacks catching and making slaves

[1] MS 'by laying it'.

[2] 'A hymenopterous insect . . . which in its habits resembles somewhat the mason-bee' (*Travels*, 538); described more fully in *Private J.*, 264–6.

of the whites in the ant community, as mentioned by Brougham in his 'Paley',[1] to say the object the marauders have in view is not 'labour', but food. When we look at the entrance into the barracks, we usually see a soldier peeping out or coming out & reconoitering, and there is always a heap of white ants' heads and legs there, which looks rather queer payment of their faithful slaves. Even the larvae get a dose of the chloroform. They do not come out of their shells if preserved in glasses or in earth. The excessive building & excavating propensities of the white ants may have led to the idea of their working for their masters. The fluid is antiseptic as well as stupefying.

The amount of vegetable matter consumed by the white ant is wonderful. No sooner does a rotten branch fall to the ground than it is covered over with a gallery, and underneath the little excavators work till the whole is removed; a thin covering of clay is left, of the exact form of the wood removed. The galleries are built in order to protect themselves from the sight of birds, and are executed in concert. Every now and then the whole body of [workers] patter the plaster with their tails, making a noise as the drops of rain do when shaken off a bush. In running up a perpendicular gallery they often go astray, but are not ashamed to go back and commence again at the point of departure from a straight line. They are so exceedingly numerous throughout most parts of Africa, and are so very prolific, some means of keeping them down is absolutely necessary. These are the black soldier ant, the red furies, another species of ant, besides anteaters and a numerous species of birds which live on them alone. They have anthills in Londa quite as large as an English cottage, and underground galleries extending in a star-like form 100 yards long in every direction. In many parts they remove all the corn-stalks from the gardens, rendering collecting & burning unnecessary, and sometimes attack even living trees so vigourously, if they had no check they could clear Africa of both vegetable & animal productions.

Have ants not a sense more than man to guide them in some of their ways?

A pallah or redbuck went past me at full gallop. I have often admired the velocity with which when pursued they can gallop. This gave several short springs of from 8 to ten feet long, then one or two of 18 or 19 feet in length. It seemed scared but not doing its utmost. If we

[1] Possibly W. Paley, *Natural Theology*, annotated by Henry Lord Brougham and Sir Charles Bell (2 vols., 1836); but I have found no mention there of ants enslaving others.

say 2 strides per second, which is certainly within the speed, and 15 ft. as the average, the rate is more than a mile a minute.[1] I believe the actual speed is double that in springbucks & hartebeests.

The ostrich when walking at leizure and feeding has a pace of 20 or 22 inches; if simply walking and not feeding, 26 inches from toe to toe of same foot. When terrified and running at his topmost speed, the stride is from $11\frac{1}{2}$ to 13 feet, sometimes 14 feet. In one case which I thought I counted,[2] the rate was 30 strides in ten seconds. Generally the eye could not follow the legs, no more than it can the spokes of a carriage wheel, but suppose we take the above, and 12 feet as the average, 10 : 30 :: 60 :180 strides per minute, $180 \times 60 = 10,800$, $\times 12$ (ft.) $= 129,600 \div 1,760$ (yds.) $= 26$ miles an hour.[3] The full speed cannot be less than that. The conviction on my mind, however, is that it is actually nearly 30 or 40 miles per hour, not so fast [as] a steam locomotive. It could never be approached by a fair end chase but for its stupidity. By crossing towards a point to which it seems running, a horseman may easily come up with it. I have seen him commence running two miles to leeward in order to prevent the slow ox-waggon from intercepting him, and pass us within one hundred yards, thinking he had performed a very clever feat, while he had free scope for 100 miles both before and behind us.

These Batoka are the most degraded-looking people I have seen in Africa. They have nothing fine about them except humanity: they are of the family of man. The knocking out of the upper front teeth makes them hideously ugly, especially when laughing or when they become old. Yet it is the fashion, and Sebituane tried to put a stop to it among his subjects in vain. When a young woman is marriageable, her teeth are knocked out as the copestone of the accomplishments.[4] Hard labour under a burning sun soon removes any little comeliness they possessed. Their dress is frightfully scanty. They raise much corn, beans, earth nuts, &c, and shew some love of liberty. Some women

---

[1] On the figures given, it is only 600 yards. DL may have mistaken 15 'ft.' for '15 yards'.

[2] '. . . by a stop watch' (*Travels*, 154).

[3] On the figures given, 25 m.p.h. would be more correct.

[4] 'The custom of removing the upper incisors and canine teeth, an operation which should be performed shortly after puberty', was formerly characteristic of all Tonga and Ila. Among the Valley Tonga it is still practised by women and girls, but no longer by men. 'They say . . . it is the law from long ago that they should not bear a child until their teeth have been removed' (Colson, *The Gwembe Tonga*, 1960, p. 18).

pierce their ears all round, and ornament them with coarse beads. They have iron rings on their legs & arms.

The men are not likely to improve either physically or mentally while addicted to frequent smoking of the Indian hemp. They like its narcotic effects, although two or three draughts are followed by a fit of violent coughing. This, which appears distressing and is in reality a most disgusting spectacle, is said to be pleasant. It ends often in rendering the victims liable to pneumonia. But though the Makololo cannot point to an old man among them who uses it, they will not abandon it. I believe it was the proximate cause of Sebituane's last illness. It is used throughout the Interior most extensively.

28th Novr. 1855. At Kaonka's villages. We have now reached the last of the Batoka subject to the Makololo. They have treated us well, the tribute which otherwise would have gone to Linyanti having by Sekeletu's orders been given to us. We have thus had a super-abundance of corn, maize, and beans (earth nuts). As usual they are living in a state of warfare with certain tribes who have rebelled, and when [I was] inculcating the duty of peace they complained loudly of having lost three villages by an attack of those called Bakanga.[1] Promised to speak with them too on the subject, only they must give no offence in the meantime. They resemble the Interior Boers exactly in petty quarrels and marauding, always protesting their intense love of peace.

Took a walk in the evening down to a large round mass of granite which has been ejected in a soft state. The outer rind inclines to peel off, but it is a large solid round mass, and the large chrystals project on the exposed surface. The rain has fallen heavily during the past day and night, and all nature sings for joy. The time of the singing of birds is come, and there are some fine songsters. Intermingled with their carols we have strange sounds. In some spots the cicadæ abound. When their hundred stridulous piercing voices or organs join they make a deafening sound. There is also a drab coloured cricket near the granite mound. The sound they make is like the drone of a Scotch bag-pipe. Seeing no hole I dug down on one. I could not concieve such a little thing should raise such a sound. It seemed to make the ground over it thrill. There were hundreds; & in the pools the many-tuned frogs poured out their merry chorus. I could still hear it when half a mile distant.

On the side of the mass a regiement of black soldiers were removing

[1] Not identified; possibly Bakonka, a widespread Tonga clan (cf. Colson, 'The Plateau Tonga', 1951, pp. 130, 131).

their eggs from the damp soil below, which probably will soon be flooded, to a piece of the granite rind which had split off but still lay on the mass. They carried them 30 feet; then, laying them down at the bottom of a fragment which had to be climbed, another party recieved them there and conveyed them home. Those returning travelled back, keeping the right side of the street. Others went among the comers, picking up any eggs which might be laid down on the path, for sometimes they only came half way to the climbing spot. They were 7 or 8 abreast, and thirty feet long. Say they are occupying each half an inch of the road, 30 ft [×] 6 = 180 inches, which multiplied by 7 gives

But It does not continue - my attention as new - It seems on oblong fir' cones. - thus - and so do many trees bulbs which we saw in

1,260.[1] A thousand is but a small swarm. All were employed. But this very laborious operation, which cost from the number of eggs a great many trips to and fro, was, wonderful to relate, performed entirely by the masters. There was not a slave white ant among them. The part they had selected, too, was one in which white ants can neither live nor work, for there was no vegetable matter on the granite, and this constitutes their entire food, nor any soil beneath the stone, and this constitutes the raw material of all their labour.

A lion began to roar at me on the rock. They are not very fierce here.

The country is beautiful—gently undulating, with green vallies and tree-covered knolls. It formerly supported multitudes of cattle. The buffaloes now bring tsetse into it. But it does not continue.

A tree attracted my attention as new. It seems an acacia growing on oblong fir cones[2] [*see facsimile*]. The corn poppy flourishes, and so

[1] DL's arithmetic is again faulty. If each ant occupied 'half an inch' of road there would be 24 (not 6) to the foot, and a total of 5,040.

[2] '. . . the leaves being like those of an acacia, but the ends of the branches from which they grew resembled closely oblong fir-cones' (*Travels*, 542).

do many trees, plants, and flowering bulbs, which we saw in the slope down from Talamongongo and Pungo Andongo.

Border territory

Novr. 29th.[1] Both yesterday and today we have travelled over an uninhabited tract of beautiful country. It is the border territory, separating those who own and those who disown the sway of the Makololo. The face of the country appears in long waves running N. & S., the course of the rainy season torrents. There are no rivers, though water stands in the pools in their beds. The grass is short and well adapted for pasturage. The native corn flourishes. My people magnify it as a perfect paradise. Sebituane was driven from it by the Matibele. It suited him exactly, both for cattle, corn, and *health*. The soil is dry & often reddish sand. Rain is needed now, and appearances say it will not long be withheld. There are few trees. Large shady ones stand where the towns were formerly. The sight of open country now is very refreshing. The hills are low. Game abounds: buffaloes, eilands and zebras, with hartebeests, gnus, and elephants. All are very tame, no one disturbing them, but we have not yet got any.

We slept last night at a watercourse. Large herds of buffaloes appeared, and some rhinoceros. During the night the lions roared very near us, but it was moonlight and no danger. Today we came early to this nullah and might have gone farther, but there is no water untill we have crossed a tract bare of trees & reach a river. Both this and the last 2 torrents run into the Unguesi, which they reach on our south. High north wind. Very cloudy, preventing observations. Temp., 6 a.m. 70°, midday 90°, ev[ening] 84°. This is moderate.

The landscape is peculiar here, from the presence of fine large shady trees dotted here and there over the surface. One close to our place of bivouac, of the ficus kind, is 40 ft. in circumference. The heart has been burned out and some one has slept in it as a house, yet it is vigorous. Have the inhabitants spared these in the midst of their levelling propensities, or are these the remains of a large primitive [forest] when the country was lower? The rest of the trees bear a stunted scraggy appearance compared to these. Is this part undergoing the process which has rendered the Basutu land in the same longitude treeless? The frequent droughts render it impossible for any except the hardiest trees to maintain their existence when young.

[1] MS '28th'.

River Kalomo

30th Novr. 1855. Today we crossed the river called Kalomo, which flows into the Zambesi below Mosioatunya to the south of this.[1] It is about 50 yards broad, and water was flowing in it. Except that, there is no constantly flowing stream in these parts. We are now in the angle between the Zambesi and Bashukulompo rivers. The Kalomo is the base of the triangle. As the Unguesi and Lekone flow west, and this south, I suppose we are now near the apex of the ridge. The journey tomorrow is over a treeless plain.

We met an elephant cow on the Kalomo, without tusks. It is wonderful to see the fear of man operating on this huge beast. As soon as she saw us she made off, her quickest pace a sharp walk.

Buffaloes abound. Large herds are feeding in all directions by day. If they were troubled by man they would retire to the densest parts of the thickets and feed at night only. We got one only, though four were badly wounded and one remained down for some time. The others came back to it, and much to the amusement of my men carried him off, half supporting him with their horns. That which we secured was shot through the fourth or 5th rib of one side, through both lungs, and through a rib on the other side, the bullet (eight ounces in weight) lying under the skin; yet he ran off vigourously, and was secured half an hour afterwards only by the people driving him into a pool of water and killing him with their spears. The bullet hole was much larger on the farther side of the bone than on the near, or that by which it entered. The whole herd rushed past us as we stood on a large anthill, and had for a leader an old cow, on whose withers twenty or thirty Bufagi Ani were sitting.[2] The rest of the herd kept up four or five abreast, so as to allow her exactly a length before the first rank. A species of Ardea accompanies them too, and seems attracted by the flies, which in turn are drawn to the herd by the smell of the animals & their droppings. The foot of this animal was 19 inches in circumference and $5\frac{1}{2}$ broad, $5\frac{1}{2}$ long; horns 33 inches from tip to tip accross forehead, helmet $11\frac{1}{2}$ broad on the brow measured perpendicularly.

2d December 1855. Remained near small hill called of Maundo.[3]

---

[1] The confluence is in lat. 17.57 S, long. 26.24 E (Livingstone SE–35 NW).

[2] 'On her withers sat about twenty buffalo-birds' (*Travels*, 545), i.e. oxpeckers (see above, pp. 50, 285).

[3] Not named on maps consulted.

Many honey birds called us, and we found much honey when we committed ourselves to their guidance. Enquired if any of my men had ever been led by the tsetlu[1] to anything else. Only one could say he had been led to an elephant; had not searched farther. This was my own case when led to a black rhinoceros. After killing him it was too dark to go & see if the honey were beyond him. I always regret this, but think the fact, that the majority of people have been led to honey only, proves that the animals met in the route have been so by mere accident, and to impute intention to lead into danger to the little guide is the same as if a man in following it should turn off in a fright on coming to an anthill, animals & anthills being in many parts equally common.

Hostile village

3d. River Mozuma.[2] Missed an occultation with great regret, for after waiting some hours the morning light obscured the star γ virginis quite.

Next day, 4th, we reached the first village of rebels or independant Batonga. We sent two men before us to inform them who we were and our peaceable purposes. The headman came and spoke civilly. But when it was nearly dark the people of another village arrived and behaved very differently. They began by trying to spear a young man who had gone for water. Then one came howling in the most hideous manner and at the top of his voice. His eyes were prominent, his lip covered with foam, and every muscle of his frame quivered. He came near me, and having a battle axe in his hand alarmed my men, but they were afraid to disobey my orders to offer no violence to any one. It seemed to me a case of extasy or prophetic frenzy voluntarily produced, as in the mysteries of the oracle priests of old. I felt a little afraid, but would not shew it before either my own people or strangers, and kept a sharp look out on the battle axe, for it appeared a sorry way to leave the world to get one's head chopped by a mad savage, though it is perhaps preferrible to hydrophobia, cancer, or delirium tremens. I at last beckoned to the civil headman to remove him, and he did so, taking him by the hand and drawing him aside. He pretended not to know what he was doing. I would fain have felt his pulse to see whether the

[1] Tswana *tsetlho*, honey-guide (see p. 273).

[2] Monzuma; joins the Zongwe (a feeder of the Zambesi) in lat. 17.16 S, long. 27.25 E (GSGS 2465, SE 35). DL struck it in lat. 16.56 S, and says that Sebetwane and the Kololo had once lived thereabouts (*Travels*, 548, 686).

violent trembling were not feigned, but the flow of perspiration shewed that it was real, though it continued fully half an hour and gradually ceased.

I have no doubt but this state of violent action of the frame is induced in the same way that hypnotism & other mesmeric states are. They are believed to be inspired, or to be Barimo, and probably succeed in inducing the state by solitary practice in the forests before exhibiting before their fellow-countrymen. It is remarkable this system has not been tried in Europe. It would answer better than clairvoyance. (See page [364].)[1]

Our second batch of visitors took no pains to conceal their contempt for our numbers, asking some of our Batonga if there were no other parties, if we had not brought our shields; and then tried to lead us towards the Bashukulompo, who are the fiercest race in this quarter, saying to each other in a tone of triumph, 'They are a godsend' (lit., 'God has apportioned them to us'), 'They are lost among the tribes', 'What can they do without shields among so many?', 'They have wandered in order to be destroyed'. We prepared against a night attack, and the discharging of our guns must have had some effect, for our enemies did not appear this morning. Our civil headman came along with us this morning. Crowds hovered around us in the forests, but he went & explained, and we were not molested.

We remain tonight (4th) by a little village under a low range of hills called Chizamena.[2] Country is generally more woody, but trees are not in general large. They are often broken off by elephants at a foot or two from the ground, and many seem pollarded from that point. This animal never seriously lessens the number of trees. Indeed, I have often been struck with the very little damage he does. His food consists more of roots than anything else; grass he never touches. The open parts of the country are studded over with anthills, exactly as haycocks are in harvest or manure heaps in spring. In the woods they are as large as haystacks, and being more fertile than the rest of the country the people cultivate maize, pumpkins, and tobacco, on them. Indeed, they are the chief garden ground (a common size is 40 or 50 ft. in diameter & 20 or 30 ft. high), and being so very numerous make one feel, in looking at the face of the country, as we do when we meet a fine woman whose face is deeply pitted. The face of nature seems deformed by smallpox.

[1] MS '625' (reference inserted on p. 593).
[2] Not named on maps consulted.

Friendly Batoka

Afternoon. Great numbers of people come from all the surrounding villages with presents of maize & masuka. They never saw a white man before, and they express great joy at the first appearance of the phenomenon being a harbinger of peace. The women are better clothed than the Balonda, but the men go in puris naturalibus. I asked an old man if he did not feel a little ashamed to go in that state. He looked and laughed with surprise at my thinking it indecent, feeling himself above such weak superstition. It is difficult to convey the exact impression he seemed to feel. It closely resembled the sentiment of young men who affect to despise the antiquated notions and narrow-mindedness of humble & sincere believers in the Bible.

5th Decr. 1855. We find the country swarming with inhabitants, who come in great numbers to see the white man and generally bring presents of maize and masuka. They throw themselves on their backs on the ground and roll from side to side, slapping their thighs as expressions of thankfulness and joy at prospects of peace. They resemble the Transvaal Boers very much in their expressions of intense eagerness for peace. I am not aware whether in their case, as in that of the Boer, they find it so very often necessary 'to conquer a peace' by stealing cattle and children from tribes which in no single instance ever molested them.

The whole country we have passed over bears evidence of having been once densely peopled. Sebituane found so many cattle among them his people could not manage them, and when the Matibele made their appearance he called upon the owners to resume possession. The Makololo would not look at the sheep & goats. And yet these were the leavings only of a chief called Pingola, lately deceased. He swept accross the whole country inhabited by his cattle-loving countrymen, devoured both oxen, cows, & calves, and never retaining a single head. He seems to have been actuated by simple love of conquest, and he effected it by carrying numbers of smith's bellows with him, heating the arrow heads before shooting, and when a wound was inflicted on either men or cattle great confusion ensued.[1]

The country is well adapted for cattle & health. It is covered generally with forest not densely planted. The masuka trees cover large

[1] Except that he 'came from the north-east' (*Travels*, 553), nothing more is known of Pingola; modern Tonga do not even have any traditions of his raid (Colson, *The Cattle-keeping Plateau Tonga*, 1953, p. 4).

patches, and the ground is so strewed by the pleasant fruit my men keep eating constantly as we march. We saw a smaller kind of the same tree called Molondo, which is only of the size of large marbles, and has a tender skin and slight acidity of taste mingled with its sweetness. Another, not now in fruit but said to be good, is named Sombo.

The method of salutation is to me very disagreable, the more especially as the men are stark naked. The women throw themselves on their sides. The Batoka are more degraded than the Barotse. They have less self-respect; savage and cruel under success, but easily cowed and devoid of all moral courage. The majority of my company are of this tribe, and a more reckless set one cannot concieve. We have to keep a strict look-out against being involved by their thieving from the inhabitants, in whose power we undoubtedly are. But it is more diffi-cult to manage their tongues. When the people come to make their obeizance, they make wicked remarks in their own language. And some even point to villages, saying, 'I killed a man there', 'I broke all the pots of that village', &c &c, within hearing of the villagers, and this, too, though I believe if they now saw danger the greater part of them would immediately run off. When they performed the valiant deeds mentioned, they were in company with the Makololo as a conquering army. They are eager to recount their soldier deeds. I called them together and spoke to them about their folly, intimating that in the event of disregarding my orders it might be necessary to treat them as children and apply that which Solomon says is appropriate to the backs of children and fools. I hoped it would not be necessary, and that they would behave as men ought. I think they will obey.

[December 6th].[1] Came to another village, or rather series of villages, and here we remain for the night. A man came running to us with his hands and arms firmly bound behind his back, entreating me to relieve him. I declined interference, till we came to our tree, and then enquired of the headman the man's offence. The prisoner had come from the Bashukulompo, and the headman gave him a wife and garden. One supply of seed was also given, and when more was asked & declined he threatened to kill his father-in-law, and had been frequently seen skulking about at night, apparently with the purpose of assasination. I declined to pray in his behalf unless he would himself entreat his father-in-law and promise not to attempt violence. He re-fused at first, but afterwards agreed. The father-in-law wished to take

---

[1] Date given in *Travels*, 553.

him to the village & release him there, but the man cried out bitterly, 'He will kill me; don't leave me, white man.' I then ordered out a knife, and one of [the] villagers released him. If they had wished to kill him they would have done it before we came. His arms were cut by the cords, and his lameness, he said, was caused by blows.

They supplied us plentifully with earth nuts, maize, corn, &c, and all express abundant satisfaction at our message. Some when they come near call out, 'We are tired of flight, give us rest and sleep.' We direct them to Jesus our Lord as their saviour, and hope we will be able to open a path for commerce, whereby they may both avoid the guilt of selling their children and get merchandise for ivory.

Chief Monze

11th December 1855. At village of Monze's sister. We spent Sunday last[1] with Monze, the chief of all the Batoka we have seen.[2] He came wrapped in a large cloth of the Mambari, and rolled about in the dust, screaming as they all do. The sight of great naked men wallowing on the ground, although intended to do me honour, is very painful, and makes me thankful that my lot has been cast in such different circumstances from those of so many of our fellow-men. It is scarcely possible to restrain them, but they promise to appear at our next visit with some little covering. Monze supplied us most liberally with maize, earth nuts, corn, a goat & fowl, and seemed highly satisfied with our presents.

I asked about 150 of his men if they would like a white man to live among them and teach them. All expressed high satisfaction at the prospect of both a white man and a white man's path. They would protect him. I asked this question because it seems of great importance to have one somewhere in this healthy quarter to whom we could in sick-

---

[1] '. . . Sunday the 10th' (*Travels*, 554); correctly, 9th.

[2] He was then living 'near the hill Kisekise' (*Travels*, 554), i.e. Chisekesi, lat. 16.26 S, long. 27.29 E (WAC 3177). Selous, in 1888, found him settled 'about eight miles' north-east of the hill; he was 'a little wizened old man, blear-eyed, and getting very infirm, but very chatty and friendly; he remembered Dr. Livingstone's visit quite well, and did not speak of it as though a long time had since elapsed' (*Travel and Adventure in S.E. Africa*, 1893, p. 211). The present Monze 'is recognized, with many reservations, as senior chief' of all the Plateau Tonga. This, however, is due to Government action. In the old days the Tonga had no 'chiefs', only headmen of villages or neighbourhoods, some of whom (like the man DL mentions) might acquire widespread influence as custodians of rain shrines (Colson, 'Plateau Tonga', 96, 154, 157, 158–9).

ness retire, & who will moreover serve to keep the way open to the coast.
This is the farthest point east of the Mambari and farthest west of the
Ambala,[1] or people who come up the Zambesi for ivory but not for slaves.

The country is open and pleasant to us, who have had our view so
often obscured by forest. Here we can see 20 miles over gently undulating downs, dotted over with large single trees or clumps of great
& small evergreens. (The green open lawns would in other lands be
termed pastoral, as well as in this.) Wood is certainly scarce. It would
be difficult to find materials for building. The streams are not perennial. I doubt if there is one suitable for irrigation. But the grass is
short, and though not thickly sown is very fine for cattle and sheep.

The population is not very large, and is spread over a wide extent of
country, and this in order that should an enemy appear in any direction
only a few people could be attacked before the alarm spread. Even the
chiefs live almost alone, and they all appear as if living not in villages
but in their gardens. This mode of living has been adopted within the
last few years. Everywhere we come on the vestiges of large towns and
extensive cultivation. My people say the whole country is so fertile it
would be all garden ground for maize & earth nuts, which require
richer soil than the common corn. It swarmed with inhabitants when
they first came, and all were rich in cattle. A few goats alone remain
after the plundering of both Matibele and Makololo. They are
humbled now and in a state favourable for the reception of the gospel,
and the gradual restoration of their former prosperity in cattle in connection with Christian missions would operate favourably on their
minds. The language is a dialect of the Sichuana, pretty far removed
from that tongue, but many Makololo understand it and a missionary
would soon learn it through that medium.[2]

Monze came on Monday morning with a piece of a buffalo which
had been killed by a lion. On leaving I put a handkerchief round his
child, which he had brought to shew me. It pleased his people wonderfully. We crossed the Mokoe,[3] which runs west into the Bashukulompo

---

[1] A name often applied to the Nsenga of Mbala native district (Petauke District),
'after a species of tall, stout grass characteristic of this district' (Lane Poole, *Native
Tribes of the Eastern Province of N. Rhodesia*, 1949, pp. 35, 41). For a similar
instance, cf. 'Luvale' (above, p. 72).

[2] 'The language is a dialect of the other negro languages in the great valley; and
as many of the Batoka living under the Makololo understand both it and the Sichuana, missionaries could soon acquire it through that medium' (*Travels*, 555).

[3] Makoe (*Travels*, 556), i.e. Magoye; it joins the Kafue on the flats west of
Mazabuka.

river, and slept at Monze's sister's village, who also is called Monze. Both are feminine in appearance. The foolish custom of knocking out the upper front teeth makes all look very ugly, communicating to faces otherwise comely somewhat of the physionomy of a kind of dog, much liked by costermongers, which has the under teeth protruding beyond the upper. Yet it is the fashion, and when some boys were looking at themselves in a mirror and laughing, the men said, 'See the great ugly upper teeth', and the boys as if ashamed closed their mouths.

The men of a village came, and as they had the Bashukulompo mode of dressing the hair we witnessed it for the first time. A circle of about 8 inches in diameter is left, the centre of which is the crown of the head. The hair of this portion is plaited and woven into a cone with an obtuse apex, bent in some cases a little forward, and 8 or 10 inches high, giving somewhat the appearance of a dragoon's helmet, for the rest of the head is closely shaven. One man had his prolonged into a point a full yard high.[1] It is said to be painful at first, for the scalp is tightly drawn up with the cone, but they become used to it. Formerly all Monze's people were so ornamented, but he discouraged it. I wish he would put a stop to knocking out of the teeth too. Sebituane, whom all knew as a man not to be trifled with, ordered its discontinuance in vain. Fashion prevailed in spite of him.

12th Decr. Slept last night at Monze's sister's place. This morning presented the appearance of a continued rain having set in from the north. At Kolobeng these were always from N.E., & at Kuruman too. It cleared up, however, and she came a mile or two with us, and on parting told us she had given orders to the people of a distant village to send food to the point where we should sleep. As they expressed it, 'They would now sleep without dreaming of any one pursuing them in order to spear them'. We have now come to rocks which closely resemble those of Angola, but dipping to the N.E.

It is not often jail-birds turn out well, but we found the prisoner whom we released some distance beyond Monze was the first who appeared to welcome us, and presented a large present of corn and meal. After praising us for our kindness he set off and brought large bundles of grass, wood for our comfort, and a pot to cook our food in. He belongs to the village of Monze's sister.

12th Decr. 1855. We crossed the Nakachinta, a small stream flowing westwards into the Bashukulompo and arising among ranges of

---

[1] The fanciful sketch in *Travels*, 557, should be compared with the photographs in Smith and Dale, *Ila-Speaking Peoples*, i, frontispiece and pp. 62, 88, 90, 91, etc.

hills called Chamai.[1] It being very rainy we went only about two miles beyond, and got an observation of Achernar which shewed we were in 16° 11' south. This morning we went forward in spite of the rain, and our two men from Monze's sister did not make their appearance. We have thus been obliged to introduce ourselves, and bear the suspicion which always attaches to people in these circumstances. We crossed two streams which never dry and flow in the same direction with the Nakachinto and Mokoe, viz. into the Bashukulompo. The hills which flank that river appear on our right now, from 15 to 20 miles off, and the plains beyond the Bashukulompo appear as a dark blue low ridge 30 miles distant. The country is very fertile, but contains but little forest except on the hills, which are covered with it. Water boiled yesterday at 204° shews we are not yet down as low as Linyanti. The people continue to supply us with presents of food.

[1] Neither stream nor hills are named on maps consulted.

XVI

THE ZAMBESI REJOINED

Killing an elephant

13th Decr. 1855. We have now left the country of masuka behind, as well as many other trees & plants identical with those on the slope down from Tala Mungongo. The most remarkable feature on the trees too, viz. the orchilla weed and other lichens, with moss on the ground.

A bird called Mokua Reza, or 'Son-in-law of God', calls out in the woods before rain, 'pula, pula (rain, rain)', and seems to be a cuckoo, for it is said to throw out the eggs of the white-backed Senegal crow & lay its own instead.[1] This crow has a bad repute, for when rain is withheld and his nest known it is destroyed, in order to dissolve the charm by which he seals up the windows of heaven. Another bird makes its loud note heard just before rain, & at no other time. All the birds now join in the mornings in full chorus, and two at least have fine loud notes.

We have rains every afternoon. Here violent thunder showers among the hills filled the Mbai,[2] on whose banks we sleep, so suddenly five men who went to the other side for firewood were obliged to swim back. The nullahs we have passed are all subject to these sweeping floods. The temperature is lowered by these everyday rains to 68° at sunrise and 74° at sunset. More frequently it stands at 72°–74° at sunrise, upwards of 90°–96° at midday, and 80°–84° at sunset.

14th. The people have by some means got a knowledge that we have medicine with us, and much to the disgust of my men, who wish to keep it all for themselves, bring their sick children for cures. Found the hooping cough here yesterday.

In coming to this place, which appears about 5 miles from a range of hills called Kaenia,[3] we saw much large game. The buffaloes select open spots, often eminences, for their standing places by day, and often feed in the forenoon, shewing they know only of danger from the spears of the people. I missed zebras three times, then went to a single

---

[1] Cf. Torrend, *Bantu-Botatwe Dialects*, 62: *Mukwe wa Leza*, '(lit., God's son-in-law)' = 'rain bird, or black and grey cuckoo, supposed to announce the rain'. The name is also used for the red-billed hoopoe, *Phoeniculus purpureus* (Dept. of Game & Fisheries, N. Rhodesia, 2.i.1962).

[2] Not named on maps consulted.　　　[3] Not named on maps consulted.

buffalo which was lying down. My loose arm makes me a bad shot,[1] but I shot this one three times. Three elephants then drove me off. They seemed to be attracted by the noise. On ascending a knoll I tried a long shot at the last, and to the great joy of my people broke its foreleg. They soon came up with it and brought him to a stand, full of spears. I brought him down with one shot into the brain, and right glad I was to see the joy manifested at such an abundant supply of meat. We give them the rest of a day to prepare it. We are on the side of a fine green valley, studded here and there with trees and cut by numerous rivulets which are generally of steep banks.

An elephant and calf appeared in the morning at the end of the valley about two miles distant. Many of the men set off to it, saying to some who remained, 'Our father will see today what sort of men he has got.' I went higher up the side of the valley in order to have a good view of their mode of hunting. The goodly beast, totally unconscious of their approach, stood for some time suckling her young, which might be two years old; then went into a pit containing mud, and both rolled about in it, the little one frisking about his dam in elephantine fashion, flapping his ears and tossing his trunk incessantly. She kept flapping her ears and wagging her tail, as if enjoying herself extremely.

Then the piping of her enemies began, which is performed by blowing into a tube or closed hand as boys do into a key. Both opened or expanded their ears and listened, and then left their bath. As the crowd rushed towards them in every direction, the little one ran forward, then, seeing the men, returned to his dam and always ran to the other side from that on which the enemy was. She passed her proboscis over it as if to assure it of safety. She frequently looked back to the men, who kept up an incessant shouting, singing, & piping; then, looking to her young, ran after it, sometimes sideways as if her feelings were divided between anxiety for her offspring and desire to revenge the temerity of her persecutors. They kept about one hundred yards in her rear, some however kept at that distance from her flank, and when she crossed a rivulet they rushed on her while still in its deep bed and threw their spears. She now appeared with her sides red with blood. The calf ran very fast. (It is never a gallop in either old or young, only a quick walk.) She seemed now to think no more of her

---

[1] DL's left arm had been badly mauled by a wounded lion at Mabotsa in 1844; it healed well, but was subsequently injured again twice during building operations (cf. *Fam. Letters*, i. 90–1, 104; ii. 60).

young, fleeing for her own life, and her pace becoming slower. She turned now and made a furious charge back among the men, who vanished sideways, so she went through the whole party and came near no one except one who wore a piece of cloth on his shoulders. She charged three or four times, but except in the first instance never went 100 yards.

I sent now to request them to spare the young one, but it was speared in a piece of water before my messenger came. It might be two years old. The dam often stood after she crossed a rivulet, and faced the men, who continued spearing her till they had no more weapons. At last, making a short charge, she staggered round and sunk down on her belly dead.

I did not see the whole hunt, having been tempted away by the appearance of the sun and moon unclouded, & when I had just completed the observation they were covered again. I turned away from the spectacle of the destruction of these noble animals, which might be turned to so much good account in Africa, with a feeling of sickness. This was not relieved by the filthy lucre propensity, though the ivory is all mine. I regretted to see them killed, the meat not being absolutely necessary. I did not feel sick the day before when my own blood was up. We ought perhaps to judge acts always more leniently to which we have no temptation ourselves. In drunkeness, for instance, we 'ken about the drinking, but naething o' the drowth'.

The first elephant was a male, not full grown, but one full grown bull in company seemed to be not a foot higher, or just the size of a Limpopo female. . . .[1]

An impression was made on my mind, by the sight merely of the animals of the districts south of the tropics and those commencing from 20° S. and northwards, that the inhabitants of the more temperate and more sterile clime were decidedly larger in bulk and more numerous in species than when nearer the equator. I expected that the more luxurious the vegetation the larger would be the size of the animal. But such certainly is not the case. The elephants of the Limpopo are said by all who have seen them to be much larger than those on the Zouga,[2] a full grown male being in the south about 12 ft., while one I measured on the Zouga was only 11 ft. 4. To a gentleman well

---

[1] I have here omitted detailed measurements of three dead elephants (MS 610–11).

[2] In the north-east of Bechuanaland Protectorate; nowadays known as the Botletle River.

acquainted with both,[1] the latter seemed equal in size to cow elephants only, though their tusks were much larger than those of their more bulky bretheren. The khoodoo seemed much smaller, and so did tsessebe and some of the smaller antelopes. Zebras are certainly no larger, nor are buffaloes. The greatest difference prevails among the domestic animals, the cattle of the Batoka, for instance, being nearly two feet lower than the aboriginal cattle of the more temperate south. The same difference exists among the sheep, goats, and domestic fowls, guinea fowls, and even dogs.

In the districts bordering on the sea coast, for instance, which come under the influence of the sea air, as near Benguela, Mossamedes, and Ambriz, they are large again, and there they are reared under the same conditions, all the natives choosing the larger and stronger males for propagation, an arrangement which prevails in nature, for it is only by overcoming his weaker rivals that the wild males obtain possession of the herd. Invariably he can shew his scars, no matter to what race he may belong. The elephant we killed yesterday had an umbilical hernia as large as a child's head, got probably when expelled from the female herd. The cow was scarred in three places by man, two of the wounds on her side still emitting pus, and there was an orifice, 6 inches long and patent, into her proboscis and about a foot from the point, which would interfere with her power of lifting water into her mouth.

The elephants' tusks from the N.E. of Angola were much larger than those in the south, but this does not argue larger animals, a large animal being by no means requisite to carry a large tusk. We have one which when measured from the point round the convex part is 8 ft. 3 long, but a rod put straight from point to root measures only 7 ft. 2. If we subtract 2 ft. 4, as the distance from crown of the head to the space below the eye where the root of the tusk is inserted, a small male of 10 feet 4 in. would have room to carry it a foot from the ground, while if he were 11 ft. 4 he would carry it nearly 2 feet high. It would have room to grow besides, as might have been in this case, for it is only 16 in. in circumference at the lip.

Food of large animals

In estimating the amount of food necessary for these and other large animals, sufficient attention has not been paid to its quality. The elephant, for instance, never touches grass of any kind except when in

---

[1] Identified in *Travels*, 564, as Oswell (see p. 277).

seed, & some sorts yield food resembling millet to man. (After crossing the feeding places of elephants hundreds of times, I met with evidence of eating grass only once.) The food consists of the branches of a considerable variety of trees, of various fruits as those of the palmyra, masuka, &c &c, and more particularly various roots of trees, and tubers and bulbs. He digs with both his forefeet and tusks. The latter are often seen broken by the operation of pressing up strong tree roots, for he eats many which are upwards of two inches in diameter. He is in truth a very dainty feeder, particularly fond of certain sweet-tasted trees & those which contain much gum, mucilage, or starch (as mohonono & maoka,[1] mimosa), various acacias, and bushes which yield sweet berries. The destruction he causes in forests is by no means great. It may be described as very partial thinning. Even in parts of the country where he abounds and is undisturbed, the majority of the trees he has operated on appear as pollarded low down and not destroyed.

Then it is well known that the benefit derived from food is not in proportion to the amount of ingesta, but the amount converted into chyle & absorbed. The alimentary canal of the elephant seems to act not so much by digestion as by extraction of the nutritious matter from, & not digestion of, the ingesta. Every one since Bruce[2] who has travelled in countries where these animals exist must have observed the great amount of undigested woody matter in the droppings. Indeed, they are nearly all woody matter together, and where birds have drawn it asunder it appears as oakum or cut tow, and from its well ground appearance proves the non-digestion is not from deficiency in the teeth. And not only the woody matter is excreted whole; the seeds of fruits, their rinds, and even leaves, are similarly undigested. They are, notwithstanding, generally in good condition and contain great quantities of internal fat. This applies more especially to those inhabiting more temperate parts.

The black rhinoceros lives also exclusively on branches of trees and occasionally on roots, and he shews the same peculiarities in his egesta, but in a less marked degree. Various antelopes, too, resort to bushes for food. Some even dig bulbs, as the kukama.[3] Indeed, the animals whose chief food is grass are not numerous. The white rhinoceros eats grass

---

[1] *Acacia karroo*, Tswana *mooka*, mimosa thorn (Miller, *Woody Plants*, 22). For 'mohonono', see above, p. 329.1.

[2] James Bruce (1730–94), explored Abyssinia 1769–71, author of *Travels to Discover the Sources of the Nile* (5 vols., 1790).

[3] The Tswana name for the gemsbok, *Oryx gazella*.

chiefly, and so does the buffalo and zebra, but it forms only the chief, not the only, means of subsistence or means of pleasing the appetite. The giraffe never eats grass. The springbuck & gnu always do.

But though there are immense numbers of all these animals in the country, I never lighted on a spot 'eaten off' as may be seen in the vicinity of Colonial farms. The springbucks cannot be influenced in their migrations southwards by want of grass, for the desert from which they go is so well covered with it, the Bushmen and Bakalahari[1] who inhabit it annually burn off hundreds of miles of it, in order that the fresh grass springing up may attract the game. The grass is burned off annually so extensively, the atmosphere is for months during the winter season tinged with it, and no part of the country can be seen which does not bear evidence, in the blacked bark of the trees, of having been visited by flames. The grass where not visited does not rot as in wet climates, but remains discoloured & easily pulverized till the following year. The springbucks, impelled by the impulse, leave a grass country for one in which it is comparatively scarce. Thousands perish from hunger, and none ever return. Their places are supplied by others from the northern part of the desert. There is no migration towards either the north or east.

The same peculiarity of stomach is observable in the hippopotamus, but there is more flocculent matter in their droppings. Places much frequented by them shew the short soft grass in which they delight cropped close, but a great deal is left in the vicinity long & seeded.

Semalembue and his people

18th December 1855. We passed through the   pass yesterday[2] and reached the residence of Semalembue, otherwise Mainza, at midday. He is the chief of these parts,[3] and his village is close under the range Bolengue & at the gorge through which the river of the

---

[1] BaKgalagadi, the earliest Bantu-speaking inhabitants of Bechuanaland; found mainly in the Kalahari (Kgalagadi) Desert, whence their collective name.

[2] Blank space for name. 'Passing the rivulet Losito, and through the ranges of hills . . .' (*Travels*, 566). The Lusito flows east to join the Zambesi in lat. 16.11 S, long. 28.50 E (GSGS 4695, sheet 1177).

[3] '. . . an influential chief in that quarter' (*JRGS*, 1857, p. 364). Not identified. The map in Smith and Dale's *Ila-Speaking Peoples*, i, facing p. xxv, shows that the region between the Lusito and Kafue rivers is inhabited by the 'Bana-Mainga'. That is also the name of an Ila clan, of which Mainga (DL's Mainza?) 'seems to have been once the head' (i. 288).

Bashukulompo passes. Here it is called Mohowhe,[1] and the Zambesi Makoe. The confluence is two days distant. The river is a little more than 200 yards broad above the gorge, and full of hippopotami, the young of which may be seen lying on the necks of their dams. The range is broken into many parts clustering above and beyond each other, and each has a different name.

Here below we have reached the same level as Linyanti, and if we take Mosioatunya as the commencement of the ridge, and this the bottom of the eastern descent from it, the breadth is about 3° of longitude or 180 miles. It would seem to extend in a northerly direction and perhaps a little to the east of the real meridian, for Ben Habib, who accompanied the Makololo against Sebolamakuea, pointed to a ridge on their east and said, 'It is a descent from that all the way to the sea, and that is not more than ten days distant when you have ascended it.' I prefer to call it a ridge, for it is not generally furnished with hills, though these indeed flank it, and to my mind it resembles a long ridge made by the plough more than anything else. 'Fringe' would do if it were broken up into hills or mountains. It is a healthy portion of the country, and though nearly destitute of fountains or perennial streams is fertile and abounds with good pasture. It probably will be the 'point de apui' for the civilization of Africa. I thank God for honouring me to explore it, and pray that my attempts may result in good, though I may not live to see it.

On the 20th I ascended one of the range of hills through which the river flows. It is called Maboe-a-sula,[2] or 'Stones stink', and though not the highest in sight is certainly not 100 feet lower than the most elevated. The boiling point of water shewed it to be about the same level as Linyanti, and its altitude above the bed of the river below only $1\frac{1}{4}$ degrees. The intervening spaces in this range have not been removed by denudation. The hills seem all to have been raised by granite (of large chrystals), for dykes of it may be seen thrusting up the hills of mica schist and quartz or sandstone schist and making the strata fold over on each side as clothes on a clothes-horse [see facsimile].

The hills are not more than 600 or 700 feet high, and yet this is the celebrated cordillera of Africa! Those to the south which obstruct the navigation of the Zambesi, and called Lupata or 'Spine of the World',

[1] 'Kahowhe' (Travels, 566); 'called by the natives Kavuvu, "Hippopotamus River" ' (Smith and Dale, i. 3). The Bolengue (Balengwe) gorge is in lat. 15.55 S, long. 28.45 E; DL gives lat. 15.48.19 S, long. 28.22 E (Travels, 568).
[2] Not found on maps consulted.

are about the same height. Lupatá is synonymous with Litáko, anglicised into Lattakoo, 'Walls',[1] and from the same reason, there being numerous dry stone dykes in both situations; and possibly the rocky sides of the hills here may have led the people to speak of them as wall-like hills, but the idea of a spine to the world entered the head only of him who wrote about them. This range extends about 30 miles north, and is then succeeded by plains and the country of the Babisa.[2] It reaches no farther south than the Zambesi 50 miles from this, so in addition to being small it is a very interrupted chain. There is, as surgeons say, a loss of continuity. But I must add no more, for in addition to spoiling the poetry of the thing for the geographers I fear I shall increase the anxieties of the geologists, letting them know that their world presents symptoms of being afflicted with 'weak spine'.[3]

Dᵒ quartz or sandstone illust trata fat... on each side clothes-horse ~~~. The hills 600 or 700 feet high and yet

Semalembue paid us a visit soon after our arrival, saying he had often heard of me and now that he had the pleasure of seeing me he feared I would sleep the first night at his village hungry. He then handed [me] five or six baskets of meal [and] maize, and an enormous one of earth nuts. Next morning he gave about 20 baskets of meal, &c &c. I could make only a poor return for his kindness, but he accepted my apologies

[1] 'The word [Lupata] is nearly synonymous with Litako, anglicised into Lattakoo (now Kuruman), viz. walls, or rather dry stone dykes. Pata, or 'mpata, is applied to any defile in hills, particularly if it has perpendicular or wall-like sides. There is one called Mpata, through which the Zambesi comes, near Zumbo' (*JRGS*, 1857, p. 385; cf. below, p. 370).

[2] An extensive group of tribes found chiefly in Luwingu, Chinsale, and Mpika Districts (N.E. Rhodesia).

[3] According to dos Santos, 1609, the name at which DL jeers is of native origin: 'the grand and celebrated mountains of Lupata . . . extend across a great part of this Ethiopia, and being very high, and crossing many lands, the Kaffirs call them the world's spine (lhe chamam os cafres espinhaço do mundo)' (Theal, *Records of S.E. Africa*, vii. 80, 262–3).

politely, knowing that there are no goods in the country from which we came, and professing great joy at [the] words of peace we spoke. He said, 'Now I shall cultivate largely, for we have the prospect of eating and sleeping in peace.'

He was accompanied by about forty people. All are large men. The hands are large, and they have much hair on their heads. Sometimes it is drawn all together up to the crown and tied in a large tapering bunch there which towers aloft. All the front and round by the ears is shaven close to the base of this tuft. Others draw out all the hair on one side into little strings. A great bunch hanging on one side gives them the appearance of having a cap cocked jauntily on one side of the head.

They require no explanation of the existence of a Deity. The interpreter speaks of 'Reza',[1] and they understand what is said at once. Like negroes in general they have a strong tendency to worship, and I hear that Semalembue gets a good deal of ivory from the surrounding tribes on pretence of being some one great. He transmits this to some other chiefs on the Zambesi, and recieves English cotton goods in return.[2] They heard of Pereira passing to their N., but never saw a white man before. Never went down the river. The statement that the Portuguese had a road to the east from Caconda is erroneous.[3] The Babisa come here for trade in ivory alone. They went to the Matibele, but were robbed and escaped with their lives only.

Semalembue said he ought to see us over the river of Bolenge (Bash[ukulomp]o), so we were accompanied by him through the hills to the ford. I put a shirt on him, at which he seemed greatly delighted. I am a poor judge of distances on water, for I set this river down as 200 yards above the gorge and here thought it much narrower, or about 150, but wading through two-thirds of it to the canoe I found even this portion 250. The remaining part was at least 100 more. But it was shallow over the two-thirds, and the remaining part not more than five feet deep. The rains had tinged the water slightly white. They are just set in now.

We went along the bank, every available spot between river and hills being hoed with their wooden hoes. Their little villages met us

---

[1] A widespread Central African name for 'God'; other forms are Leza, Oreeja, Urezwa, etc. The 'interpreter' was Sekwebu (*Travels*, 567).

[2] '. . . which come from Mozambique by Babisa traders' (*Travels*, 567).

[3] 'If, as has been asserted, the Portuguese ever had a chain of trading stations across the country from Caconda to Tete . . .' (*Travels*, 531). Caconda, lat. 13.43 S, long. 15.03 E, is in Angola. I do not know where DL saw the statement; it is not in Bowdich, his usual source of information about the Portuguese in Africa.

at every turning. They are compelled thus to hide themselves from the observation of enemies. The country on the plains & vallies is excellent for their purposes, but fear drives them to maintain a constant war with the hippopotami which swarm in the river. This they do by pit-falls very neatly covered. We shot several, and as usual they were covered with scars. Even the cows were so marked by the teeth of their companions. Young bulls, as we found at Mosioatunya, are often killed in these frays, and all seem to be a quarrelsome race. The young when only the size of terrier dogs sit on the necks of their dams in the water, their little saucy looking heads cocking up between the parents' ears. When older they sit on their backs. . . .[1]

20th. We have been detained a day by skinning and eating the hippopotami. The men and myself all enjoy good health. This is partly owing to our getting all into cover usually before rain. It falls gener-ally in the afternoon, so by making shorter stages than formerly much greater comfort is enjoyed, for all set themselves to build sheds as soon as we come to a stand, and in an hour we are all sheltered. The rains come most frequently from the east, and in the afternoon clouds always come, though it may not rain, in that quarter. I attribute my better health now to having wheaten bread constantly. I did not take it in the other journey, because I wished to avoid lading the men more than absolutely necessary. The parts hitherto travelled are more salubrious too. There are fewer streams to be crossed, and no stagnant sedgy marshy banks.

22d Decr. 1855. We are among the hills now, five distinct ranges of which are visible between Bolengo and Komonga inclusive. The Bashukulompo river flows between Bolengo and Sekonkamena ranges, and the Funze between the Sekonkamena and the next.[2] All are quite covered with trees, and are extremely beautiful. The sides of the range present the appearance which the tide leaves on mud banks exactly. Elephants climb up strange places in search of their favorite roots, and often overturn trees from a foot to 16 inches in diameter. They eat roots 4 inches in diameter.

[1] I have here omitted detailed measurements of 'a full grown old cow hippo-potamus' (MS 623).

[2] 'We can see from this hill five distinct ranges, of which Bolengo is the most westerly, and Komanga is the most easterly. The second is named Sekonkamena, and the third Funze' (Travels, 570). The names Komonga and Sekonkamena do not appear on maps consulted. The Funze (Funswe) joins the Kafue in lat. 15.50 S, long. 28.30 E (Lusaka SD–35 SE).

Prophetic afflatus

(See p. [347]).[1] Numerous instances have occurred of persons pretending to the prophetic afflatus, and all commence their utterances after a period of violent action of the voluntary muscles, sometimes by striking the ground violently with a club, or stamping or leaping with surprising agility. One, named Tlapane, guided by one utterance the policy of Sebituane for years. His name [was] Tlapane, and office that of senoga[2] or 'speaking with the barimo'. He said, looking eastwards, 'There, Sebitane, I behold a fire which will scorch you. The gods say, go not thither.' Turning to the west he said, 'There I see a city and a nation of black men. Your tribe is perishing and will be consumed, but you will govern black men, men of the water. They must not be killed, they are your tribe. When your warriors have captured red cattle, know they belonged to your future subjects. And thou, Ramosinini, your villages will perish utterly, and so will Mokari if he removes from your village. You, Ramosini, will be the last to die. I myself am called hence and cannot stay much longer. Other men have been caused to drink water, I have been made to drink the urine of the rhinoceros.'[3]

He himself soon afterwards died. Was always in the habit of retiring, no one knew whither, when the moon was full, and returning about new moon quite emaciated. Probably he went to some cave and remained in the hypnotic state which seems to afford pleasure to certain habits of body, as we see hysteria does, and the state of the moon shews he must have had a smack of insanity. All he said on the above occasion shewed an observant shrewd mind, & nothing else. Of the firearms down the Zambesi he must have heard, and also of the Barotse in the west. The policy he recommended was wise and humane. Sebituane followed it implicitly, and spared even the Barotse chiefs, though they attacked him first.

Another man of the Makololo tried it, but made a mistake in his calculations as to the successful inheritor of the chieftainship: denounced the birth of Sekeletu, and when he unexpectedly came into

[1] MS '593'; see above, p. 347.

[2] Tswana senogi, diviner, prophet.

[3] In the published version of this prophecy (Travels, 87), 'urine' is replaced by 'bitter water'. DL is our only authority for Tlapane, all later accounts of whom (e.g., by Ellenberger) were borrowed from him. Mokari (Mokgari) and Ramosini (Rramosinyi) were perhaps among the original leaders of the Kololo; I have found no other mention of them.

power the prophet was an object of vengeance and was cast into the river.

Prodigious quantities of large game

27th Decr. 1855. We have got through the hills now, and the sight of the river as it winds away to the confluence, with the long range of hills on the other side of the Zambesi, constitutes as fine a picture as I have seen in Africa. A glorious scene. It seemed, from hundreds of buffaloes, zebras, and lordly elephants feeding majestically, to be like what must have been seen by angels when megatheria fed undisturbed in primaeval forests. When we descended we found all the animals all remarkably tame. The elephants stood fanning themselves with their large ears beneath the trees as if they did not see us at 200 or 300 yards distance, and large pigs came and gazed [at] us in wonder, as if asking what new thing is this. They are little disturbed by man.[1] The people are great cultivators and, as such generally are in Africa, have but little courage. Here they are Babimpe,[2] and allow their teeth to grow. Never have had any intercourse with white men, or even with Bastards. The Babisa alone have visited them.

The roughness of the rocky hills knocked up the oxen in four days, and heavy rains compelled us one day to return several miles to our sheds. There was no grass where we were compelled to halt, so wet to the skin we were fain to retrace our steps. These rains are from the east.

A land tortoise was caught, which measured accross the belly 9 inches, length 14 inches. It contained many eggs, and being considered a delicacy is always given to the principal person in the company. . . .[3]

31st. The numbers of large game, especially elephants and buffaloes, are quite astonishing. Pigs are seen every few hundred yards and seem very little afraid of man. I never saw elephants so tame as near the Chongue,[4] but they became more troublesome as we came near the villages of Tombanyana,[5] where they are hunted or rather speared from stages on trees. The country became covered with broad-leaved bushes pretty thickly planted, and we had several times to shout to

[1] 'The people live on the hills, and, having no guns, seldom disturb the game, (Travels, 571).   [2] See above, p. 27.

[3] I have here omitted detailed measurements of two elephants and two buffaloes (MS 628–9).

[4] 'I never saw elephants so tame as those near the Chiponga' (Travels, 573). The Chipongwe joins the Kafue in lat. 15.56 S, long. 28.43 E, about 8 miles west of the 'Lesser Chongwe' (Lusaka SD–35 SE). For the Chongwe, see below, p. 367.

[5] 'Tomba Nyama' (Travels, 575); apparently a local headman.

elephants to get out of our way. A cow with three young ones, of different sizes, charged through the centre of our extended line and recieved a spear for her temerity. The buffaloes came trotting to look at our oxen, but shooting a fine cow soon made them retreat.

Back on the Zambesi

The rains from the east are deposited on the hills on our right very frequently, hence their covering of green trees and their fertile vallies. We saw we were coming near our Zambesi by the numbers of water fowl in the vicinity. On the day we reached [it] I shot 4 geese with two shots and might, had I followed the wishes of the men, have secured a meal of geese for the whole. I never saw a river with so much animal life around, on, & in it. Game, fish, and fowl, seem to find abundant support from it. The people say its fish and fowl are always fat. This agrees with my experience.

On the 30th we were again gladdened by a view of its goodly broad waters,[1] and got observations besides, the which we have been quite unable to get from constant rain and cloudiness for many days past. We were, however, about ten miles east of the confluence there. The Zambesi is here very much like what it is from Katimamolelo to the confluence of the Chobe, viz. flowing between flat reedy banks with many long islands and sandbanks in it. But it is now much broader. One would try to make his voice heard accross it in vain. Its flow is here more rapid, 6 miles an hour, and, what I never saw before, the water is discoloured brownish-red, and as it is rising a great deal of wreck, reed, sticks, and trees, are carried along.

The islands are all inhabited as places of safety. We are now opposite that of Tombanyana; is about 2 miles long, $\frac{1}{2}$ or $\frac{3}{4}$ broad at its widest part, and contains, besides a human population, one of buffaloes, more than 100, which never leaves it. The human and animal inhabitants understand each other, for when the former think they ought to avenge liberties committed on their gardens, the latter or the leaders come out boldly to do better.[2] The small space to which they have confined themselves shews how luxuriant the vegetation is

[1] In lat. 15.50.49 S, '8' or 10' below [the Kafue] confluence', which DL gives as lat. 15.53 S (Travels, 687). The Kafue joins the Zambesi in lat. 15.56 S, long. 28.54 E (Lusaka SD-35 SE).

[2] In 1860 DL found Tombanyama living on the mainland, 'having resigned the reedy island, where he was first seen, to the buffaloes, which used to take his crops and show fight to his men' (Narrative, 216).

in this region, for were they in want of more pasture they swim well, and the breadth on this side is not more than 200 yards. The ranges of hills appear now to run parallel with the river, which is running east & by south, and are about 15 or 20 miles apart. The river divides the Batonga and Banyaia.[1] These abound in buffaloes, but no communication takes place between them. They are kept down by killing when the island is partially flooded. They are then approachable in canoes. They have been on the island from time immemorial. The island is named Menyemakaba.

5th January 1856. Detained two days at Tomba's by continuous rain. He volunteered the loan of a canoe when we left to enable us to cross the Chongue, which we found about 100 yards broad and flooded.[2] We crossed many gullies and through some thick jungle, which will require cutting down on our return. The path lies along the left bank of the river, which here flows at the rate of 6 or 7 miles an hour, carries much wreck, and is very muddy. This never happens above Mosioatunya. The vegetation is exceedingly luxuriant. The people have reaped their first crops already. The Kabompo was just beginning to rise in December & January 1853-4, hence this rise must be owing to rains west of us. Indeed, we daily see the clouds from the east resting on the hills and depositing their fertilizing showers in the vallies. It fell a foot in one night, which could not be if the rise were owing to rains in the north.

The people profess to be delighted to hear our message of peace. Formerly they possessed large herds of cattle, but now the tsetse has followed the buffaloes into the very spots in which cattle were pastured. We see none now as we travel along the bank, though buffaloes, zebras, pallahs, and waterbucks, abound. Pigs are in great abundance, and so are khoodoos and the oryx on the hills. Got a buffalo with a large piece of skin torn off his flank, it is believed by an alligator. He was rolling in a pool of mud and seemed to be enjoying himself extremely. There are no elephants now. The natives make stages on

[1] BaNyai. Posselt (*Fact and Fiction*, 120) says they 'were not a tribe, as the name connotes servitude or tribute, hence a tributary people'; but elsewhere (p. 135) he states that according to 'some Natives' the name, meaning 'inferiors or slaves', was applied to a group of Rozvi defeated in a struggle for the chieftainship, whereas others maintain it 'dates back to immemorial times' and 'means "messengers", a term generally exclusively applied to the messengers of a chief'. See below, p. 418.

[2] '... which we found to be about fifty or sixty yards broad and flooded' (*Travels*, 575). The Chongwe (distinct from the Lesser Chongwe, above, p. 365.4) joins the Zambesi from the NW in lat. 15.42 S, long. 29.21 E (Lusaka SD–35 SE).

trees and wait for the passing of the animal, and kill him by large spears from above.

The rains are warm. At sunrise the thermometer stands at from 82° to 86°; midday in the coolest spot, viz. my tent under a shady tree, 96° to 98°, sunset 86°, 9 a.m. 84° to 86°. This is different from the Interior. Rains bring down the thermometer to 70°–72°, 68°, in the morning, 80°–84° midday, and 72°, 74°, 76°, evening. Feel first mosquitoes here.

6th January 1856. Our course lies between the range on the left bank and the river. Each village furnishes a couple of men to take us to the next, and [they] are useful in shewing the parts least covered with jungle. There is no footpath, communication being carried on by means of canoes. The people are large muscular men having large ploughmen's hands. When we come near a village, we see both men, women, and children, employed in weeding their gardens. They are great agriculturists. Indeed, most Africans are. The idea that this employment tends to develope a brave patriotic population, if applied to Africa, is fabulous, and so is the theory of the political economists that food which requires most time and labour for its production is best adapted for civilization. Those who have to spend most of their time in toiling for a subsistence, either by agriculture or hunting or fishing, are the least advanced in civilization and even in manufacture of necessary utensils.

We have rains every day now. Considerable cloudiness, but the sun often bursts through with scorching intensity. All call out against it then and say, 'O the sun! That is rain again.'

White ants working continuously all last night and all today in removing my grass from under me. They never tire as other mortals do.

Mobala visited us today, giving corn & two fowls.

Selole's hostility

10th January 1856. We passed Mobala in peace, but after a few hours reached Selole or Chilole, and found he not only considered us enemies but had actually sent an express to raise the tribe of Mobu-ruma,[1] with the information that Mobala and all the villages beyond

---

[1] Mburuma, official name of the chief of the Ambo (Kambosenga) in Feira District, Central Province, N. Rhodesia (*General List of Chiefs*, 6; Lane Poole, *Native Tribes*, 57). The man DL mentions was killed in 1860 by 'a Portuguese half-caste' (*Expedition*, 163, 399–400; cf. below, p. 384.2). Selole and Mobala were apparently local headmen.

were utterly destroyed by our firearms. All the women of Chilole had fled, and the few people who came near us exhibited symptoms of terror. The party who came to assist him from Mburuma saw Mobala come into the town, and immediately suspecting deciet came boldly to us and told the hoax which had been played upon them, and then went home.

We followed, but the men attacked some elephants for provisions, and a large one fell into a hole and could not extricate himself for some time. When he managed to rise [he] was like a porcupine with spears, but fell not. They called upon me to finish him, as he could no longer charge. I fired 8 large & 4 small bullets into him, but we were obliged by night to leave him and he managed to die where we could not on the following day discover [him]. We thus lost a day, to the great chagrin of my men, who need meat much, and though I have exerted myself greatly, and the country is full of game, as always happens my loose arms makes me such a bad shot I kill nothing. The more hunger, the worse my success invariably, & now when my plates are melted up I can try no more.

We reached Moburuma's this morning. His brother came to meet us. Women and children generally out of sight. The ladies however are no loss so far as viewing the human face divine with pleasure is concerned, for they pierce the upper lip and draw it out, inserting a shell or large piece of reed in it and giving themselves an ornithorhyncus air. Both lips stick out very far, both are said to be elongated. What hideousness fashion can make poor mortals perpetrate. A present of meal, maize, native corn, &c, was brought by a large party fully armed, and shewed great suspicion. Sekuebu had to order them to place their bows, arrows, and spears, at a distance. Moburuma did not come.

We have heard rumours of a man named Seyatomba having been killed by Selole, hence his hostility. They say he came proclaiming peace as I do, but stole their children and bought ivory with them. We are supposed to be following the same calling. Slavery is toto et ubique a curse and a blot. They volunteer to give us canoes. This is to part me from my men, and is thought cunning. Sinkantaba is said to be north of this, and has twice attacked Tete, which they name Nyunkue.[1]

---

[1] See below, p. 421. 'Sinkantaba' suggests the Ngoni chief Zwangendaba, but he had died near L. Tanganyika c. 1845, and there is no record of his having attacked Tete (Lane Poole, 1, 5, 7). The reference may be to Soshangane, another Ngoni chief (d. 1856), who is known to have attacked several Portuguese settlements in Moçambique (see below, p. 436.1).

We are now at the end of the ranges which run on each side of the Zambesi. The gorge through which it passes is named Mpatue.[1] If we pass unscathed now, we may hope to return with ease and without those looks and acts of suspicion which make it unpleasant to come near a village. May God direct our steps. The chiefs seem to usurp his authority, for when we told Moburuma's brother of our ill success yesterday he said, 'The man at whose village you remained allowed you to want meat, for had he only come and asked from Moburuma he would have given him a little meal, and having sprinkled that on the ground as an offering you would have found your elephant.'

Suspicious conduct of Mburuma's people

11th January 1856. We started for Mohango pass[2] this morning, and Moburuma's brother put us into the way. We are now nearly through it. The conduct of these people has been very suspicious. The loan of a canoe to convey me and the goods was pressingly offered several times. This was in order to separate me from my men. We stated no suspicions, but declined civilly to accept it. Then men were sent in the morning after us as guidés to the Loangoa,[3] and they said Moburuma had come to our bivouac with meal after we had left. When we had marched about 6 miles, we were brought up under a tree with the notice, 'Moburuma says you are to sleep under this tree'. On declining this also, we were told that we must wait for some corn which the people of a village at hand were seeking for us. As none appeared in an hour, I went forward again, but this seemed to disarrange their plans. One was observed running back to Moburuma, and in a short time all left us, because we declined travelling according to their dictation. I dislike a suspicious person myself, but there was evidently a project afloat here to attack us when entangled in the pass. Our passing nearly through before they were aware seems to have been unexpected. How precious to have an all-powerful Friend and Protector who can controul the hearts and hands of men. May this be the set time to favour poor Africa, and may I, the most unworthy of all his servants, ever be grateful to him for allowing me to be a pioneer of mercy.

[1] Mpata gorge, lat. 15.38 S, long. 30.00 E.

[2] Not named on maps consulted.

[3] Luangwa, a major tributary of the Zambesi, which it joins from the north in lat. 15.37 S, long. 30.26 E, between the towns of Feira (N. Rhodesia) and Zumbo (Moçambique).

13th January 1856. At Ma-Moburuma's, at the confluence of the Loango and Zambesi.[1] We found the pass long and difficult, between 20 & 30 miles, and such was the roughness of some parts we slept two nights in it. On the second day we wandered, and when we recovered the path our guides came up to us. We went on to another village, but declined sleeping there. It is so disagreeable to be suspected. On reaching the villages of the mother of Momburuma, the chief of our guides was so influenced by our explanations he gave in a favourable report, and the women and children did not flee. We discovered that we were called Bajunka, i.e. Bastard Portuguese,[2] who come thus far in boats or canoes. One of them called Siriatomba, son-in-law of Sekolole, left with a strong party and advanced beyond the island Meyamekaba and then attacked a village of Matibele, making the majority prisoners. Returning, it was believed by his father-in-law, in order to set up chieftainship on his own account, a party was dispatched to meet and kill him. This having been effected,[3] his people dispersed among the tribes we have passed, and Mpendé[4] says, 'No Mozunka will henceforth pass me up the Zambesi'. It seemed necessary to disabuse their minds of the idea that I was of the Bazunka tribe, so I directed Sekuebu to explain the difference, and the sight of my bosom and arms and hair convinced them of the reality of the difference. Their suspicions are much allayed, and we are promised the loan of canoes on the 14th to cross Loango.

Great numbers of men and boys have come to see the white men, and marvel greatly at the sight of books, watch, looking glass, & revolver. They readily understand the little instruction given on divine things when the Supreme Being is spoken of as Reza. They are a strong muscular race, & both men and women cultivate the ground, which is a rich soil and contains so much comminuted talc it seems as

[1] In *Travels*, 687, DL locates her village in lat. 15.37 S, long. 30.22 E, 'about 10 miles from Zumbo'.

[2] 'Bajunka' (Mazungu) was a name already applied to the Portuguese in the 16th century (cf. Monclaro, 1569, in Theal, *Records of S.E. Africa*, iii. 192, 193, 242, 243). DL says 'it probably means foreigners or visitors,—from *zunga*, to visit or wander,—and the Portuguese were the only foreigners these men had ever seen' (*Narrative*, 331).

[3] Siriatomba was the nickname (meaning 'don't eat tobacco') of 'an Italian named Simoens'; Sekolole was a chief 'living north of Tete' (*Travels*, 578). A Portuguese report, 1853, mentions 'Simões', who was killed while raiding for ivory in the vicinity of Zumbo (quoted by Eça, *Guerras no Zambeze*, i. 276).

[4] See below, p. 380.

if mixed with grease. They eat their corn only after by steeping in water it has begun to grow. They decline eating it if simply boiled without having undergone the sprouting or germinating process. This spot is of great beauty, quite enclosed in hills which are nearly covered with trees. The vallies are occupied by gardens of native corn.

We are obliged to hurry along, for all the oxen are bitten daily by the pest tsetse, which now inhabits extensive tracts once covered by herds of cattle. These were all swept off by Mpakane[1] & others, and the insect returned with the game. Coming after successive marauders we have to bear all suspicions, and when we passed along heard our guides remarking to men in gardens, 'All very fine, words of peace; but lies, as Bajunka are great liars.'

[1] See below, p. 375.2.

XVII

FROM ZUMBO TO CHICOVA

Crossing the Loangwa

14th January 1856.[1] At the confluence of the Loango and Zambesi. Thank God for His great mercies thus far. How soon I may be called to stand before him my righteous Judge I know not. All hearts are in his hands, and merciful and gracious is the Lord our God. O Jesus, grant me resignation to thy will, & entire reliance on thy powerful hand. On thy work[2] alone I lean. But wilt thou permit me to plead for Africa? The cause is thine. What an impulse will be given to the idea that Africa is not open if I perish now. See, O Lord, how the Heathen rise up against me as they did to thy Son. I commit my way unto thee. I trust also in thee that thou wilt direct my steps. Thou givest wisdom liberally to all who ask thee. Give it to me, My Father. My family is thine; they are in the best hands. O be gracious, and all our sins do thou blot out. A guilty, weak, and helpless worm on thy kind arms I fall. Leave me not, forsake me not. I cast myself and all my cares down at thy feet. Thou knowest all I need, for time and for eternity.

It seems a pity that the important facts about the two healthy longitudinal ridges should not become known in Christendom. Thy will be done.

Here there are the ruins of an old church rudely built of stone. The bell (undated except I.H.S.[3] †) lies broken by a dwelling house of the same materials, also the font in the edifice and the stand for the cross of wood. There are the remains of what may have been a fort, but all is occupied by gardens now.

The people behave very suspiciously, collecting from all sides and keeping at a distance from us though professing friendship. They will have us completely in their power when we are parted in fording. They are silent as to the cause of the removal of the Portuguese hence, although we question them. There is now no intercourse

---

[1] The entries for this and the following day were published, incompletely and not quite accurately, by Blaikie, *Life*, 181–2; cf. also Debenham, *The Way to Ilala*, 117 (brief extracts). Seaver, *David Livingstone*, 256–7, combines portions of the journal entry with relevant passages from *Travels*, 584–5.

[2] 'word' (Blaikie, 181).

[3] Jesus Hominum Salvator (Jesus Saviour of Men).

except through the Babisa. They will not furnish us with more canoes than two. I leave my cause and all my concerns in the hands of God my precious Saviour, the friend of sinners.

Evening.[1] Felt much turmoil of spirit in view of having all my plans for the welfare of this great region and teeming population knocked on the head by savages tomorrow. But I read that Jesus came and said, 'All power is given unto me in Heaven and in Earth. Go ye therefore and teach all nations. *And lo, I am with you always, even unto the end of the world.*' It's the word of a gentleman of the most sacred and strictest honour, and there is an end on't. I will not cross furtively by night as intended. It would appear as flight, and should such a man as I flee? Nay, verily. I shall take observations for lat. & long. tonight, though they may be the last. I feel quite calm now, thank God.

15th January 1856. Left bank of Loangua. The natives of the surrounding country collected around us this morning, all armed. Children & women were sent away, and Moburuma's wife, who lives here, was not allowed to approach, though she came some way from her village in order to pay me a visit. Only one canoe was lent, though we saw two tied to the bank, and the part we crossed the river at, about a mile from the confluence, is a good mile broad. We passed all our goods first on to an island in the middle, then the cattle and men, I, occupying the post of honour, being the last to enter the canoe. We had by this means an opportunity of helping each other in case of attack. They stood armed at my back for some time. I then shewed them my watch, burning glass, &c &c, and kept them amused till all were over except those who could go into the canoe with me. Thanked them all for their kindness and wished them peace. Perhaps after all they were influenced only by [the intention][2] to be ready in case I should play them some false trick. They have reason to be suspicious of whites.

In looking east from the confluence we see a hill about 20 miles off, called Tofulo. Is this Fura?[3] On the range on the left bank there are many ruins, which I hope to see tomorrow. The people say the whole of both banks were once inhabited by Bazunka, and we tonight

---

[1] This paragraph is also published, with some minor alterations, by Campbell, *Livingstone*, 1929, p. 221.

[2] Beginning of new page in MS; words in brackets supplied from *Travels*, 585.

[3] Mt. Fura, now called Mt. Darwin, lat. 16.45 S, long. 31.39 E; at its foot was Massapa, 'the principal and richest' of the early Portuguese trading fairs in the country of Monomotapa (Axelson, *Portuguese in S.E. Africa*, 6, 7). 'Tofulo' (Metuafuro) is nearly 10 miles NE of Zumbo (GSGS 4355, SD 36/4).

sleep beneath a mango tree of their planting which is fifteen feet in circumference.

Zumbo

16th January 1856. This morning we passed along under the range called Mazanswe, and found the ruins of five or six stone houses,[1] all facing the river and high enough up to give a pleasant view of the broad Zambesi. They had all been built on one plan, and each has a large stone-wall court surrounding it, shewing they were large slave establishments. In some the rafters & beams had fallen in but were entire. Trees grow on the walls, of the ficus family, 2 feet in diameter, & there are some inside the house walls of equal size. The work has been performed by negro masons, for the stones are often not placed so as to cover the joinings below, hence there are corners with a seam from top to bottom. Much clay has been used as mortar, and now when rains moisten it the walls come down by wholesale. There are remains of houses of smaller pretensions, and a large wall on the top of a hill on the other bank (right) may have been a fort which commanded a considerable population. The church is at a central point, as both sides of the Loangua & Zambesi were well peopled & cultivated. The last of the population withdrew suddenly, by means of their boats, on hearing of the approach of Caffres under Changamera, 'Ngabe,[2] and Mpakane. Sekuebu was among the last named. They never came to the confluence, though they carried off all the cattle of Moburuma and others and left the country to the game and tsetse. We have seen 7 mango trees and several tamarinds, but though the chiefs claim all the fruit they do not propagate them. We saw no inscriptions whatever.

The men whom Moburuma sent to see us accross the Loangua were highly pleased with a red baize cloth for Moburuma and a handkerchief and few beads for themselves. These Sekeletu gave to enable me to buy a canoe.

[1] '... and found the ruins of eight or ten stone houses' (*Travels*, 586). Mazanswe (Madzansua) is a mile or so east of Zumbo (GSGS 4355, SD 36/4).

[2] Nxaba (son of Mbekane), one of the Ngoni leaders who had migrated from Zululand *c*. 1824. In 1831(?) he annihilated 'a flourishing settlement of Portuguese' in 'Manikaland' (see p. 426.3); he then gradually made his way westward to Barotseland, where he and most of his followers were killed by the Kololo (Bryant, *Olden Times in Zululand*, 424, 454, 460–1, 471–2; cf. *Private J.*, 27 n.). 'Mpakane' may have been a name sometimes applied to him, after his father; this would both explain the reference in *Private J.*, 26, to Sebetwane's having been attacked by 'a large party of Matibele under one called Mpakane', and also account for Sekwebu's presence among the Kololo.

We thought we had got rid of the hills at Mazanswe, but another block appears before us, perhaps on the opposite bank. Tsetse and hills have destroyed two riding oxen, and when the little one I now ride knocks up I must foot it. The bush was very dense today, and when coming along three buffaloes broke through our line, sending my Sinbad the second[1] off at a gallop. When I could manage to glance back, I saw one of the men up in the air at least five feet above a buffalo tearing along with a stream of blood running down his flanks. When I came to the poor fellow I found he had lighted on his face. No bone was broken nor was his skin pierced, though he was carried on the horns of the animal about 20 yards. When the beasts appeared he had thrown down his load and stabbed one in the side. It turned suddenly upon him, and before he could use a tree for defence carried him off. Elephants & buffaloes frequent these thickets. There are a few black rhinoceros, but we never actually saw one. No white. The footprints are all of the other.

The Zambesi is very broad, more than a mile, but islets and sandbanks are frequent in it. Old sandstone, with shingle in it and dipping southwards, forms its bed. Tonight we sleep at a village on an island about 200 yards from this bank. The heat by night is much greater than in the higher country. It seldom falls lower than 80° at sunrise, and the air feels steamy. Water unrefreshing from its temperature, and more is required. I now drink four times more than formerly. Yet it is a mercy there are scarcely any mosquitoes. Indeed, I imagine that which I thought were such are a small black hard insect which abounded farther up the river, whose bite is akin to that of the mosquito but not so bad.

17 January 1856. On starting this morning from the island Shibanga,[2] we were pleased to see a person with a jacket and hat making towards us with a present of rice. He comes from the east for purposes of trade. The Portuguese or Bastards of Tete or Nyunkue have been fighting with Kaimbwa,[3] but peace having been restored they are now desirous of reoccupying the station at the confluence, which I now understand is called 'Zumbo' or 'Mazumbo'.[4] The hills

[1] In conscious allusion to the *Arabian Nights Entertainments* story of 'the old man of the sea', DL had given the name Sinbad to the ox he rode on his journey to Luanda (see *Miss. Corr.*, 292; *Travels*, 345).

[2] Presumably one of the three small islands a few miles east of Zumbo, shown (but not named) on GSGS 4355, SD 36/4.

[3] Not identified. Cf. below, p. 383.

[4] 'I could not ascertain from the present inhabitants the name of the station. From two Portuguese traders I have met since I learn that it is Zumbo' (15.ii.56

of Momburuma they name 'Kariva', and Mpata is 'Uairo'. He advised crossing the river, as Tete is on the right bank and the distance along the left bank is much longer than the other on account of the bend of the stream to the S.E. He declined to lend his canoes through fear of offending the lords of the river. We are in consequence obliged to go to Pangola's village to obtain leave and canoes. After an hour's march we remained some time at the village of Zungo, who gave us a present of corn and, what is better, a recommendation to his brother-in-law Pangola.[1]

The country is covered with dense bush and rank reedy grass. The bushes are very thorny and tangled, making one always stoop or stop till the men break or hold the branches aside. The heat at the same time is intense. It was 91° in the shade at sunset. One cannot get a draught of cool water even in the mornings. There is a holm ajacent to the river studded with villages and gardens, but only partially cultivated. On it grows the rank reedy grass. There is a second and third on which bushes and trees abound. The path runs sometimes on the one, and sometimes on the other. Boats are essentially necessary for the Zambesi, & with these we could have now been near Quilimane. The hills took a great deal of time. We have not yet left tsetse behind.

18th January 1856. We yesterday rested a short time under a wide spreading ficus, and buffaloes and the water-antelopes being near the men tried to get some by surrounding them, but being too few the animals soon broke through the circle. They however saw some hippopotami in a small lake, and as we are all in need of meat I fired and struck a cow just below the ear. This morning they speared it twice and I fired about ten times, but missed most provokingly. This excessive bad shooting arises from being unable to steady the arm, thanks to old Leo at Mabotsa,[2] and has been a source of great annoyance both to myself and others, who expected me as a white man to be able to kill sufficient for my own use. The men speared the calf yesterday. We have been spearing and shooting this beast the whole day, and yet she lives.

We had a visit from Pangola today, and have got the promise of

Maclear). It is located in lat. 15.36 S, long. 30.27 E (GSGS 4355, SD 36/4); DL gives lat. 15.37.22 S, long. 30.32 E (*Travels*, 585, 687). Originally occupied by the Portuguese *c.* 1720, it was abandoned in 1836, and reoccupied in 1862 (Sousa, *Distrito de Tete*, 1927, pp. 26, 40).

[1] Zungo, 'a fine frank fellow', lived on the island next to Shibanga (*Travels*, 589); Pangola, whom DL met again in 1860, was a 'vassal' of Mpende (*Narrative*, 198).

[2] See above, p. 355.1.

canoes to enable us to cross the Zambesi. They all express satisfaction with our message of peace and good will, and say nothing about the smallness of our return presents when they give us food. We explain that we have come from a country in which there are no European goods, and they readily agree to the truth of the statement. In few other countries would 115 sturdy vagabonds[1] be supported from the generosity of the headmen. We have made friends, and hope to be able by suitable acknowledgements on our return to secure a continuance of their favour.

19th January 1856. At Pangola's.[2] Two of his lords came to our place of bivouac, and tried to play something into their own hands by pretending there were no canoes, but we insisted that my friend Pangola was willing to ferry us across and was prevented by them. They soon agreed to give canoes, and then I gave each a handkerchief and piece of my best riding ox, which sprained his ankle on the hills. They brought two bundles of maize and a fowl from Pangola. The maize is as large as the seed maize brought from the United States to the Cape, and grows in the wonderfully rich soil on the banks of the Zambesi. The grass is as rank as any I ever saw, and though they are agriculturists, both male and female, they can cultivate only a small portion of the extremely fertile valley.

How different the appearance of this land is to that of Kolobeng and southwards. There we waited anxiously during months for rain, and a mere thunder shower was the only result. On rare occasions we had a continuous rain, and that was remembered as extraordinary long afterwards. Here we have thunder showers which make the water stand on the ground some inches deep. The very plants in that dry land have no fragrance; they cannot afford to part with a particle of their moisture. The insects are few too. Here they swarm.

The south sides of the southern hills are bare or covered with bushes only, but the northern sides have trees. Here the hills are all covered with forest and beautifully green, especially when a mass of fleecy cloud runs along about midway up. The summits and bottoms are then very lovely to behold. I shall never forget the dry sultry eastern winds of Kolobeng, the yellowish cloudless sky, the grass and all the plants drooping from drought, the cattle lean, the people dispirited and our own hearts sick from hope deferred, with the shrill whistle of the

---

[1] '. . . 114 sturdy vagabonds' (*Travels*, 590).

[2] There is a native village named Pangura (=Pangola) in lat. 15.36 S, long. 30.43 E (GSGS 4355, SD 36/4).

rain doctor in dead of night proclaiming faith in nostrums and incantations undiminished. How different the feelings when one beholds smiling vallies adorned with plenty, and hears the merry chorus of happy songsters saluting in the pleasant dewy mornings the rising sun. It is a mistake to suppose the intertropical birds as devoid of song.

The hills are near the river only on the left bank. Beyond, or on the north, there are treeless plains and no tsetse. The insect abounds much along the river, and though the people formerly had cattle they were kept among the hills, & goats alone on the holms of the river.

The villages behind the range belong to Pangola. The lords did not know any of the Portuguese names mentioned by Bowdich[1] except Zumbo, nor did they possess any knowledge of silver or gold. Iron is worked by some of the villages in front of us.

In reflecting on the geological changes which have taken place in this country, one gets a better idea of eternity than by any other process I know. If we look at the valley of the Quango, for instance, we find it about 1,000 feet deep & about 100 miles broad; how long, I know not. It has been produced entirely by denudation through a solid mass of keel or clay-slate. Some sort of eddy has left the hill Kasala untouched, but with the same height and horizontal strata of the sides. The Quango is annually discoloured by the same operation which it has been carrying on for ages. But though it carried down as much mud annually as our own Thames, what myriads of ages were requisite to bring the hollow to its present depth. The mind becomes lost in trying to fathom it. But then there is a fixed point at which we arrive, and makes the difference between this and the ordinary ways of thinking of the infinite. We come to the time when the enormous mass began first to be deposited stratum by stratum while primaeval seas performed the Quango work on other rocks, and away beyond that we go again into the hot chrystalizing ages of the Earth's history. By means of these stepping stones into the past, and after getting by the process a sort of glimpse at the eternal by these landmarks of time, we may well bow with humility and a sense of nothingness before the Everlasting Jehovah.

20th. Remain at Pangola's vil[lage]. We are to cross the Zambesi tomorrow. Many of the Batoka who were brought up under the island lords have still much of the slave spirit. They care not how much they trouble us by disobedience to orders. When told not to

[1] *An Account of the Discoveries of the Portuguese in the Interior of Angola and Mozambique*, by Thomas Edward Bowdich, 1824.

place temptation before the villagers, they obey by casting down the ivory of Sekeletu whenever we approach a hamlet and running towards it in order to beg food, though hitherto they have had as much as they can eat. The ivory is thus in danger of being lost. But what do they care for that? Talking to them is of no avail. That vile slave spirit seems to run in the blood. The Barotse are superior to them decidedly. It is grievous to behold their perverseness. It must have been to cure them of the degradation their own slavish spy system engendered that Sekote and others hung the heads of offenders on poles. The chiefs often encouraged private assasination in order to furnish heads for ornament.

Difficulties with Mpende

22d January 1856. At Mpende's, opposite the hill Kamoenja. Another high conical hill appears due north of us, and is called Chanyuné.[1] It seems about the highest I have seen in these parts. It may be said to consist rather of two cones, the northern one being a little lower than the southern.

Pangola did not treat us well, for having promised to ferry us accross the river he sent guides to take us to his farthest village, and when there we discovered he had given no orders to his people to lend their canoes, and they will not without some authority. We have thus been forced to come on to Mpendé, and it is understood he is unfavourable to intercourse with white men. When we came he sent merely to see what we were, and the guides from the last village were sent back to call their masters the headmen. No message was sent to us, which looks ill in African affairs. But we are engaged in the service of a good and powerful master. I commit my way to Him.

We make very little progress. Mazanswe is still in sight. The speed of our tsetse-stricken oxen is about 2 miles an hour, and they will soon require to be slaughtered. With canoes we could get on rapidly, for the river flows more rapidly here than above the falls. We are further delayed by being obliged to stop at every village and send notice of our approach to the headman, who comes and recieves an explanation of our objects and some little religious instruction. They give a little food, and recieve a little of the remnants of our beads & handkerchiefs. Though this devours much time it is all in the way of doing good, and

[1] The names given for the two hills do not appear on maps consulted (but see p. 383.2). Mpende was a chief of the Manganja, a division of the Nyanja group of Maravi; they inhabit the lower Shire R. as far as the Zambesi, and across into Tete and Sena districts (Tew, *Peoples of the Lake Nyasa Region*, 31; *Narrative*, 198).

they generally express satisfaction with what is said. If any suspicion exists, it must be because we appear over good to people who have generally been visited for disreputable purposes.

The ajacent country is planted thickly with bush, sometimes with mopane. We are somewhat wiser now than in our former journey, for when rain approaches we stop, cover the goods & ourselves with little sheds of grass, and remain till the rain passes over. Yesterday we happened to be among mopane when a thunder shower came over us. The men called me to avoid all mopane trees, for, said they, 'the lightning hates much that tree, it is very dangerous to be near it in thunder'. This must be the result of much observation, as in the case of the other tree used at Cassange as a protective against the electric fluid.[1]

23d January 1856. At Mpende's. This morning at sunrise a party of his people came close to our encampment, using strange cries and waving some red substance towards us. They then lighted a fire with charms in it, and departed uttering the same hideous screams as before. This is intended to render us powerless, and probably also to frighten us. No message has yet come from him, though several parties have arrived and profess to have come simply to see the white man. Parties of his people have been collecting from all quarters long before daybreak. It would be considered a challenge for us to move on down the river, and an indication of fear & invitation to attack if we went back, so we must wait in patience and trust in Him who has the hearts of all men in his hands. To thee, O God, we look, and O, thou who wast the man of sorrows for the sake of poor vile sinners and didst not disdain the thief's petition, remember me, and thy cause in Africa. Soul and body, my family, and thine own cause, I commit all to thee. Hear, Lord, for Jesus' sake.[2]

When three of the Batoka went last night contrary to orders to beg food, a man in the chief's village went round about each of them making the same noise as a lion. When done they called, 'Clap your hands to him'. They did so, and by the chief's orders some chaff was given to them, as if it were food. Other things shew unmistakeable hostility.

Afternoon. After long discussion with his counsellors Mpende has

---

[1] See above, p. 217. In *Travels*, 165, DL calls the tree 'morala', which Hiern (*African Plants*, i. 461) lists as a 'local' name of *Gardenia jovis-tonantis*, whose branches the natives 'fix . . . on the roofs of their huts, as a protection against damage by lightning'.

[2] This paragraph was published by Blaikie, 182.

been compelled to adopt peaceable measures. A man named Sindesé-oa-lea[1] was the chief advocate on our side. We passed him yesterday, and when we were parting he said to his people, 'Is that the man whom they wish to stop? After he has passed so many tribes, what could Mpendé say to refusing him passage?' He came with a boy only, and would not countenance Mpendé at all in his project. I thank God heartily for this termination, for in the event of a skirmish I must resign my mission. We would have been victorious, I have no doubt. Indeed, the Batoka were rejoicing in the prospect of securing captives to carry the tusks for them. We now, said they, will get corn in plenty, and clothes too. Several have since come and desired to see my watch, &c &c, but their morning purposes were dark enough. I gave my men an ox, and sent a leg to the chief. This may have helped to mollify him.

In the evening Sekuebu went in order to broach the subject of the sale of a canoe, to carry one of the men who is so ill as to be obliged to be carried by his companions. When he told Mpende that his companion had sent him to say one of his children was very ill, without giving him time to finish his story he remarked, 'That man is truly one of our friends, see how he lets me know his affliction'. Sekuebu adroitly took advantage of the turn the conversation took and said, 'He highly appreciates your friendship and that of Mburuma, and as he is a stranger trusts in you to direct him'. He replied, 'He ought to cross to the other side of the river, for this bank is hilly and rough and longer'. 'But who will take us accross if you do not?' 'Truly', replied Mpende; 'I only wish you had come at midday, but you will cross. My people will ferry you over'. This is much more than we expected. He was proud of the leg of ox, and regretted he had but little food to give me, also that he could not himself visit me, being restrained by the lion-man from following his own inclination. He was prevented also by the same enchanter from accepting a bit of red cotton check I had, as it would arouse strife, said the same oracle. Promised nothing would detain him when I returned.

Next morning, 24th, he sent two of his principal youths, related personally to himself, to order the people of a large island to ferry us accross. They delivered their message faithfully, but we had afterwards trouble with the headman of the island, who played us falsely. Another man at its eastern end, however, behaved manfully and brought his canoe. We then having the means of approaching the rebel ordered

[1] Called Olea in *Expedition*, 255, where DL says he died 'last year', i.e. in 1859.

him to give a canoe too. He skulked away, but we took it and immediately began to transport the whole party over to an island, and having made the canoes secure by placing them on the bank and setting persons to sleep in and around them we went to sleep.

We commenced again by moonlight, but though we were 455 yards from the northern bank we were 800 from the southern one. It is at least 1,200 yards from bank to bank, and at present there are 700 or 800 yards of water flowing at the rate of $3\frac{3}{4}$ miles per hour. The late rise, which is now fast receding, must have been the result of local freshes alone. It has fallen more than 2 feet as we came along, and the water, though still muddy enough to deposit a film at the bottom of vessels in a few hours, is not nearly so red as it was. Nor is there much wreck now. It is therefore not the period of Zambesi inundation yet. Here it never rises more than four feet, and there is no appearance of three successive levels for the river here. The banks are composed generally of old micaceous sandstone, sometimes with pebbles in it, dipping down on both sides to the river. Nodules of clay slate appear in it having concentric laminae, and there are fragments of silica wood often seen. The forest near Chongue of that fossil wood is very remarkable.[1] Is this indeed a growth on that antient silurian stratum?

A very remarkably shaped hill called Chanyuné stands about 7 or 8 miles to the N.N.E. of this. It is pyramidical in form, and farther west appears as a double cone. Another on the N.E., Motemua[2] (from its likeness to an axe), is in Kaimbua's country, who lately fought with the Bastards. They work much iron there.

We were nearly the whole of the 25th in crossing the broad Zambesi. The people are well supplied with English cotton goods by the Babisa, who come from Mosambique with goods for trade. We are now nearly on the latitude of that place,[3] & but for the wish to secure water carriage might make a shorter journey by cutting through the country of the Basenga.[4] The Babisa are said to be so fond of a tusk that they will sell a newly-married wife for one. I am sincerely thankful to have got accross the river, for if one refuses his canoe all do. They sagaciously remark, 'Why did so-&-so not lend his canoes?

---

[1] In *Travels*, 572, the forest is said to be near the Chipongwe (see above, p. 365.4).

[2] Matemoe, lat. 15.34 S, long. 31.29 E (GSGS 4355, SD 36/4). The description of 'Chanyuné' suggests that it may be 'Cone', lat. 15.32 S, long. 31.16 E (ibid.).

[3] The island (and town) of Moçambique is in lat. 15.02 S, long. 40.45 E (*Africa Pilot*, III, 266).

[4] Nsenga, a tribe of the Maravi cluster; they live north of the Zambesi, between the Luangwa and the Luwiya (*Manual of P.E.A.*, 1920, p. 114; Tew, op. cit., 31).

He must have had some good reason'; and no reward will induce them to swerve. Our last beads were expended today, and I sent back one of my two spoons as a thankoffering to Mpende. He was much pleased with a shirt I gave. Others give presents of food, I suppose in expectation of a return, but readily believe us when we explain all our goods having been expended in our long tour. We have not yet got an uncivil word.

Portuguese traders

29th January. Having come early to Mozinkwa's,[1] I was agreably surprised by seeing two Portuguese traders come to salute. They belong to Tete, and give a very black account of the natives in these parts. One of them was lately robbed by the people to whom we have come. Their names are José Anselmo Santa Anna and Davida da Costa. Very friendly they have been, and it is most refreshing to meet with Europeans.[2] They say that they have great difficulty in managing the negroes on the river, who demand payment for leave to pass them. They have just now concluded a two years' war with them. Powder and lead and guns are contraband, both here and at Mosambique. Many robberies occur, and they are always suspicious of each other.

It is a most unhappy state of affairs and bodes ill for our success, but we look to the Great Jehovah who has all hearts in his hand. We have had no cause for discontent as yet. The chiefs fear me, and when I was coming down the river they spread the report that the son of God was on the way. I wish I were indeed a true child of the living and merciful one, through Jesus Christ our Lord. The chiefs are not permitted to come near me, though they wish it. Mozinkwa promises me the loan of a canoe to carry my sick [man] down the river.[3] I gave a shirt to

[1] Headman of an island in the Zambesi (*Travels*, 595; cf. *Expedition*, 254). He subsequently became 'odious to his countrymen', who put him to death (*Narrative*, 196).

[2] In *Travels*, 597, these men are referred to, very briefly and anonymously, as 'native traders'. The first is described by name in *Expedition*, 399–400, as 'a Portuguese half-caste' who was 'the chief agent in the assassination' of Mburuma (see above, p. 368.1). There is much more information about him in *Narrative*, where he is mentioned only by his native name 'Sequasha' (pp. 193, 201–2, 205, 327–8, 339); cf. also Stewart, *Zambesi Journal*, 63–4, who calls him José Santana. David da Costa is mentioned in a list published by Eça, *Guerras no Zambeze*, ii. 576, as a merchant, born in Portugal, who in 1868 was among those furnishing men for the attack on the rebel leader Bonga (see below, p. 424).

[3] But cf. *Travels*, 596: 'One of my men, after long sickness, which I did not understand, died here' [at Mozinkwa's].

Mozinkua, having nothing else to bestow. The whites complain bitterly of the blacks, and they again of the other, as destroying them by purchasing their children. They say Tete is full of their children as slaves.

The laws of these tribes are very strict. If any one kills an elephant, the tusk and half of the body on the ground belong to the lords of the land, and the hunter must wait their good pleasure, for should he begin to cut up the animal all becomes the property of the proprietors of the soil. They claim, too, certain parts of a buffalo.

Provisions are said to be scarce in front, and my men are naked and require clothing. I intend to purchase some cloth for them with the tusks they have slaughtered, unfortunately all little ones. We are now ten short stages from Tete. If we had canoes we could manage well in a third of the time which it takes us to wind along the banks of tangled jungle. All the oxen are dead of tsetse except 2, and the riding ox is so weak from the same cause as to be nearly useless. (Killed same day; knocked up.)

Finished letter to Sir R. Murchison today.[1]

31st. Detained by very heavy and long continued rains *from the west*.

1st February 1856. We passed our two friends on this day, purchasing for 28 lbs of ivory two pieces of white American calico & one and a half of coloured, it being, it seems, absolutely necessary to pay tribute to that amount to three chieftains in front before reaching Tete. I have the goods by me in case of necessity, but mean to try persuasion first, my object being neither more nor less than the advantage of all the tribes. They have thus far behaved better than I could have expected.

Mr Anselmo gave me a guide, who was to carry one of his tusks home for him, but he absconded next morning. One of my men, too, fled from us. He is one of Mokuine's people, who have the largest infusion of the slave spirit of any in the party. He said one still with me had killed both his father and mother, and he never wished to return to the country of the Makololo. This is probably true, so I gave instructions if such were really his wish he might remain, but he must not be sold as a slave.

The people here anxiously invite my men to remain, and they probably intend to sell them after I am fairly gone. They complain bitterly

[1] Dated 'Hill Chanyuné, on the banks of the Zambesi', 25.i.56, it was published in *JRGS*, 1857, pp. 357–67.

of seeing their children forming powerful villages for the whites after they have sold them. Their finest daughters are sold to be concubines, and though the prices are recieved they feel bitterly afterwards. Both my friends had young women from these parts, and one has three wives. It was odd to see Europeans clothed with a piece of calico around the waist alone. They were very kind in presenting my principal men with cloths and beads. The blacks cannot form any very high idea of our virtue from the specimens they see of Europeans.

There is no medical man in Tete, nor yet a chest of medicines. I left mine at the waggon.[1]

2d February 1856. We came a few hours on foot to Mosusa's village at Chowé R.,[2] which is a brackish stream affording salt to the inhabitants in its sand. It is about 100 yards broad, and only occasionally flows. We were detained all the rest of the day by continuous rains, which now curiously enough come from the west. During most of the journey the east wind prevailed so much we always placed the door of the tent to the west, in order not to get it filled with smoke, as happened when it looked east. We have now to reverse it, for both rain and wind come in the opposite direction. The rich reddish-brown soil is so clammy it is very difficult to walk, but my riding oxen are all dead, and we have no canoe. New shoes don't improve matters.

The people cultivate amazing quantities of corn and maize, earth nuts & pumpkins, also cucumbers. When the plants fail in one spot they transplant others into it. Build high stages with huts on them as watch houses in the gardens. This is necessary both on account of the spotted hyaena, which is here very fierce, but also as a protection against elephants. Mozinkua had his upper lip bitten off by a hyaena, so his teeth are bare.

Liberality and politeness of the people

I must express my admiration of the great liberality of these people to mine. They go into their villages and rarely return without some corn or maize. Some dance, and one, a natural bard, sings and jingles his bells, and never in vain. The real politeness with which presents of food are given through nearly all the tribes makes it easy to accept the gifts. Suppose an ox is presented: 'Here is a little bread' is the phrase employed, or it is whispered to my principal man to say for them.

[1] At Linyanti, where he recovered it in 1860 (*Narrative*, 296, 297).
[2] The Chowe (Choe) joins the Zambesi from the south in lat. 15.42 S, long. 31.36 E, where there is a village called Msusa, i.e. Mosusa (GSGS 4355, SD 36/4).

When meal is given, an apology is invariably made about its smallness, or regret expressed that they had not notice of our approach in time to grind more. And so all the way down the river. All readily accept of our excuse of coming from a land where there are no goods for sale, saying they are perfectly aware of the fact.

I always give a good present when I have it in my power, something really useful and its usefulness known, for the honour of old England, and have found the benefit of the procedure afterwards when run out. They say, 'If he had it, we know he is liberal'. How such persons as the commanders of the Niger expedition could have the face to give 'a small present', 'a trifling present', &c &c, and deliberately pen their stinginess,[1] is to me unaccountable, seeing scores of crimson silk dresses were sold by auction afterwards. As the miser who tried to cheat old Charon was proposed to be punished by sending back to the world to see the use his heirs made of his riches, it might have been beneficial to send the donors to act as auctioneers in Rag Lane.

African ladies recieve a small gift very gracefully, handing [it] quickly to an attendant, who then becomes the owner, without any remark. They laugh afterwards, saying to those near them, 'Is that a white man? There are niggards then among them too.' Those accustomed to frequent visits of white men or slave dealers change considerably. This is in part owing to our asking to purchase everything, and giving the food they bring to our servants.

It is as much the law from time immemorial for the chief to feed all strangers as it is among the Arabs. It is one of the arguments for polygamy they employ. A man with one wife only could not feed strangers. The present given is by way of compensation. We spoil it by being purse-proud, giving the present and then saying, 'Tell him I want to buy so & so'. But for this aboriginal law I could never have come thus far. I intend, if spared and able, to repay all my friends abundantly. Although I have now nothing to give, I never pass a chief knowingly. He is gratified by my politeness, and so are my people by his generosity.

The range of hills on the left bank near the confluence of Kafué possesses at the bottom a forest of silicified trees, all lying as if the elevation of the range had made them fall towards the river. I could

---

[1] DL must have been thinking of the gifts made to relatively unimportant persons (cf. Allen and Thomson, *Narrative of the Expedition to the River Niger in 1841*, i. 190, 210, 248, 284, 287, etc.); official presents to chiefs, e.g. at the signing of treaties, were in comparison very substantial indeed (i. 257–8, 315–17, etc.).

not detect on what they were reclining, for they are nearly the only rock visible there. Higher up the rock is mica slate and perhaps clay slate. But from the Loangua downwards the bottom rock is old primitive sandstone, with banks of shingle and pebbles embedded. Opposite Chanyuné fossil trees again occur all along the bank, lying on the same rock, but there are nodules of clay slate too, and I believe the trees grew in that, which when removed to form the soil left the harder rock with fragments of silicified wood thereon. It is like fir wood, and an ordinary-sized tree standing on end measured 22 inches in diameter and twelve laminae in the inch. On the opposite bank from this the Basenga live, and work in iron, which in all this region from the Batoka eastwards occurs in tears, which when broken often shew streaks of pure metal. It is excellent & easily worked. The range on the other side is remarkably furnished with conical hills in successive tiers or ranges.

4th February 1856. Detained by rains. As in going north, we have with great regularity a heavy shower without wind just about daybreak. It often clears up after that and admits of our moving on a few miles. Then about midday a continuous rain sets in, which continues several hours. There were three large elephants on the island opposite us yesterday, and one not more than half grown. This is not common, the young males remaining with the cow herd untill the age of puberty, when they are expelled. As soon as the weather clears up, the chorus of singing birds bursts out into song which is very agreable. Cicadae and crickets help most vigorously to swell it by their monotonous stridulous notes. The birds are not remarkable for gorgeous plumage.

The liberality of the people is wonderful. The girls call out to my men, 'Dance, and I will grind corn for you'. Those who can work willingly on the terms, and return laden with food. Being nearly naked, too, they excite compassion. Here the people have great abundance of clothing, bought from Tete and the Babisa traders. A party of the latter was lately robbed and plundered by Mburuma. A few escaped, but many were killed. We passed in safety, thank God who gaurds us night and day.

The women here pierece the upper lip, but insert a small button only. They are thus not so hideously ugly as those farther up the river. The men tatoo their bodies variously, and drawing their hair out into rolls a foot long wind the inner bark of a certain root round each. This gives it stiffness. When tied behind it often reaches below the bottom of the shoulder-blade. Others tie it at the crown. The bunch then stands straight up. The women seem to care less for ornamenting the hair than the men.

Missionary enterprise needs stability

Our missionary enterprise is one of the characteristics of the age. The tendencies of our times turn strongly towards such schemes of benevolence, and are we to learn only by the experience of the present? I see that both on this river and at the other side of the continent the church and trade flourished together. Has the one declined in consequence of the decay of the other? Will our missions decay with the witholding of contributions from Europe, as the churches & monasteries have here decayed with the loss of support from rich merchants whose souls were cared for?

We seems to want an element of stability which the ancient establishments for the propagation of civilization and Christianity had. The monasteries when pure were perhaps what we now need more than our present missionary institutions. The best lands belonged to them, because they had most knowledge and could make the best use of them. This was no hardship, no injustice to the inhabitants, who had thus normal schools of husbandry brought into their vicinity. Fruit trees and most of our vegetables and many flowers were introduced by the monks, who like modern missionaries did not disdain to hold the plough. They were, as mission stations now are, the schools in which serfs were taught, the hospitals or dispensaries for the sick, and almoners for the indigent poor. How close the resemblance. But they go no farther hand and hand together. The monasteries became the nurseries of learning, the schools of Europe, rich and self-supporting. Mission stations are pauper from their commencement to their old age and decay.

Can we learn nothing from the monasteries? Do we indeed see nothing in them but the laziness and pollution of their decline? When their work was pretty well finished in Europe there was a necessity for their abolition, but in the heathen world some modification of the self-supporting plan on which they worked seems necessary. It would be heresy to mention the idea of purchasing lands like religious endowments among the stiff Congregationalists; but an endowment conferred on a man who will risk his life in an unhealthy climate, in order thereby to spread Christ's gospel among the heathen, is rather different, I ween, from the same given to a man to act as pastor to a number of professed Christians. The former [is] the appointment of

L   389

godly men, who have the power to cancel it and are in fact frequently called upon to change its reciever, the latter [is made] by men who may easily be preached asleep.

The tendency to go astray from rectitude is the peculiarity of all earthly things. And I cannot see that there is any greater tendency to error in a revenue derived from abroad, and under the supervision of Directors, than there is in one derived from voluntary sources at home under the same vigilant oversight. What missionary cares for what the contributors think and say of him? He deals with the Directors alone. I would treat a letter from a private contributor as if it were anonymous. Some may think it creditable to our principles that we have not a single acre of land, the gift of the Colonial Government, in our possession. But it does not argue much for our foresight that we have not farms of our own equal to those of any Colonial farmer. A good deal of mumbling and grumbling occurs among settlers and others if they see a number of poor Hottentots settled on any spot near them, and endless annoyance is given by empounding their cattle & other shabby ways not practised towards each other. It is our fault such are in the vicinity at all. The Hottentots are expected to go soldiering against Caffres too, and the farmers claim the privelege of remaining at home.

District of Chicova

7th February 1856. We slept last night at Boroma's village or rather lot of villages, each surrounded by most extensive patches of cultivation. He did not make his appearance, but a substitute behaved civilly. In consequence of the continuous rains which detained us, the Zambesi is again flooded and great quantities of wreck float down the stream. It is probable that the fresh occurrence of rains sufficient to flood it are frequent enough to make observers at Quilimane think it is in active flood through its whole course. It is very broad, and begins to make southing at Boroma's or rather at the hill on the opposite side named Chori Chori.[1]

This morning I sent to say I wished to proceed on my way. The answer returned by his chief wife and mother was that they expected me to remain & consequently no food was yet ready, but they sent a

---

[1] Boroma's village is now several miles south of the Zambesi, in lat. 15.47 S, long. 31.43 E (GSGS 4355, SD 36/4); his people are Tavara, a Shona tribe of the Korekore cluster (Santos Junior, *Algumas Tribus do Distrito de Tete*, 1944, fig. 25). Chorichori, 'a great cluster of conical hills' (*Travels*, 602), is not named on maps consulted.

basket of corn and a fowl. Boroma was seized, it was said, by the barimo, which may mean that he was drunk, and no one could see him. He grunts on these occasions like a lion, and they say he is now changed into one of these animals.

There is no very large empire among the negroes. One named ¹ may be an exception. He lives south-east of this. The form of government may be called a mixture of republicanism and monarchy. When a chief dies his son does not succeed to the chieftainship, for the same reason that the youngest son of the Scotch Highlanders was the heir. A brother or cousin is chosen by the chief men, who proceed to his residence, though he may be in a different part of the country, and bring him to where the late chief's body is lying still uninterred. A grave is then made and much beer brought. The new chief pours much of the liquid into it as an offering to the barimo. Goats and kids and sheep are slaughtered there in abundance, and the blood poured into it also. He is then praised for his cleverness in doing the needful properly, and called chief. The same process is gone through when he dies. His son does not inherit either.² They hold the graves sacred, and we have been told not to cut down certain trees, as there they went to worship the barimo.

We came [in] 2 hours to the rivulet Mpata,³ and here remain for the night. It seems to come from the south-east, and is a sandy stream of forty yards wide.

8th February 1856. Came to Pinkwe,⁴ and as the Zambesi fills all the rivulets far in we are obliged to strike farther into the country in order to avoid them, and strike accross a part of the great bend to the south which begins here.

9th. Left the river this morning, and came through about ten miles

¹ Blank space in MS; name not give in *Travels.*

² This mode of succession, said to be characteristic of the Nyai, is more clearly and accurately described as follows in *Travels*, 617–18: 'The chief is elected, and they choose the son of the deceased chief's sister in preference to his own offspring. When dissatisfied with one candidate, they even go to a distant tribe for a successor, who is usually of the family of the late chief, a brother, or a sister's son, but never his own son or daughter.'

³ Impata, joining the Zambesi in lat. 15.38 S, long. 31.53 E (GSGS 4355, SD 36/4).

⁴ 'We marched along the river to a point opposite the hill Pinkwe (lat. 15° 39′ 11″ S., long. 31° 48′ E.)' (*Travels*, 602); 'Pinkwe, or Mbingwe, otherwise Moeu' (*Narrative*, 192); located on DL's maps on the north bank of the Zambesi. The only name resembling it on modern maps is Fingoe, a lofty hill in lat. 15.08 S, long. 31.56 E (GSGS 4355, SD 36/4).

of mopane tree country. Wherever this tree flourishes the soil is hard and baked, generally shallow too. Its form is very upright, and during the heat of the day the leaves, which are in pairs and seem one divided, nearly close, and thus having their edges to the sun give very little shade. They have few branches low down, so one sees far among them. There are many buceros nests in holes in them, and today I noticed a squirrel had placed a great number of fresh leaves over a lot of seed. It is not a cold winter makes it do so here; probably it is a provision against the time when the trees generally are not in seed.

There are a great many silicified trees lying on the ground among the mopane. Some are broken off horizontally, others are lying prone and broken accross into a number of pieces. One was 28 inches of semi-diameter, or four feet eight in diameter. The wood must have been soft like that of the baobab, for there are only six lamellae to the inch; $28 \times 6 = 168$ years. Between each concentric ring the silica is deposited almost pure, and these stand out between the lamellae, which have been more easily worn away than it. I found also a piece of palm tree transformed into rust of iron, the pores being filled with silica. They all lie upon primitive sandstone, but there are nodules and mounds of a clay slate which may have been the soil for these ancient forests. Above all lies scattered generally a calcareous tufa. The R[ive]r Bangue[1] reveals a hard igneous looking rock on edge, strike south.

We found a white edible berry in abundance. It resembles in size the currant, but pure white; the seeds bitter. It is named Monuana (=finger). Another fruit, Mokorongua or Mohororongué, is a pleasant-tasted black plum having a bright red or light purple colour. The people eat that and another named Kalongua, but not so good.[2]

The wood is scarce near the villages, not from want of trees. These are abundant, but generally in a green condition. All that can be used as fire wood are immediately appropriated to that use. Many trees, and more especially a species of acacia yielding a fruit as large as a walnut, are sacred as places of prayer, chiefs and other men of influence being buried near them. We have been warned not to cut them down. This feeling has preserved many venerable trees, more especially of the Ficus family, which is remarkable as being sacred or medicinal among all negro tribes.

We remained last night with a very obliging and intelligent man

---

[1] Joins the Zambesi in lat. 15.40 S, long. 32.02 E (GSGS 4355, SD 36/5).

[2] Monuana = Byrsocarpus orientalis (Miller, *Woody Plants*, 17); mokorongua = Cleistochlamys kirkii (Wild, *Botanical Dictionary*, 65); kalongua, not identified.

opposite Pinkwe. When told of our dislike to purchase slaves, he re-marked that he was a subject of Gōsa, who is the most influential chief in these parts,[1] and that when Gōsa sees any article of merchandise which fascinates him a messenger is sent to him and such-like headmen for children, & should he want those of others he must send his own. On enquiring what would be the punishment supposing he should refuse, he replied a party would be sent to plunder him of everything and they would drive him off Gōsa's lands, saying 'You have been placed here for no other purpose than that of bringing forth children for Gōsa.'

The general colour is a dark brown or deep olive. The Bakoba or Bayeiye are the darkest people I have seen. They are the Quakers of the African body politic, and according to a tradition 'their fore-fathers made bows of castor oil plant branches, which breaking they abandoned fighting entirely.' They become the slaves or subjects of whatever tribe gains the mastery of the lands through which their river runs. Every one goes into their villages to get food, yet they generally fare well, for when out fishing or hunting they keep a pot boiling in the canoe and stop beside a bunch of reeds, dine, then come home, looking quite innocent in denying the possession of food to their visitors. They are in general miserably poor. The success of such principles seems to depend as much on the diffusion of principles of justice among the natives of Anglia as upon the rectitude of the peace principles themselves.

The Banyeti are famed as smiths and workers in wood and basket work. They are said to have been always liberal, and so kind no one could ever pick a quarrel with them. The poorest person who comes to them is treated well, and they being great agriculturists they have always plenty to spare.

10th February 1856. A plant called Mokuri[2] abounds among the mopane. It seems inclined to be a creeper (rather, a climber), but is rather a drooping shrub. The people percuss the ground all round at distances varying from 2 to 4 feet, and find by the difference of sound where a number of large tubers are deposited. Some are quite a foot below the surface, but are readily detected by the percussion stone.

---

[1] He was principal chief of the local Tavara (see p. 390.1), a tribe living between the Zambesi and Ruya (Luia) rivers (Posselt, *Fact and Fiction*, 117; Sousa, *Distrito de Tete*, 95). There is a village of his name in lat. 15.52 S, long. 31.52 E (GSGS 4355, SD 36/4). He is not mentioned in *Travels*.

[2] Not identified.

They resemble turnips in taste; contain a great deal of sap and a sweetish gummy matter which makes the lips feel sticky. (It strangely determines to the knee joints like Thōma,[1] which causes pain in all the joints!) The Batoka know it well.

We are among the people of Gōsa. Chicoba or Chicova is on our east, and is a location formerly occupied by a Portuguese. It is not a district nor kingdom.[2]

12th. Yesterday morning we came to a sand river about 60 yards broad and named Nake.[3] The bed at the point we crossed it was of shale easily broken, and I found a piece on the opposite side containing a thin seam of coal. Both shale and coal burned well, and I have no doubt but coal exists somewhat farther up the river. The dip is to the south, and a dyke of basalt near the ford seems to separate the part having the coal from the rest of the country. The rock I imagined to be primitive sandstone must belong to another class, for here it lies above the coal. Thus coarse sandstone, clay slate, sandstone slate and shale above the coal. The main bed may be farther down the stream or in the direction of the hill Bungwé,[4] which is on our east, with Chicova behind its northern end. We had to cross the Nake several times, the path winding along its sandy bed on account of the thick brushwood on the ajacent lands. Several salt or brackish springs appeared, and the water from the recent rains felt a little more than tepid. The sandstone formed the bed occasionally. We have still to cross the Nake three times, then get quit of it. We are detained today by a continued rain. The gardens on the banks are very large, and the grain very large in its growth.

The great chiefs on this side the river are said to be he of Dande,[5] Boroma, and Gōsa. The others are all partially or wholly subject to them.

[1] 'A scented medicinal shrub' (Brown, *Secwana Dictionary*, 305); not identified.

[2] Early Portuguese reports often referred to Chicova (Chicoa) as a kingdom with rich silver mines (cf. Bowdich, *Portuguese Discoveries*, 129; Axelson, *Portuguese in S.E. Africa*, 5). The village of that name, in lat. 15.36 S, long. 32.21 E (GSGS 4355, SD 36/5), was first occupied by the Portuguese in 1614 (Sousa, *Distrito de Tete*, 25).

[3] Probably the river known nowadays as Dague (see below, p. 398.1), which joins the Zambesi in lat. 15.39 S, long. 32.06 E (GSGS 4355, SD 36/5).

[4] Lat. 15.47 S, long. 32.10 E (GSGS 4355, SD 36/5).

[5] Danda, a subdivision of the Ndau group of Shona; they live south of the Zambesi and west of the Messenguezi (*Manual of P.E.A.*, 116; Rita-Ferreira, *Indigenas de Moçambique*, 47).

13th February 1856. We are compelled to remain here another day. We had an indifferent guide from the village, where our guide from the river left us—an inveterate talker, and always stopping and asking for pay so that he might go on with a merry heart. He led us purposely into inextricable thickets [and] then into the bed of the Nake, so that we might not see the path, and completely tired us all out. I paid him well with 6 feet of blue cloth and wished him to leave, but he kept to us pertinaceously, untill Sekuebu heard him telling others to allow him to lead us astray, as we were a stiff set. I then gave him some beads, told him 'he was a mere tongue and must leave us'. It is in general best, when a scolding is necessary, to give it with a present and end by good wishes kindly expressed. He went off smiling, and my men remarked, 'His tongue is cured now'.

We came through immense gardens of Caffre corn, maize, beans, earth nuts, pumpkins, and cucumbers. The country on our left is thick tangled jungle all the way to the hill Bungué. We expect soon to get out of it and reach Nyunkue, as Tette is universally named by the natives.

In the afternoon the Nake filled and exhibited the usual characteristics of these sand rivers in flood. The flow is very rapid, and a vast load of sand and gravel is borne along a great distance, though the freshet may be of only a few hours duration. When crossing the Zingesi[1] we felt thousands of particles of coarse sand striking the legs, and the slight disturbance caused by our footsteps caused deep holes in the bed. If I followed another person this made it so much deeper for me; though he was only half thigh deep, I was breast deep. The sand rivers are the means of removing vast masses of disintegrated rock before it becomes fine enough to form soil.

Ever since boyhood my imagination has been haunted by the idea of a river running into sand and becoming lost. I have often longed to see and examine such a wonderful phenomenon. But now I begin to doubt if there is really in Africa a sight corresponding to my preconcieved idea. The nearest approach to it is in such rivers as the Kolobeng, flowing into and becoming lost in the sand river Motsemotlabe.[2]

[1] Probably the Messenguezi (Umzengezi), which joins the Zambesi in lat. 15.43 S, long. 31.14 E (GSGS 4355, SD 36/4).

[2] The Kolobeng (after which DL's mission station among the Kwena of Bechuanaland was named) joins the Metsemotlaba ('sandy water') in lat. 24.38 S, long. 25.38 E, and the latter joins the Notwani (Ngotwane, a tributary of the Limpopo, in lat. 24.28 S, long. 26.07 E (WAC 3300).

When we came to the Kolobeng, we found it five or six yards broad and two or three feet deep with a quick current. It ran into the Motsemotlabe sand and disappeared. The sand however being coarse, water may be found by removing the sand, and it then may be observed still flowing. The game know this, and rhinoceros dig for drink. But this, I imagine, is scarcely what is meant by a river becoming lost in the sand, for the Motsemotlabe has well defined margins, flows in the rainy season above the sand, and in the driest part of the year deposits its water in pools before joining the Notuané.

The Nake is fifty or sixty yards wide. Ought such to be placed in the map? Here its flow is northerly.

The rock which I though primitive sandstone is probably of a more recent formation. It contains beds of shingle, pebbles and coarser sand gradually gliding into a slaty sandstone. The mica in both shews it must have been formed by the wearing away of the hills of mica schist behind. These exhibit the peculiar appearance, on a grand scale, which banks of mud shew when left by the tide, or places composed of clayey soil destitute of vegetation when worn by the rains. They have also a wonderful number of peaks or conical projections both above and below the general height of the ranges. Here we begin to see flat or table-formed hills and ranges. Mounds and nodules of a sort of clay slate, of variegated colours running often in circles, appear often on the sandstone, and may have been formed by the eddies or still places caused by the silicified trees. Above that lie patches of hard chalk with pieces of pure flint. Is this chalk a guide to the formation of the trees? How curious the pores of the palm should be selected by the silica, and the wood by the rust of iron.

The bed of the Nake shews quartz with large pores and striæ as in the volcanic bombs, also porphyry with fine white round chrystals not so large as millet seed. Chicova is said to have had silver mines, but I am not acquainted with the appearance of the ore. Basaltic dykes bursting through the sandstone, clay slate, and shale, may afford metallic veins. The natives, however, have no silver ornaments, and those of tin they invariably assert come from Nyunkwe. It is not very probable that all silver ornaments and knowledge of the metal could have entirely vanished in the course of one or two generations. A bed of good coal would be of more value here than one of silver, for it might be taken down the Zambesi and sold to English steamers. As the dip of the overlying rock is to the south, the bed may be in that direction. The shale seemed quite horizontal. The presence of the silicified trees & coal shews that this part of Africa, at least, was once under the sea. How wonderful I have never been able to detect a single shell.

We sent the last fragment except one of our cloth to Nyampungo,[1] with the request that we should be furnished with a guide to the next chief. After long conference with his chiefs the cloth was returned, with the promise of supply, but requesting some beads in addition. I gave the last of these, and he desired us to remain over today. He presented a little rice only, saying he had no fowl to give me. Others come here to beg rain. A red cloth here would be a crime, as it would drive off the rain.

The people here call themselves Bambiri,[2] and an old man, father-in-law of the chief, says he has seen books before, but never knew what they meant. Seems much pleased with the little knowledge we can communicate. They never digged silver, but say there is gold, dalama, in the sand of the rivers Mazoé and Luia, which unite in the Loenya.[3] It is got by washing. This is the first time I have [heard] the name of gold among the natives of Africa. It is not Portuguese,[4] though many words have been adopted from that language: 'Inde, Inde', ainda ainda.[5]

[1] 'The head-man of these parts. . . . This man is supposed to possess the charm for rain, and other tribes send to him to beg it' (*Travels*, 605). Inhampunga, 'king' of Boquiza (Vuchiza), is mentioned by Bocarro (*c.* 1640) as a vassal of Monomotapa (Theal, *Records*, iii. 266, 356). There is a village of his name (Nhampunga) in lat 16.03 S, long. 32.04 E (GSGS 4355, SE 36/2). The people in its vicinity are chiefly Tavara (Santos Junior, *Tribus do Distrito de Tete*, fig. 25).

[2] 'Here they call themselves Bambiri, though the general name of the whole nation is Banyai' (*Travels*, 604). The Mbire are nowadays classed as Zezuru (central Shona), but Posselt says that they 'at one time formed part of the Monomotapa empire' (*Fact and Fiction*, 120).

[3] The Mazoe is joined by the Luia in lat. 16.34 S, long. 33.13 E, and itself joins the Luenha (Ruenya), a tributary of the Zambesi, in lat. 16.32 S, long. 33.26 E (GSGS 4695, sheet 1176).

[4] *Ndarama*, the Shona word for gold, is said to be of Arabic origin (Hannan, *Standard Shona Dictionary*, 427).

[5] The Portuguese adverb *ainda* is commonly translated 'yet, even, moreover, besides'; *inde* is the word for 'yes' in Nyanja and related languages (Scott, *Mang'anja Dictionary*, 192, 737; Courtois, *Diccionário Portuguez-Cafre-Tetense*, 430).

XVIII

APPROACH TO TETE

Insects and Birds

14th February 1856. Left Nyampungo this morning and wound up the Molinje, another sand river, which flows into the Nake.[1] Volcanic porphyry with serpentine in a green rock & red clay slate abounded. The chrystals in the porphyry are minute, round, and pure white. When we had got clear of tangled jungle we got into mopane and could walk with comfort. The country is soaked with water everywhere.

When Mvungue hills[2] bore on our right an elephant was espied and, before I knew, the men who still have spears were all in full pursuit. Though a bull it soon was killed, the people of the country saying they never had seen such desperadoes before. Hunger made all eager, and when I came up it was dead. By the law of the land the under tusk and half of the animal belongs to the lord of the soil. We have been obliged to send all the way to Nyampungo, to give information to a certain person who has been left there by its real owner to watch his territory,[3] before we can touch it. If we began cutting up before he came we should lose all. Fortunately the under tusk in this case is short and broken, the upper (ours) large and thick. It is an old animal, and never charged. 'God gave it to us', say the men; 'He said, "Go up there, men are come who will kill and eat you."'

We came through grass today which reminded me of the valley of Cassange. Insects are very numerous. Centipedes with blue legs and myriapods with yellow ones run about everywhere, but they are not yet large enough to excite the feelings of horror which such insects produce in man. I suppose the feeling which makes the larger animals, indeed all the animated creation, flee from man is of the same [kind]. An elephant may think, 'There comes the disgusting biped which ruins our peace', as we do when we call out, 'A snake, a snake, or hundred legs, kill the vermin'. Several of the men have been bitten by insects, but no ill consequences have ensued other than pain and swelling. I was roused one night by hundreds of a reddish ant biting me

[1] The Molinge joins the Dague in lat. 15.55 S, long. 32.09 E (GSGS 4355, SD 36/5).

[2] Mvunga, lat. 16.05 S, long. 32.16 E (GSGS 4355, SE 36/2).

[3] '. . . the owner himself living near the Zambesi' (Travels, 608).

furiously. They had been attracted into the bed by some fat on my gun, and I must have disturbed them by my movements.

Yesterday I observed a great number of insects like grains of fine sand moving on my boxes. On examination with a glass, there were four species apparent; one of green and gold prinning its wings, which glanced in the sun with metallic lustre, another clear as a mite,[1] a third of vermilion colour, and a fourth black. These are probably the insects which consume the seeds of every plant that grows. The Mohorongwe is often covered with fine eggs of such little scavengers. There are great numbers of distillers. The saliva-looking mass abound on the grass, and the insects themselves, generally beautifully green with transparent wings, come spring[ing] to the lamp at night. A species of butterfly with perpendicular wings lights on our clothes, and applying a long flexible proboscis to them squirts from its tail drops of water, as if to melt anything soluble for food. Twenty or thirty drops don't exhaust its store.

The birds of the tropics have been described generally as wanting in the power of song. I was decidedly of opinion that it did not apply as a general rule to Londa, where indeed birds are remarkably scarce. The canary, for instance, is not heard amid the loud and merry hum. Here the chorus or whole mass of music made by the birds is decidedly louder than in England. I say not it is more harmonious. It always sounds as if they were singing in a foreign tongue. Several resemble the lark, and that bird is not awanting. Two have very much resemblance to the mavis. One is like the chaffinch, another is like the robin in his notes. Then there is a mocking bird besides. And several curious abrupt notes are unlike anything English, yet loud enough. One says distinctly 'peek, pak, pok', another gives a single note like a stroke on a violin string or that said to have been emitted by the vocal Memnon,[2] succeeded by a coarser return note of the breath. The Mokua-Reza utters a scream[ing] set of notes like our blackbird when disturbed, then concludes with 'pula, pula' (rain, rain). To me the words seem to be 'weep, weep, weep'. The loud screaming cry of pheasants, the 'pumpuru, pumpuru' of turtle doves, and 'chiken, chicken, chick, chirr, chirr', of the honey guide.

---

[1] '. . . clear as crystal' (*Travels*, 609).

[2] Mythological son of Eos (the Dawn). 'The Greeks called the statue of Amenophis III, in Thebes, that of Memnon. When first struck by the rays of the rising sun it is said to have produced a sound like the snapping asunder of a cord' (*Brewer's Dictionary of Phrase & Fable*, 1952 ed., p. 604).

But in hot dry weather all at midday are still. They roost and go to sleep in shady spots. Let, however, a good shower fall, and all burst forth at once into merry song and loving courtship. Early morn and cool evenings are the favourite times for pouring forth their loves. They launch out their merry lays on the sunny earth and among the green glancing leaves and boughs most untiringly, yet never had an Aristophanes to reduce their songs to verse. The fact of many of our birds and animals having a classic as well as modern interest is not borne in mind sufficiently when those of other lands are compared. They want interest, though superior.

I have been disappointed in the plumage of the birds of the tropics. The majority are decidedly in sober dress. I suppose collectors have tried to select the gaudiest as the most valuable, and thus conveyed the idea that the majority possess gorgeous plumage.

Observed today (14th) the footprints of a black rhinoceros and calf. We saw the same among the hills of Semalembue. They are remarkably scarce. The white is extinct in these parts.

A fungus or mushroom makes its appearance all over the country after the rains. Its crown is a foot broad, and stalk an inch and a half in diameter near the crown, tapering to the end of the root often 18 inches long. It grows in & on anthills exclusively, and is delicious either raw or cooked. In trying to preserve the sporules they became putrid and smelled like rotten meat in the course of one day. Another kind, with some brown on the top, is liable to produce pains in the stomach as if poisonous.

There is a well marked difference between this and the western side of the continent in regard to ferns and mosses. From Londa westwards every part which has been cultivated is covered with a mass of ferns or a certain allied plant sufficient to prevent the growth of other vegetation, and on the Chihombo I found tree ferns growing. In Londa, too, the ground is covered with three varieties of moss, and the trees are white with lichens. We observed a trace of the same vegetation when descending from the ridge, but here we never see a fern nor a patch of moss, though we do see green cryptogami and fungi, resembling those called mouldiness, on the ground. This smells strongly as we turn aside the rank vegetation in our path, and sometimes it gives a hot sort of blast on the face. Everything is damp, and we often come upon extensive masses of decayed or decaying vegetable matter, yet we have no fever. Great numbers of small ponds, too, are dried up if the rain holds up for four or five days.

The illustrious Humbolt says small stagnant pools liable to be dried up are more dangerous than a large surface, and cites the case of Vera Cruz & Carthagena, which seems fully to bear him out.[1] But the Kalahari Desert seems to be the counterpart, for whenever the rain falls it is collected into numerous small pools, which again are surrounded by a sandy soil which raises high the temperature of the ambient air. And yet there is not a trace of fever known. This miasma is a most puzzling affair. Cassange is situated on an open elevation of clay slate, in the midst of a valley 100 miles broad, and no marsh near. A trickling rill supplies the people with water. Yet intermittent fever prevails extensively. Pass on to the banks of the Quango, where there is abundance of marsh constantly drying up and sometimes dry, and there is less fever considerably. Yet it is connected with marshes somehow or other. A nor-west wind causes fever in Cassange. Fortunately it does not often blow.

The chief Nyampungo is afflicted with the disease called 'Sesenda' and 'Mbingua', a species of Lepra, and his toes are hidden, so is one of his hands. The disease is not connected with Manassa,[2] which the foeda mulier may give to her husband and is well known to the Barotse. His father told us they had always lived in their present position. Never had cattle. 'Who said he would give us the medicine to enable us to keep cattle?' We found the reason of not having cattle today in abundance of tsetse. One man was pretending to be a lion as we passed, lying up in his dovecot house and grunting in leonine fashion. They believe here that certain men possess the power of metamorphosis, and that they will kill those whom they dislike, or their cattle, and then become men again. Alligators also. This belief is very extensively prevalent.[3]

---

[1] Vera Cruz is on the east coast of Mexico (Gulf of Campeche) and Cartagena is on the north-west coast of Colombia (Caribbean Sea); Humboldt visited both places during his travels in C. and S. America, 1799–1804. DL must have been citing him from memory; the statement mentioned is not in *Cosmos* (see above, p. 258.2).

[2] 'Sesenda' = (Ila) *cinsenda*, leprosy (Torrend, *Bantu-Botatwe Dialects*, 331); 'mbingua', see above, p. 283; 'manassa' = (Lozi) *manansa*, syphilis (Jalla, *Dictionary*, 145).

[3] It is described more fully in *Narrative*, 159–60; cf. *Expedition*, 168, 169, 251, 254. For other African examples, see Willoughby, *The Soul of the Bantu*, 1928, pp. 156–8.

N̲yaole

As we heard the version of the two traders, we now get the native account of the disturbances between them and the Portuguese. A real Caffre chief came with his people to Tete, and requested permission to live in their country. He was pointed to a location, and his mother built and planted thereon. But he was pursued by another Caffre, and being in distress sent to Tete to request assistance. This was not granted, and single handed Nyaolé not only beat but killed his enemy, and secured most of his people to augment his own tribe. The Tete people, hearing of his success, sent a demand for the prisoners to be given to them. But Nyaole replied, 'Nay, I asked for your assistance and you refused, the people are therefore mine.' The Tete people upon this refusal went to fight Nyaole, but were defeated and driven off with loss. 'This will never do, to allow the prestige of our arms to be despised and lost.' Greater preparations were made for a second attack on Nyaole, but it ended like the first in defeat and shame. And this was not all, for Nyaole followed them, took their cattle and burned their houses, and shut them up for two years in their fort. Communication with the sea was thus cut off. But Nyaole died, and his son being milder than his father they are now at liberty.[1] Here beyond Tete they say, 'We never had any quarrel with the Bazunko, they are our wives & furnish us with clothing.'

If a slave runs away, the owner pays some goods to the person to whom he has fled. He is then brought back, all the slaves of the tribe collected, and in the sight of all he is put to death and thrown into the river. Slave buying was not introduced by Portuguese.

February 15th, 1856. Heavy continued rains would have prevented

---

[1] This garbled account refers, not to 'a real Caffre chief', but to Joaquim José da Cruz (a mixed-breed of several different strains, including Siamese and Portuguese), whose native name was Nyaude ('Nyaole'). He 'pursued a policy of aggrandizement on the Zambesi', where 'his ambitions brought him into conflict' with another mixed-breed, Pedro Caetano Pereira, 'who had overrun the left bank . . . from Lupata Gorge to Zumbo. Both men freely stopped shipping to Tete, claiming fees for rights of passage'. The rivalry between them led to open warfare in 1853, when Pereira attacked Nyaude's stronghold at Massangano (see below, p. 459), 'and was driven off after a long siege'. The following year Nyaude's 'private army scattered a small government detachment sent to punish him for insubordination'. He died in June 1855. (See Duffy, *Portuguese Africa*, 1959, p. 88, from which the quotations are taken, and, for more detail, Eça, *História das Guerras no Zambeze*, i. 177–378; cf. also *Travels*, 631, where Nyaude is more correctly described.)

our movements today. But we have another cause of delay. Our elephant of yesterday has not yet been cut up, because the lord of the soil has not yet come to give the requisite permission.

A large caterpillar is frequently seen. It is covered with long grey hairs, and itself being dark coloured it resembles a porcupine in miniature. If one touches it the hairs enter the pores of the skin and remain there, giving sharp pricks. There are others which have the same means of defence, and when the hand is drawn accross them, as in passing a bush on which they happen to be, it resembles the stinging of nettles. The first is called Lezuntaboea.[1]

The men sent to give notice of our elephant's funeral came late in the afternoon. I expected some foul play, as we were strangers, but they had been detained by the heavy rains and a full river. They brought a basket of corn, a fowl, and a few string of beads, as a thank-offering for our having killed it, and said they had thanked the barimo for our success; then added, 'There it is, eat it.' They brought a large party to eat their portion, and they divided the carcase in a friendly way. My men are delighted with the feast, which by lying unopened is now pretty far gone. When fighting it yesterday, one of the men took out his snuff-box and poured out all his snuff at the root of a tree as an offering for success,[2] and the man who remained with me went forward and uttered loud prayers for the success of our 'braves' in the combat. It is impossible not to admire their devout belief in the actual existence of unseen beings. God grant they may yet know the God of Love.

Tubé=shrew mouse, eats vegetables=Tundua. Kongone, a small mouse which kills others. Sichuana Mochori, carnivorous mouse, which expels all others from a house.[3]

18th February 1856. We passed along the short range called Vunga, and find it to be an erupted red porphyry. Many holes in it shew the existence of air or other elastic fluid, for sometimes silica fills their walls and chrystalizes round towards the centre. In one instance a little tuft of asbestos is thus formed. It is curious to observe the various forms the silica assumes—minute round globules, globules of different forms and

[1] Lenje *sicisunta-boya*, kind of hairy caterpillar 'detested by everybody' (Torrend, *Bantu-Botatwe Dialects*, 95).

[2] He was a 'Banyai elephant-hunter' who happened to be present (*Travels*, 607; cf. *Miss. Corr.*, 307).

[3] Tubé (*thube*) is the Sotho name for the short-snouted elephant shrew (Roberts, *S. African Mammals*, 23); the others mentioned I have not identified.

so arranged as to appear like fossil wood, serpentine, red yellow and green chrystals sometimes in a shell or diffused with pieces of clay slate in its substance.

We have two men as guides from Nyampungo, who give a sorry account of the people of Tete. Nyaole treated them, after getting the upper hand, as slaves, beating them publicly &c. A new governor promises to do better. Senhor David, who informed me he had been robbed, is said to have abused one of Mozinkwa's people with his tongue, and his companion came and gave him a sound beating, the other, Senhor Anselmo, looking calmly on and saying he deserved it. The beaten man then paid a fine, and now says he was robbed. This is strange treatment for a European to recieve at the hands of natives.

The people have several times invited my men to spend the night with their daughters. The object of this is to secure children for themselves. A man may come from another tribe to live with a young woman whom he fancies. He must perform obeisance to the mother-in-law every time he comes near her hut, and always keep her well supplied with firewood, not an easy matter along the river. Though his wife bear him many children he can claim none of them, and must depart at last to his own tribe childless. One of the Bastards has a child at Nyampungo's, but cannot claim it. They say they wish seed from my men who are able to kill elephants, as it must be good, but my party have hitherto been very wary and fear a snare.

There are many of the buceros here, and I have seen several extracted from their nests. They are reported here to enter during this month, and the male plasters the females up, leaving only a space $\frac{1}{2}$ an inch broad and 4 long by which she is fed. In every case I have seen, the hole is prolonged two or three feet up, and she avoids pursuit by running up to the top. She moults or denudes herself of feathers, hatches her eggs, and when these are fully fledged emerges. The male feeds her for three months, and the period of corn ripening is known by her appearance with the young. Their food consists of beetles, gryllae, and other insects. They are much attached to a particular nest.[1]

The men killed five or six buffalo calves from a herd we came up.[2] The large game is disturbed only by people sent from Tete to hunt. I feel the marching on foot considerably during the heat of the day.

In Brazil each coffee tree is supposed to yield about 2 lbs annually.

[1] The bird described here (and also on p. 407) is the red-billed hornbill, *Lophoceros erythrorhynchus* (cf. *Travels*, 613–14; *Private J.*, 109, 283–4).
[2] '. . . killed six buffalo calves out of a herd we met' (*Travels*, 615).

Some, however, yield as much as 8 lbs. But taking the lower figure, a missionary would have enough and to spare with 100 trees in full bearing.

The Portuguese and Spanish colonies do not seem to contain the elements of prosperity in themselves, as do the British. Much of this may be attributed to the employment of forced labour, and desire to amass a fortune as speedily as possible and then return home. Labour is not popular. And the offspring of the whites and blacks is not energetic. They all take to trading instead of tilling the soil. That would be looked upon as beneath them. It is confided to the blacks entirely.

I intend to say nothing publicly against the slaving propensities of those whom I visited. I lamented the existence of slavery when among them, and did not hesitate to discuss the subject when with them, and was invariably replied to with candour. Those who say behind the backs of their hosts what they feared to do when in their presence may act otherwise. But while admitting the evils of slavery it is not marvellous they approve the better and follow the worse. How very few of our own contemporaries get out of the rut in which society runs, and how few comparatively were out and out anti-slavery men before the Act was passed, the credit of which all now eagerly appropriate. At the Cape, for instance, there are numbers who so far from approving the freedom of the Hottentots mumble forth lamentations against the whole body of them, because England has decided they shall live under equal laws with the whites.[1] And some even, who would hesitate to put their names down for out and out slavery, give the curious shallow sentiment currency, 'the liberated Africans are better here than they were in their own country'. Let it be fully expressed it means, 'Slavery is better for them than freedom in their own land'.

Fruit trees

19th February 1856. We came slowly along, for being on foot I have to halt for rest every hour or two. This is necessary also for the men, for if we push on they lag behind. I am always ahead of them considerably. We crossed several running rivulets. The Kapopa is the largest, and flows to the south-east. Where we sleep it is named the Ué,[2] and it flows over and between banks of a soft red sandstone mixed

[1] In 1828 the Government of Cape Colony had issued an Ordinance cancelling various restrictive laws hitherto applying to Hottentots and other coloured people, and giving them political equality with Europeans (Theal, *History*, v. 502-3).

[2] 'We crossed the rivulets Kapopo and Ue' (*Travels*, 616). The Ue joins the Metangua (a tributary of the Luia) in lat. 16.15 S, long. 32.37 E (GSGS 4355, SE 36/2; the name Kapopo does not appear on that map).

with white do. in streaks and lime (tufa). The sandstone is evidently alluvial, and is often cut into 12 feet deep.

The country is uninhabited but game abounds, as we see by the footprints of elephants, black rhinoceros, and buffaloes. The elephant seems very fond of Mokoronga and stands long under one tree, carefully picking each of the fruits off the branch and swallowing it. He does not masticate the seed, in this respect imitating exactly the native mode of filling the stomach with indigestible matter. He is very dainty in his habits. The grass is often cut off just below the seed.

The Mokoronga is said by the inhabitants to be very wholesome and strengthening. 'It is fat entirely', fat being in their estimation the perfection of all food.

Another fruit attracted my notice. It grows in a cup, acorn fashion, only the rim spreads out gracefully. They say it is not edible itself, but the women eat the bark of the tree in order to make them bring forth light-coloured children. Fairness is a test of beauty with them as much as it is with us. When saying anything flattering to Sekeletu they call him 'White Lord'. The tree is called Chokabakadzi.

Many trees of much use are probably known to them by tradition. One, named Shekabakadzi, is known as being superior to others for making fire by friction with the point of another stick, and women even may readily produce it when benighted. It appears now with a great profusion of berries hanging, like currants but not edible. I recieved the foregoing information on asking the use of the fruit.

Another, called 'Ndongo' by the Makololo, 'Dongolo' by the Bambiri on the Zambesi, and 'Ntomboloa' by the Batoka, resembles in appearance a small apple, and when ripe becomes black and is said to be delicious.[1]

At Linyanti average temperature during October and November, the hottest months before rains, was at sunrise 63°, highest 70°, lowest 62°; sunset 88°; noon 93°, highest 97°, lowest 90°. This was in the coolest spot I could find under the eaves of a large hut, the thermometer protected. In the waggon it was often 110°, 112°. The temperature on the Zambesi during January & February has been at 79° on the average at sunrise. This is the period of greatest cold, radiation being at its greatest from the sun's rays shooting accross the

---

[1] 'Chokabakadzi' I have not identified; 'shekabakadzi' (Shona *sikavakadzi*) = *Vernonia amygdalina*, also *V. colorata*; 'dongolo' (Shona *mutongoro*, Tonga *intumbulwa*) = *Uapaca kirkiana* and other spp. (Wild, *Botanical Dictionary*, 35, 39; Torrend, *Bantu-Botatwe Dialects*, 227).

atmosphere and producing similar to what occurs when certain chemical substances are in solution. The lowest was 75°. At sunset the average was 85°, at 9 a.m. the average 82°. About 3 p.m., the hottest part of the day, the average was 90°. The highest average in January 88°, the highest in February 94°, a thunderstorm followed. It seems to be becoming a little cooler now as we descend, and there is considerable evaporation. Before February we never could get a cup of cool water. A wet cloth round a vessel had not cooled it in the morning. Within the valley the temperature always falls below 70° in the course of the night.

Test of witchcraft

Our guides willingly give Sekwebu information respecting their customs here. If two persons die at nearly the same time, the wise ones begin to fear and say, 'We have a witch among us for certain'. They then dig a certain piece of wood, which they keep under ground, allow it to lie all night in the field at some distance from the village, and in the morning the entire population go to it fasting. Some medicines are drunk by all, and the person who is first purged is the witch. It is no doubt a device of some knowing one who understood the effect of fear on the bowels, as some other of the same craft understood the effect of fear in restraining the saliva, when he introduced the test of chewing and then spitting out a little rice. The individual proved by this test to be the witch is then burned in a large fire made for the purpose.

A man suspecting his wife puts a pot of water on the fire, and when it boils desires her to shew her innocence by putting her hand in the water. She confesses rather, and the paramour must pay with the child of his sister or brother. The children thus are not those of the father or mother at all.

We passed today the nest of a buceros just ready for the lady to enter. It was plastered so as to leave a hole the size of her body and of a heart shape. Another had laid one white egg like that of a pigeon, and when handled laid another. She had four impregnated, but small, in her ovarium; others, of a white colour, were not impregnated. She often hatches two, and before they are fledged other two. The male then complains of being tired providing for the five, and the lady and two elder ones come out. The hole is replastered, and the young cared for as before till able to move about too. They expel their excreta with force enough to make it alight a full yard from the hole, and this often proves a means of discovery.

Monina's village

20th February 1856. After two and a half hours' march this morning we came to Monina's village,[1] and recieved as usual a hearty welcome from an elderly man, who at once sent a large basket of green maize for our refreshment. Soon afterwards he came himself and talked very kindly to us. 'You are tired from the long way you have come, but you are now at home and must rest yourself.' He is very popular, and great numbers come to him from different tribes because of his liberality.

The country ajacent is mopane, and game abounds so much the zebras and buffaloes feed in sight of the gardens, a proof of the inefficiency of the bow and arrows for expelling the large animals. Last night a wonderful number of hyaenas came about us. A young buffalo had been killed by a lion, and our men secured the fragments. They were thus disappointed of an expected feast, and kept up a doleful howling over it. When they had plenty of elephant they kept up as good an imitation of loud laughter as one can concieve a beast capable of making. Our guide remarked, 'They say you believe you cut all the flesh off, but we too have eaten our fill.'

Many animals are killed nightly, but not so very many as one would expect in thinking of the great numbers of different sorts which occasionally fall a prey to the carnivori. The latter have a very efficient check to multiplication in buffaloes, zebras, kukamas, and giraffes. The buffaloes and kukamas often kill them with their horns. We saw one yesterday which had expiated his temerity by a toss into the air by a buffalo cow. And zebras and the giraffe give but one of their tremendous kicks behind to settle him. In the case of the zebra it is, however, rare the spring knocks one down. Occasionally the horse of the herd runs back and gives him a settler while busy with a mare on the ground.

Boroma, Nyampungo, Monina, Jira, Katalosa, and another,[2] all acknowledge the supremacy of one called Nyatewe, who is reported to have placed them where they are and decides all disputes respecting

---

[1] '... close to the sand-river Tangwe', lat. 16.13.38 S, long. 32.32 E (*Travels*, 617). For the Tangwe, see below, p. 415. I have found no other reference to Monina.

[2] '... and Súsa' (*Travels*, 617), i.e. Soswe, official name of the Mbire chief (Posselt, *Fact and Fiction*, 35). For Katolosa, see below, p. 445; Jira and Nyatewe I have not identified.

land. Boroma's people are addicted to infanticide, the infant being buried while yet alive. When one dies here, he is interred by the people of ajacent tribes alone.

The lake Maravi is simply a continuation of Nyanji grand beyond the hill Morombola [*see facsimile map*], and it is said to be connected

with the Zambesi in Cazembe's country. This river he heard spoken of as the Luambesi, and the Loapola as the Loapura. Canoes can ascend the Shire to the lake. The people Mujaos being friendly with white men, there would be no difficulty.[1]

[1] 'Nyanji grand' is apparently a partial translation of *Nyanja mukulu*, 'great lake', identified in *Narrative*, 80, as 'Lake Shirwa' (Chilwa, in Nyasaland). Of the rivers named, the Luapula flows into L. Mweru, and the Shire from L. Nyasa (Maravi) into the Zambesi (see below, p. 462); 'Luambesi', according to Debenham (*The Way to Ilala*, 152), is the upper Kafue. The 'Mujaos' are the Yao, a large group of tribes east and south of L. Nyasa; for 'Morombola', see below, p. 462.

So far as I can at present understand, there are no such things as nations or kingdoms in the interior of Africa. If we could call the different divisions in Europe in the ninth and tenth centuries by the name of nationalities, then may those in Africa be so termed, only here there is much respect shewn to hereditary descent from certain families. Beyond that it is the strong hand of the warrior which decides power and influence. Again and again a chief more energetic than his neighbours bursts over all bounds, and carries all before him by conquering. But when he dies his extensive conquests revert to their former state of comparative independance. Here we have an arrangement which would have pleased the author of the Cyropædia perfectly, for all the children of chieftains or those related to the ruling family come to Monina, live entirely at his expense, and are educated (trained) by him. They never marry while with him, and the other headmen are careful to send the ivory which they can secure to him, and he purchases clothing &c, distributing all to the young men, scores of whom are always seen in his village. They supply also men to till the ground for them. Their affections are supposed to be gathering around this man only, and not around their parents.[1]

21st February 1856. At the village of Monina. Sent him an offering of two yards of useless print, which we got from Senhor David when we could not help ourselves to better, and a hoe. He said he was not in need of hoes, and the print was not cloth but a mere rag. He had absolute power over the passage, and though he prevented us from proceeding no one would say anything. In the morning his little boy Boroma, to whom I gave a knife, brought a pint of honey for me. The father came soon afterwards. I offered him a shirt, and he remarked to his people, 'It is evident he has nothing; if he had, his people would be buying provisions, but we don't see them going about for that purpose.' His council did not agree to this, and he went away.

We don't give up hopes of his goodness yet. But it is rather hard to be suspected of dishonesty. Of course he does not know us. When I have it I am only too proud to give liberally, and now feel sorely the necessity of giving little or nothing. Perhaps the feeling arises because

[1] The *Cyropaedia*, a 'romantic account of Persian education' by Xenophon (*c.* 430–354 B.C.), 'was a thinly veiled attempt to bring the Spartan ideal of education into the Athenian world, especially its two dominant characteristics – the moulding of character from infancy for a specific civic purpose and the insistence that education is the concern of the state' (Castle, *Ancient Education and Today*, 1961, pp. 79–80). For the native custom, see also below, p. 418.

we are more anxious about appearances when really poor than when conscious of having enough. If I had passed any one with a present of three buttons or a handkerchief, I think my first idea after getting home would [be] conscience money for the Lord Chancellor or some one else. Certainly not publication, as if I had done something excessively clever.

Monageñ lost

With much sorrow we found that Monageñ, one of my companions,[1] had left us during the night, and not a trace of him can be discovered. It is supposed he is afflicted with insanity, and in a wide country full of wild beasts behind us we fear the worst. I sent to inform the chief of it, and he at once sent to all the gardens, desiring the people to look out for him and should he come near them to bring him home. He added, 'We never catch or kidnap people here, it is not our custom, it is considered guilt among all the tribes.' This I knew without his assurance. Monageñ had an attack of pleuritis but recovered from it, and lately complained of his head only. He was in good spirits yesterday, and last night even. His servants are strangely apathetic, and did not report him till we missed him ourselves.

When the men sent to search for him came home, they attributed his insanity to having been the person who laid violent hands on Mokuine, the chief of a large party of my men. They say, 'He was said to have been killed by Moshobotuane, but Monageñ was the individual who put forth his hand upon him and slew him'. This sort of insanity happens not unfrequently among them in similar circumstances. Though in general they merge their individuality in the chief or those who command them, when, however, a man tries to distinguish himself and murders a man of note, he is thrown on his own individuality, and common people make remarks which perpetually bring the affair to remembrance.[2] This iteration on the conscience ends in insanity, and in a wide country the fleeing person is never heard of.

Monageñ was perfectly well to appearance, but lately became afraid of the party Bamokuiné, and hearing their remarks said, 'They

---

[1] He was the Kololo headman in charge of the Toka from Mukuni's village (see above, p. 331.1).

[2] 'When one of these people kills in battle, he seems to have no compunction afterwards, but when he makes a foray on his own responsibility, and kills a man of note, the common people make remarks to each other, which are reported to him, and bring the affair perpetually to his remembrance' (Travels, 620).

want to kill me'. On the evening before he ran away he eat nothing, and during the night got up and said to one who was awake, 'Don't you hear what these people are saying? Go and listen'. He then went out behind and never returned. The country is so full of hyænas and lions it will be a miracle if he escapes. The people make huts on the trees when they travel. If he comes to any village they will take care of him. I feel his loss greatly, for he was a most sensible obliging man. We could have spared others better.[1]

Prevailing winds in Africa

22d February 1856. The prevailing direction of the winds in all that portion of Africa north of Kuruman is clearly easterly, and the time of greatest activity and force is between 9 a.m. and 4 p.m. There is not much variation in this throughout the year. But at the end of winter (June and July) they blow with a strength and regularity sufficient to attract the attention of the most careless observer. Clouds appear daily following the sun at the same time, and the 'preparation' for rain goes on untill the end of October or November, when the rains commence.

This windy time is so well known, the people living on the Leeambye hasten to cross to their gardens before the waves arise, and I have been obliged to place the door of my little tent to the west all the way down in order to prevent the smoke being blown into it. In coming south from Cassangé I gave the order, 'Always place the door in the direction in which we are going', for the same reason. Between four and five the wind falls, and in the calm the temperature also, so the evenings in and near the valley are always delightful and the nights refreshing. In Angola a sea breeze was observed to set in every day between nine and ten on the coast. At Golungo Alto it came between one and two, maintaining the same westerly or west-south-westerly direction. As we receded farther from the coast its activity became apparent later in the day, with the same calm nights and mornings. At Pungo Andongo the winds were variable, but the rains and thunder-storms came so regularly from the north the sides of the houses front-[ing] it were all denuded of whitewash. At Cassange a westerly or N.W. wind was the ill omen of fever, as one day's exposure to it is

---

[1] In 1860 DL learned, from the man he had left behind at Mozinkwa's (see above, p. 385), 'that poor Monaheng had fled thither and had been murdered by the headman for no reason except that he was defenceless' (*Narrative*, 196).

invariably followed by cases. In my party one day's blow laid three of my men up of fever.

As there is no cordillera to stop the course of the winds westwards, the surface of the land heated by the sun's rays combines with the rotation of the earth to give *one* direction to the air. The heated surfaces causing an influx of air from the Atlantic meets that from the Indian Ocean, but not half way accross, because the eastern wind has both the rotation influence and sun's rarification on its side. The western current has sun's heat alone to stir it. Rotation influence is against it, hence its short course. I imagine the ascending current from both sides is mainly caused by the sun's heat, so when that declines we have our delightful cool African evenings.

During the rainy season we have very often two strata of clouds, the lower one almost always going west, the upper one sometimes going east, sometimes west, and much slower than the other. When the lower tier, as the natives say, 'turns back from the west', we have a continued rain for days together. The quantity of rain is graduated, as it were, by the eastern current of air. The farther east the more moisture. At Kolobeng, on the borders of the Kalahari Desert, the hills are covered with trees as if the air, forced to rise, parted when rarified by its altitude with the last portion of its moisture (though invisible to us except by its effects) before going over the Kalahari. During three years at that station, the amount of rain was $4\frac{1}{4}$, $5\frac{1}{2}$, and 4, inches, but these were exceptional seasons. 7 or 8 would be a good season. The former sums may indicate the rain of the Kalahari.

A remarkable wind occasionally blows during the winter months, which is remarkable for its cold and effects. The general direction it assumes is from the south, and it extends as far up as Cabango, sowing wintry aspects all the way. It is piercingly cold and disagreable. The leaves of the majority of trees are withered by one night of it. The tender shoots of real evergreens are killed. At Lotembua all the manioc on the southern aspects of forests was denuded of its leaves, and the grass was yellowed by it even at Cabango. This wind gives the wintery aspect to all the Interior. A period of rest follows. If there has been a good rainy season the year before, there is a gradual bursting forth of trees & plants & grass as we have in England. If it has been a year of drought, the first good shower makes the vegetation rush up so rapidly, five days suffice to give a tinge of greeness to the country, and ten give the landscape a brilliant new aspect. It is much more lovely than in cold slow-growing England.

Here we see changes almost daily, and the change though so quick does not proceed simultaneously among all the trees and plants. Many of the former retain their old clothing either withered or quite green, but not growing untill at or a little before the rains, when the old foliage is pushed off by the new. The evergreens renew their leaves too, and several, keeping on the old dress, send [out] new branches with red brown or fresh green young leaves. Some discolour their leaves before pushing them off, if indeed it can be called discolouration, so bright an orange I have often mistaken a tree so bedecked for one in full blossom. Other leaves are copper coloured, others as black as ink, and others pink or crimson.

Much of these effects is produced by the aforenamed wind, which, if not from the Snewbergen,[1] must be the cold current from the pole taking what we should think ought to be its invariable course, viz. flowing in from the Antartic circle towards the equatorial regions to supply the place of the heated atmosphere of the torrid zone. I have sometimes thought that I could see a gradual verging to the south-east in the winds between Kolobeng and Kuruman, but had not sufficient time for observation. I never knew the cold withering south wind blowing for a shorter period than two and a half days, and it continues through the night often.

Another remarkable wind, resembling the harmattan, blows occasionally previous to the commencement of the rains, but not at any other time, and comes from the north. It is exceedingly dry and hot, strongly electric, and in former times bore large quantities of reddish sand along its course. This was deposited on furniture, which shrunk and cracked at the same time. A bunch of ostrich feathers held to it shews all the piles divergent, and if the hand is applied they all rush to it, clasping the fingers and emitting a crackling noise. The skin cloaks of the natives at the same time emit sparks by night. On re-marking it to the native whose cloak was the subject of observation, he said, 'This (effect) did not come among us with the white man, we saw it of old, we and our forefathers.' Humbolt mentions Otto von Guerrike as the first who observed the spark and heard the crack in Europe,[2] but the human race in a dark skin observed it for ages before, but with the eyes of oxen. This wind is often the precursor of rain. The thermometer standing at 84° during the day at Kuruman, and

[1] Sneeuberg ('Snow Mountain'), a lofty range of mountains between Richmond and Graaff Reinet, central Cape Province.

[2] See above, p. 279.

96° and upwards at Kolobeng, are also precursors of this refreshing phenomenon.

During these winds alone have I experienced the heat disagreable by night in the centre of the continent. But no sooner had we come into the basin of the Zambesi than we felt that the night never became cool. Water was always lukewarm, and a wet cloth around a vessel through the night had not cooled it by sunrise.

It may be added that the winds, though generally from the east, are not invariably so, and when a change takes place it is most frequently from the east round by north, to west, south, and quickly back to east again. The rains follow the course of the sun with admirable regularity, especially in the north. The day when they cease and commence can be predicted with tolerable certainty. This regularity diminishes the farther south we go.

(At Tete the rains come chiefly from the east, though the continued winds come from the south-south-east. We are about one day with the canoe from Lupata. During March rain has come almost daily from the east at 4 o'clock in the afternoon. There is here much thunder, and in summer the thermometer is said to rise to 108° in the house. 21st March 1856.

27 March. Heavy continued rains all day after considerable heat. The temperature will be lowered by them. Many cases of fever in days previous, of mild forms.)[1]

𝒩 yakoba

23d February 1856. Reach the village of Nyakoba after three hours' march, chiefly in the bed of a sand river about $\frac{1}{2}$ a mile broad.[2] It is like walking on snow, and is very fatiguing. It is called Tangue, and is about the largest I have seen, but water flows therein only occasionally.

The country is infested by lions to an extraordinary degree. A person never goes even a short distance alone. Having turned aside at midday, an animal sprung out of the grass taller than myself, which appeared to differ from an antelope, but I did not get a good sight of it.

---

[1] As shown by the dates, the remarks in parentheses (made on the blank lower half of a page) were added when DL was already at Tete, which he had reached on 2 March (see p. 421). For Lupata, see below, p. 459.

[2] '... a sand-river a quarter of a mile broad, called Tangwe' (Travels, 620); presumably the Metangua, which joins the Luia from the NNE in lat. 16.25 S, long. 32.53 E (GSGS 4355, SE 36/2). I have found no other reference to Nyakoba.

This abundance of carnivori is accompanied with great numbers of game of the larger sorts. The black rhinoceros abounds. Men sleep usually on the trees, and never alone if possible. They were surprised to see one of our party turn aside to hew honey out of a tree.

Poor Monageñ went off in the very worst part of the country, but the insane often pass through great danger unharmed. The people of Monina, being all young men, have a dance with spears and firearms in their hands, and a trumpet braying to the discord of a drum was seen by Monageñ on the evening of our arrival. Our present of cloth being returned at the same time must have proved the exciting causes of his insanity. We can already percieve a difference in the conduct of the people of Mokuiné, for having now their own chief and not, as they felt, a usurper who had murdered their late ruler, they go on more cheerfully, and Sekuebu says, 'We will see no more hardheadedness now.'

We were plagued by two men who shewed us the way hither, for they would not believe I had no beads. They pointed to the boxes, but having opened these the village men assented to the reasonableness of their going on to Tete, where I would pay them. It is trying to have one's veracity doubted, yet how often we act so as if we imagined that of the Ruler of the Universe was doubtful. We got them away by some beads off Sekuebu's waist and a promise to send two yards of cotton cloth to each from Nyunkwé. See 1 John 5 : 9–12.

In the way we were informed that a witch doctor who had been sent for by Monina had arrived during the night, and all his wives had gone to the field fasting this morning. They will be caused to drink a certain medicine, and those who vomit it are considered blameless, while those who are purged will be burned to death. It is probable the lot will fall on some one to whom he has taken a dislike. His accusation is that they wish him to die, so that each may be married to her own husband instead of being an eighth or tenth concubine. The Barotse, Bashubea, & others, use a similar test, pouring some first down the throat of a cock and of a dog; if it produces vomiting and not purging, it is imagined it ought to do the same in the person suspected. Our own test by water in Scotland excited more wonder in their minds than theirs did in mine.[1]

24th February 1856. We have got on better with Nyakoba than

---

[1] 'I happened to mention to my own men the water-test for witches formerly in use in Scotland. . . . The wisdom of my ancestors excited as much wonder in their minds, as their custom did in mine' (*Travels*, 622).

we expected. He is a decrepit old man, and requires to be fed. I shewed
my articles to his principal man to convince him I had nothing which
could be useful to them. N. was offended with him for not believing,
and sent me a large basket of maize and another of dourrha, with
the message that he believed my statement and would send men with
me to Nyunkwe, who would not lead me to any other village to plague
me.

The birds sing very nicely here. A canary enlivened us with song
rather louder than in Londa, and have 'cheep, cheep, chip chip, chap
chap', which reminds me of the chaffinch. Yesterday a bird which
sings loudly being near us at midday, I asked what it said. They
replied, 'It says, the boys have a club to beat me with'. It is named
Seanja in consequence.[1]

25th. Nyakoba prevailed on us to remain over today, and as we are
to enter no other village till we come to Tete, and the rain threatened
and fell, we were not very difficult to persuade. I went to see him. His
hands are either deformed or off, for he is fed and everything else done
for him. He sits guzzling beer and smoking all day, the height of enjoyment to him. He speaks very liberally, and is liked by his people for
his generosity.

A fall of rain makes the thermometer sink 14° in an hour.

Another tuber of the size of a turnip is to be found among mopane.
It is called Bonga,[2] and in winter has a sensible amount of salt in it. It
does not determine to the joints like Mokuri.

26th. We make but small stages on account of the sickness of
Sinenyané,[3] who seems to have a polypus in his ear.

27th Feby. 1856. We observed this morning a large flock of
swallows chattering on a tree and preparing for flight, I presume to
the north. They have none of the appearance of breeding, so far as I
could notice by their flight for two months past.

The country is covered over with well-rounded shingle and gravel
of granite, gneiss with much talc in it, quartz, and other rocks which
we saw in situ between Loangua and Kafué. The underlying rock is
soft red sandstone with streaks of white in it. It is so soft as to crumble
in the hand when taken up. The gravel above proves such an excellent
drain the trees are all scrubby, and there are large patches without a
drop of water, though the soil is all moist. The rivers are all of the
sandy kind, and large. Hills of considerable height rise on our south,

---

[1] Not identified.   [2] Not identified.
[3] One of DL's men (cf. *Expedition*, 69, 83, 101).

called Lokole,[1] and beyond them runs the Mazoe with its golden sands. The sea seems to have had a current in this direction, which screiving[2] round by Semalembue's made large mounds, here of well-rounded gravel & shingle. There are flints with chalk on them to be seen.

Republican feudalism

This people have a remarkable system of govt. When a chief dies, any trader who may be near or comes to them is plundered. They say, 'Who sent for you, and with whom can you trade?' Commerce instantly ceases untill the appointment of a successor, who sends word to the traders they may resume their visits. The successor is usually of the family of the deceased chief, brother or sister, but never his son or daughter. When the new chief is appointed, all the wives and goods and children of the deceased become his.

Generally the lads of all free men, when ten or twelve years old, leave their parents or rather grandparents and live with certain chiefs, as Monina, to learn lordship (*bonyai*). They are here indoctrinated and kept on rather stringent regulations. All must clap their hands on approaching a lord, and when food is cooked one of the nobles eats of it, separating portions for all the cadets, but none dare approach the dish. They remain unmarried untill a fresh set of youths is ready [to] occupy their places.[3] When they return to the village of their parents, a case is submitted to decision, and if he speaks well on the point the parents are much pleased. But should he tire of this state of absolute dependance

---

[1] Mt. Lukore, lat. 16.41 S, long. 32.43 E (GSGS 4355, SE 36/2).

[2] Scrieve, 'to move or glide along swiftly' (*Oxford English Dictionary*).

[3] In some groups of Southern Bantu youths often serve for varying periods at the court of a paramount or local chief (cf. Schapera, *Government and Politics in Tribal Societies*, 58), but I have found no other relatively recent account, for the Shona, of the system described above by DL. However, Bocarro (*c.* 1640) mentions that 'the Monomotapa' was served by 'the sons of the nobles of his kingdom', who 'from fifteen to twenty years of age' formed part of his domestic establishment; they were then replaced by others, and for several years afterwards rendered 'out-of-door service . . . and the king gives them lands from which to subsist'; finally 'they serve as ambassadors, and in such posts and offices as the king gives to their charge, until lands and large houses fall vacant, of which he makes them lords, either of such as belonged to their fathers or by virtue of new grants' (Theal, *Records*, iii. 267, 357). It may be noted in this connexion that according to Eça (*Guerras no Zambeze*, i. 108 n.) the term BaNyai (see above, p. 367) originally applied to 'the armed men, warriors in the service of Monomotapa', and was subsequently extended to include all his vassals.

on the decisions of his parents' free companions, and desire a village, the party of young Banyai are sent to him, and should he omit to shew absolute subjection to all their forms (one, for instance, recieve the clapping of hands without returning as much), the father says, 'He wants to be like me, return and burn his village and everything he has.' The children have fewer privileges than common freemen. They may not be sold, but rather than choose one of them for chief at any future time, they prefer one of themselves having only a very distant relationship to the family. It is a sort of half-hereditary republicanism. At the death of Katolosa fighting for the chieftainship is expected.[1]

We pass some villages because we have nothing with which to purchase provisions. One near which we slept last night has the chief dead in it, and the drums going all night shewed some other important person had finished his course. Had we gone to it we should have been robbed had we submitted to it, which, however, is rather doubtful. If a nation values liberty it must be willing to fight for it.

[1] See below, p. 445.

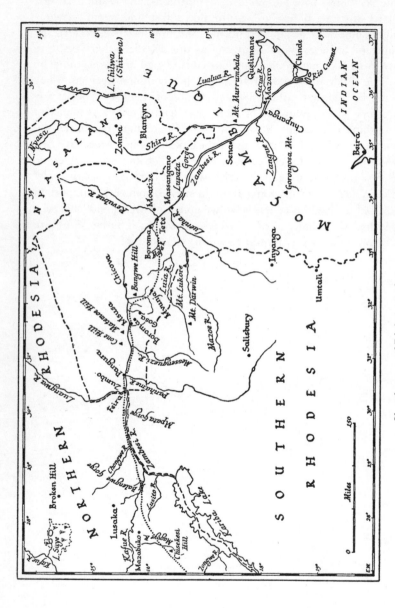

3. Sketch map of Livingstone's routes: Eastern Sector

The journey from Tete to Quelimane was made on the Zambesi and other rivers.

XIX

AT TETE

Arrival at Tete

5th March 1856. At Tette or Nyungue.[1] Under the guidance of three men from Nyakoba we passed away to the east and tried to avoid the villages, because it would cause much delay to be obliged to listen to all their reasons for believing we still had goods which we might give them. When, however, we were near Katolosa, who is the chief person in these parts, we met some men, who ran off and informed the villagers of our passage. A party followed us, and now we had to stand as culprits before an insignificant band. We had broken the laws, and must pay for it. I tried to get off as low as I could, but they outrageously demanded a tusk, and subsequently two. Rather than allow them to go forward and raise a storm against us with Katolosa, which might have resulted in our being robbed of all, we submitted to the imposition.

We now went through a very rough stoney country, often without path. The rocks were of gneiss lying on its edge, and the strike N. & S. In it occur very remarkable round holes of from 4 to 6 feet in depth. The mouth is about 3 feet broad, larger internally than at the brim. Were these not formed when the sea went schrieving along as it now does in the gulph of Florida? This continent must then have had the same shape as the east coast of America now has.

Being pretty well tired out, I sent forward my letters of recommendation to the Governor of Tete in the evening of the first. At 3 in the morning we were aroused by two officers and a company of soldiers, who had been sent with the materials of a substantial breakfast for my use and machilas[2] to bring me hither. The men had been living on roots, and I was become very weak and thin, but a rest here will set me right again. Thank God who has brought me thus far. The Governor is remarkably kind, and so indeed are all with whom I have come into contact.

[1] A Portuguese settlement since about 1540 (Theal, *History*, ii. 235), in lat. 16.09 S, long. 33.38 E (*Africa Pilot*, III, 239); DL gives the same lat., but long. 33.28 E (*Travels*, 627, 687). He had arrived there early in the morning of 2 March (*Miss. Corr.*, 302; in *Travels*, 626, he says 'the 3rd'). Nyungwe, the native name, is that of a Maravi tribe living in the immediate vicinity and westwards (Tew, *Peoples of the Lake Nyasa Region*, 31).

[2] Palanquins.

(Tito Augusto d'Araujo Sicard [see facsimile], the name of the
Governor of Tette who treated me with such extraordinary kindness
and liberality.[1] May Almighty God abundantly bless and reward him.
6th March 1856.)

Tito Augusto d'Araujo Sicard the name of the Governor of Tette who treated me with such extraordinary kindness and liberality. May Almighty God abundantly bless and reward him. 6th March 1856.

I sent forward letters for Sir R. M[urchison], Dr Tidman, Mrs L.,
Charles, Niel L. in Canada, Mr Maclear, Mr Duprat & King of
Portugal, Mr Thompson & Moffat, Paris Geog. Soc., and Mr Gabriel
of Loanda.[2]

This place is built near the river but in a sort of hollow, being over-
looked by a hill. The underlying rock is sandstone, dipping to the
south-w[est]. It overlies coal. On the opposite side of the river there
is a river called Lofubu,[3] about 60 or 80 yards broad, and at present
having a strong current with clear water. Passing up this river about
four miles, we come to another branch which comes from the east and
by south, about 20 yds broad, called Muatize or Motize, and when we
go three or four miles up that we come to a bed of good soft coal.[4] One

[1] A regular army officer, born in Portugal c. 1818, he had been commandant of
Tete several times, 1845 onwards; in office again Oct. 1855–July 1857, Oct. 1858–
Feb. 1860; died July 1864 (Eça, *História das Guerras no Zambeze*, i. 240-2, 339-
340; ii. 49; and *passim*). Often mentioned in DL's writings, usually with warm
appreciation; 'a little man, with a quiet and somewhat gentlemanly manner'
(Stewart, *Zambesi Journal*, 72).

[2] Of these letters, the following are published: to Murchison (*JRGS*, 1857, pp.
367-74), Tidman (*Miss. Corr.*, 302-3), Maclear (*PP England*, 1857, Sess. 2, XLIV,
32-5), Duprat (Eça, 'Inéditos do . . . Livingstone', 1953, facsimile and Port.
trans.), Thompson (*Miss. Corr.*, 303-4), Moffat (*Fam. Letters*, ii. 276-8), Paris
Geogr. Soc. (*Bull. Soc. Géogr. Paris*, 4me sér., xii, 1856, pp. 155-68). The Rhodesian
National Archives has a draft of that to the King of Portugal; the others I have not
traced. 'Niel L' was Neil, eldest son of DL's brother John (see p. 190.2); born in
Scotland, he had migrated with his parents to Canada, where he subsequently
became a medical practitioner (information from Mr H. S. Livingstone).

[3] 'Revubue' (*JRGS*, 1857, p. 378); 'Lofúbu or Revúbu' (*Travels*, 633); joins the
Zambesi about two miles below Tete (GSGS 4355, SE 36/2; *Travels*, 633).

[4] The Moatize joins the Revubue in lat. 16.06 S, long. 33.42 E (GSGS 4355,
SE 36/2, which also marks a 'coal mine' about four miles ESE of the confluence).

seam is 10 inches in diameter and another 58 inches, but it is probably thicker, for it is in the water. It is about 30 yards long. Above it there is lava which has acted on clay slate and also converted coal into coke.

On the left there is another feeder of the Lofubu, called Morongoze, in which there is also another larger bed of coal; also in a rivulet named Inyavu, and another called Makaré,[1] and there are many spots in the Maravi country beyond containing the valuable mineral. From their country, indeed, the Lofubu comes. Its lowest period is after September, and then there is water only of about 18 inches or knee deep.

On the Tette side of the river there are no fewer than five places at which the coal crops out, so that when the gold diggings are exhausted in Australia[2] the miners may bring their engines here, and will not want for either wood or water or coal to drive them. And the people are all willing to have intercourse with Europeans.

☞ According to Mr Tito, May June July and August are the best months for ascending the river, and no stranger ought to come into Quilimane sooner than April. November, December, January, February and March are the most unfavourable, and also at Mosambique. The river water is then believed to be bad, both by Europeans and natives, & wells are dug in the sand in preference. The amount of vegetable matter in it is certainly most at that time, in consequence of the rains. The most healthy time is that, too, in which there is neither too much nor too little water in the river.[3]

8th. Tette or Nyungwe. I am nearly quite recovered from my fatigue, and so very evident is the desire of the Commandant to serve me I find not much difficulty in accepting his kindness. I have left about 70 people with him, and will go down the river with only the more robust. He has allotted them a piece of land to cultivate, and generously supplies them with food in the meantime.

The Commandant informs me today that there is a cargo of goods on the way from Senna to this,[4] and I shall now have an opportunity to

[1] The Murrungose joins the Revubue in lat. 16.07 S, long. 33.39 E (GSGS 4355, SE 36/2); the two 'rivulets' are not named on that map.

[2] Where gold had been discovered in 1851 (*Enc. Brit.*, 14th ed., art. 'Australia').

[3] The whole of this paragraph is marked in the MS by triple lines in the left-hand margin and at the foot. (Several other paragraphs in both this chapter and the next are similarly marked, though usually with only a vertical double line in the left-hand margin. To distinguish them, I have placed the symbol ☞ at their beginning, which, as in the present instance, DL himself occasionally also does.)

[4] Sena (see below, p. 461) is about 140 miles downstream from Tete (*Africa Pilot*, III, 241).

go down in the boats on their return. He says Bonga will treat me well.[1] He has been sent here 4 times to make peace in the country. The people respect him much, and I none the less. The Maravi are more hostile, but there is abundance of coal on the lands of the Portuguese. The iron ore is very pure, and several of the rocks contain gold. Even in the village the rocks contain gold, and the Commandant prevented the people from digging in a ravine by the fort because the Zambesi would thereby be let too far in. The washings in their rude way of performing bring but little gain to the employers. The annual produce is small, because the natives take the sand from the surface only, and, though it is difficult to believe such folly, when they light on a piece they make a deep hole and bury it again, in the belief if they used it the gold would disappear. It is put in again as seed. There must be some superstitious reason besides.[2]

The most probable cause of the flood here is the rains east of the eastern ridge, for after this there is only a small rise. Last month it was 20 feet higher than it is now. At the fort of Tette the river was measured 500 fathoms (= 1,000 yards), but below it is much wider, especially below Lupata.

9th March 1856. Here we have senna, the purgative plant, and, it is said, quina also. The trade in ivory is from 600 to 1,000 arobas annually = 20,000 to 30,000 lbs annually, the gold only a few pounds.

The Portuguese Government seems to desire the formation of mining companies, for by a decree of 22d December 1852 it is legal

[1] Bonga was the native name of António Vicente da Cruz, 1832(?)-79, eldest son of Nyaude (see p. 402). An 'even worse rebel than his father', he had sacked Tete in 1853 (see below, p. 428). Thereafter he successfully resisted several Portuguese attempts to subdue him; in both 1868 and 1869, especially, he disastrously defeated strong forces sent against him at Massangano (see p. 459). An armistice was then made which lasted until his death. (Almost the whole second volume of Eça, *Guerras no Zambeze*, is devoted to his relations with the Portuguese authorities; cf. also Botelho, *História dos Portugueses em Moçambique*, ii. 189-225, and, for an English summary, Duffy, *Portuguese Africa*, 88-9). His many misdeeds included murdering six of the men DL had left behind at Tete on going to England (*Expedition*, 40, 42, 63; *Narrative*, 43).

[2] A similar observation was made *c.* 1570 by Monclaro: 'If they find a large piece of gold they hide it that it may not be discovered, and the mine is ordered to be closed, as they say has sometimes been done, after laying charms that no one may be able to dig there again. In this there is something strange, the reason of which is unknown, as they have a great love of gold' (Theal, *Records*, iii. 184, 234). Elsewhere DL comments: 'It may have been the sly invention of some rogue among them, who wished to baulk the chiefs of their perquisites, for in more remote times these pieces were all claimed by them' (*JRGS*, 1857, p. 380).

for any one, whether Portuguese or foreigner, to search for mines, and the finder has the right conceded to him of working the same upon paying some consideration to the owner of the soil if Portuguese or native. . . .[1]

9th March 1856. Went to the church today[2] to see the Portuguese troops. When they came to Senna they were a force of 105 men, but remaining there one year twenty-five were cut off by fever. Since coming to Tette only 8 have died out of seventy, though aguardente is distilled in all directions and from various plants, fruits, and grain, and they indulge largely in this pernicious beverage. In appearance they looked as well as soldiers do in Europe. Many of them were robust, and all of a good colour. The priest, a native of Goa, officiated. His voice was just audible to me who was standing near. The bending of the knee frequently, and standing with uplifted hands with the back turned to the audience, made me wonder men of intelligence like the Portuguese could submit to think this acceptable service to the Almighty. There were four or six candles burning, and a lamp also, and two soldiers with bayonets fixed presented arms at certain parts of the service. It lasted about a quarter of an hour. At some parts the priest's eye ran over the prayers, and he continued spitting as if he were chewing tobacco. He is of a dark colour and slender in make. Suffers from scorbutic gums.

A hot spring

11th March 1856. Went up the river in a boat to visit a hot spring called Nyamboronda in a portion of land named Sambo. After 12½ hours pull against the current we came to a small rivulet named Mokorozi, and then went about a mile east to another named Nyaonda.[3] It is a mere rill of water, which when rice is boiled therein makes it reddish yellow. In its bed a space about twelve feet square is so hot the natives could with difficulty stand on it. A little spring bubbles out on

---

[1] I have here omitted MS 736–41, containing many scrappy notes on 'trees and plants used as food or medicine by the natives of Tete on Zambesi'. Much of the information is given in a lengthy footnote in *Travels*, 649–50; the list is also published (in part, and not always accurately) by Gelfand, *Livingstone the Doctor*, 292–3.

[2] Sunday.

[3] These 'rivulets', etc., are not named on maps consulted, but Sousa (*Distrito de Tete*, 70) mentions hot sulphuric springs at 'Nhaondúe, bordering on Boroma'. Boroma is a large mission station in lat. 16.03 S, long. 33.26 E (GSGS 4355, SE 36/2).

one side, and in the bank and all around a great deal of steam issues from the ground. It bubbles out from small holes, too, near the spring, and there is a considerable evolution from the hole itself. It is slightly acrid but not inflammable, as I tried by lighting grass at the well. The water in the well stands at the temperature of 160° Faht., and when it flows over the hot surface of the rivulet's bed is too hot for the hand. When fish leap into it they are scalded to death. We saw a frog in that state. The stones are encrusted with a salt and the water tastes saline. Ground has been dug near to extract the salt.

It is situated at the bottom of a hill running N. & S., and in a part where, interior to certain gneiss & porphyritic rocks on edge, & strike N.E., there are many specimens of half-formed pumice, the foam of volcanoes, lava, greenstone, and quartz. The sandstone strata are broken up by a horneblend rock & by basalt about a mile below the Mufa, which is about 80 yards wide and comes in from the S.W.[1] The sandstone is broken through in various parts by eruptive rocks, and coal acted on by an igneous rock in Motize shews the period of activity in these parts to have been subsequent to the period of the coal formation.

On the 13th we went about 3 miles to the north-east of this hot spring, which is on lat. 16° 0′ 16″ S.,[2] to examine the gold washings in the Mokorozi. It is a sand river, but the banks are covered with fine groves of mango trees, among which the Portuguese in former times lived while superintending the washing for the precious metal. It is in fine scales, and unless I had been assured to the contrary I would have taken it for mica. But even now, when the rains cause the rivulet to flow, the natives wash the sand in order [to] buy cloths with the gold. It must come far, for being in this fine state of comminution only distance could effect this. In the north it is coarser, and so it is in Manica.[3] The grains being generally as large as wheat, the process of washing must be very laborious, for the water is stirred about, then a half rotatory motion given to the dish, which causes the coarser particles of sand to go on one side. These are removed with the hand, and the process renewed untill the gold alone remains. The sand is not removed

[1] It joins the Zambesi in lat. 16.05 S, long. 33.27 E (GSGS 4355, SE 36/2).

[2] In *Travels*, 687, 'hot spring Makorozi' is located in lat. 15.59.35 S. Cf. above, p. 425.3.

[3] The region inhabited by the Manyika, a Shona tribe, in and around Umtali and Inyanga districts, S. Rhodesia, and the adjoining Manica district, Moçambique.

by the water, as in California &c. (Hot well also at Mosanana, Bashukulompo c., Nakalombo hills.)[1]

14th. In returning today we came down with the current in 3 hours what required 14 hours to ascend. Got some seeds of a bush which are used & taste exactly like coffee. It resembles the sloe tree. The seeds are used as food in times of scarcity as well. Also gum copal. Also a pod of seeds named Kombé,[2] which when pounded and mixed with the juice of aloes to give it consistence is the poison used on arrows. The animal does not go far afterwards, especially if water be near, for it drinks enormously and soon dies.

On the 10th of March the river rose several feet of non-discoloured water. This must be the Interior water of inundation, for when rains happen in this quarter they cause the water to become quite brown. The wheat is sown after the rains have ended, and in hollows or damp places, as in the valley of the Nile. Four months alone are necessary for its maturation, and it has been known to yield one hundred fold.

15th. The Governor told me this morning that my men might go and hunt elephants in company with his servants and purchase goods with both ivory and meat, so that they might have something wherewith to return to Sekeletu. They are delighted with his liberality, and I too have reason to be grateful for his great liberality to me and mine. Thank God for his great kindness to me in all this journey.

It is perilous to remain any time at either Senna or Quilimane on account of the fever. A brig of war has been in three times enquiring for me and has left despatches there.[3]

[1] 'Bashukulompo c.' [country ?] and 'Nakalombo hills' are interlineations. The 'hot well' is in lat. 15.49 S, long. 26.08 E, among the Nakalomwe hills; Musanana is the name of an Ila chief living in that vicinity (GSGS 4646, SD 35; Smith and Dale, *Ila-Speaking Peoples*, i. 314 and map; Smith, 'Sebetwane', 68). DL's informant was Sekwebu (*Travels*, 568).

[2] *Stropanthus kombe,* 'from which the Zambesi natives most commonly derived the poison for their arrows' (Stewart, *Zambesi Journal*, 111 n.).

[3] Before leaving Luanda, DL had told Gabriel 'that it would be a great satisfaction to him if, through your Lordship's kindness, instructions could be forwarded to the naval Commander-in-chief at the Cape of Good Hope to order any of Her Majesty's cruizers which may be employed off the east coast of Africa, to make occasional inquiries for him at Quilimane, where he hopes to arrive about November of the ensuing year (1855), and, if requisite, to afford him a passage to the nearest place from whence he can reach England' (Gabriel to Lord Clarendon, 5.x.54, received 26.ii.55: *PP England*, 1854–55, LVI, 100). HMS *Frolic* accordingly called at Quelimane in both October and December, 1855, but failed to get news of DL (*PP England*, 1856, LXII, 100, 159, 160); subsequently (see below, p. 472) HMS *Dart* also called there.

The rains here come generally from the south-east, and the continued winds from the S.S.E. Engaged on the map today.

Am getting much better now. When I arrived I was exceedingly thin and scorched, drank very large quantities of water, and passed much brickdust-coloured urine, as if after fever. End of March, a continuance of the latter symptom makes me fear organic disease of the kidney, or obstruction of the vena porta near the liver. Haemorrhoides several times.

16th March 1856. Went to see the ceremony of Palm Sunday. After the padre read a long prayer, he blessed and sprinkled holy water on a lot of palmyra leaves, and then distributed them to the soldiers and others. The soldiers then went and, taking a crucifix, the priest closed the doors and standing outside sung a verse, which was responded to by one within. He then took the crucifix and drove the doors open with it. All entered, and after a long prayer during which, being fatigued, I came home, the affair ended. The Commandant remarked the language of every religion ought to be that of the people of the country.

Decay of commerce

17th March 1856. The possessions of the Portuguese in Eastern Africa are all in a state of ruin. There is an annual deficit of the treasury in Mosambique, and the military here have not recieved any pay for four years past, though often employed in war. When hostilities commenced with Nyaode, an officer was sent to apprehend him, but not suspecting anything he went to his residence and the soldiers, putting down their arms, were at once disarmed and made prisoners. A large party was then sent against him, and while that was at Luenya Nyaode sent Bonga with another party to attack Tette, and as all the force was at Luenya he burned nearly all the houses without resistance. The Commandant's house and 2 or 3 others alone escaped. The cattle were all carried off. Then Kisaka or Choutame[1] attacked all the villas

---

[1] 'Another half-caste from Macao, called Kisaka or Choutama' (*Travels*, 632). Choutama and Kisaka were in fact father and son, both named Pedro Caetano Pereira. Choutama's elder brother, Manoel, was the Pereira who had visited Kazembe in 1796 (see above, p. 67), and his father, Gonçalo Caetano Pereira, was a Goanese who had settled on the Zambesi *c.* 1760-70 and accompanied Lacerda to Kazembe's in 1798. He started his freebooting career about 1841, and after his death (1849) his son Kisaka (died *c.* 1858) became the rival of Nyaude (see above, p. 402.1) and a similar menace to life and property (Eça, *Guerras*, i. 249-60, 275-91; Botelho, *História*, ii. 185-6; *Expedition*, 43).

on the other bank, and carried off thousands of cattle. No goods were permitted to pass Nyaode from Senna or Quilimane for years. The Portuguese are thus quite impoverished. The trade is destroyed, and all the other East African stations languish as well. Is this the collapse after the excitement of slave trading?

They attempted to form a company similar to that in India, but gave the Govt. the power of resuming all their possessions after fifty years, and it was to cease in 99 years, everything going into the Government's hands. From the commencement the royal power was to preponderate largely in the direction, and no measure could pass without the permission of the Government. All the risk was to be incurred by the company. All the expense of building arsenals, schools, erecting botanic gardens, the propagation of the faith and defending the Portuguese possessions and keeping them intact, opening roads, improving harbours, &c &c &c &c, was to be defrayed by the company. Nothing was garaunteed by the Government, except delivering over the East African possessions into the hands of the company; and though it is abundantly well known that with all the mines, forests, rivers, harbours, trade, and other advantages, the Government now possesses, it is not able to pay its own way, the company was expected to set all agoing properly, and then when the country was rich and flourishing and well peopled by Europeans, brought at its expense, all would be handed over to the Crown of Portugal—an example of pure patriotism such as the world never expected to see. It is remarkable that all schemes of companies in Portugal have specially for their object the abolition of the slave trade and slavery, the propagation of the faith, and promotion of civilization. The foregoing scheme was propounded by a gentleman, Sr Almeida Garret, rather heady and since dead.[1]

If a company were formed for working the mines of gold or iron by coal, and the Government imposed the obligation of keeping a small armed steamer on the Zambesi, this would lead to improvements, for but a small outlay would improve the river so much that the carriage of merchandise would be practicable during the greater part of the year, and besides giving an immense stimulus to trade it would soon pay itself. The iron ore is very good and one may say half manufactured, for it has been well roasted in the operations of nature and contains a proportion of pure metallic iron. When smelted now it closely re-

[1] Probably the distinguished poet, dramatist, and statesman João Baptista da Silva Leitão de Almeida Garrett, 1799–1854, who was for a short time minister of foreign affairs in 1852 (Grande Enciclopédia, xii. 185–9).

sembles good Swedish iron in colour, but is harder and less liable to break.

The only salubrious stations are Sofala & Cape Delgado.[1]

The way the soldiers support themselves is by marrying the free blacks of the country. The wives have gardens, and feed their husbands. Their parents help them too.

Good white bread is made by using the boyaloa, here named Pombé,[2] instead of leaven. The meal is ground on a stone and contains the entire grain of the wheat except a small portion of bran. It rises so as to resemble very closely fine English loaves, and where it is possible to obtain it the water of the cocoanut makes it rise much more energetically than Pombé. I have often observed that meal mixed with native corn meal fermented in one third of the time required for leaven alone.

18th March 1856. Got good sets of observns. for longitude last night. Offered to sell some ivory to Major Tito, but he advised me to take it rather to Quilimane and there I should get a much larger price, and if I parted with it here the people might think I had paid for my own clothing with Sekeletu's ivory.[3] He said he never had a stranger in his house before, but I was welcome to everything he had. I thank my God who has put these kind feelings in his heart. May he who is abundantly able bless him and shew him mercy. He remarked on the danger of going to Quilimane now, March being one of the most sickly months.

The tree which produces the quinine grows here and at Quilimane in abundance. It really seems as if Providence placed the remedies for fever at hand where fever should most abound. I got specimens of it, and also of the coals of Morongozi, which are better than those of Moatize.

Made a copy of map to be sent to Mr Maclear. Wrote Mr Watt & Moore.[4]

[1] Both are on the coast: Sofala in lat. 20.13 S, long. 34.44 E, and Cabo Delgado in lat. 10.42 S, long. 40.39 E (*Africa Pilot*, III, 227, 302). They were, in DL's time, relatively insignificant hamlets, though Sofala (occupied by the Portuguese in 1505) had formerly been a considerable trading centre. Botelho (*História*, ii. 36) says it was abandoned by its inhabitants in 1864 because the site was 'very unhealthy' (muito insalubre)!

[2] 'The boyaloa (pombe), or native beer . . .' (*Travels*, 639).

[3] '. . . though I pressed him to take payment in ivory for both myself and men, he refused all recompence' (*Travels*, 639).

[4] David Gilkinson Watt (1817-97) and Joseph Moore (1816-93), both formerly LMS missionaries in India and Tahiti respectively but now clergymen in England, were personal friends whom DL had got to know during his student days (cf.

The streams mentioned in notes of a journey to Cazembe by Major Monteiro,[1] when put into the map according to the courses he mentions and the variation applied, shew clearly the existence of the ridge a considerable way to the north.

My men are to get land to cultivate, and then go and hunt for meat and ivory to sell on their own account. They have begun already to buy cloth with the wood they collect in the fields.

☞ Remember to bring seeds of a large pumpkin known in Portugal, and maize said to be a yard in length; also seeds of every sort, especially Cape seeds.

There is great abundance of fine wood for shipbuilding near Quilimane, and ebony abounds at Mosambique, also cloves and ginger and many spices.

19th. Went up to Karuera hill[2] to view a fizzure through which a stream falls. A fine scene is beheld from the top of Karuera. Write Earl of Clarendon.[3] Coals from Morongosi.

20th. A man who accompanied Major Monteiro to Cazembe says that the town of Cazembe is situated on the Loapola or Muapura (Luapura) River, which is there very large, and one or two days beyond or westwards there is another large river flowing to the south, which he calls Bara, and thought it went to Angola. This is clearly the Zambesi.[4]

Trade in gold

21st March 1856. Formerly the Portuguese merchants went with large companies of slaves to Mushinga range and held fairs. The female slaves sold goods for gold dust, and delivered all to their masters at the end of each week. Slaves were also employed in washing it. A tem-

Blaikie, 25, 33, etc.; *LMS Register*, 52, 55). The letter to Moore, 16.iii.56, is now in the British Museum (Add. MS 36525, f.9); the other I have not traced.

[1] Major José Manuel Correia Monteiro, commandant of Tete, had led an expedition to Kazembe of the eastern Lunda in 1831–2. A detailed account of the journey (*O Muata Cazembe*, by A. C. P. Gamito, second in command) was published in Lisbon, 1854.

[2] Caroeira, three miles SW of Tete; height about 1,600 feet (Eça, *Guerras*, i. 300).

[3] Dated 19.iii.56, this letter was published in *PP England*, 1857, Sess. 2, XLIV, 62–6.

[4] 'One man, who had gone to Cazembe with Major Monteiro, stated that he had seen the Luapúra or Loapula flowing past the town of that chieftain into the Luaméji or Leeambye, but imagined that it found its way, somehow or other, into Angola' (*Travels*, 640). The Luapula, in fact, flows into L. Mweru. The only 'large river' west of it in that vicinity is the Lufira, which, however, flows northwards.

porary church was erected at these spots, and mass performed. When the goods were expended the fairs were broken up, presents having been given to the chiefs for the privelege of gold washing. The soil everywhere near Mushinga range produced abundance of the metal. The same sort of trade was carried on at Abutua and at Dambarari, which was situated not at the confluence of the Panyanie but some way inland or S. of Zumbo.[1] The larger pieces of metal or flakes of it were the property of the chief, and sometimes so much was demanded of the washers as tribute they were unwilling to labour.

The rocks of Mashinga are said to be quartz, but soft enough to allow the women to pound it in wooden mortars for washing. The gold I have seen exists in exceedingly minute scales, indicating its having come a long way. That found at Manica and Abutua is about the size of wheat, hence the gold-field would seem to be of a semilunar form and not very much removed from the eastern ridge. The existence of a coal field in the middle of a gold one is I believe unique in the world. And when the diggings in California and Australia are exhausted, here is another mine, combining the advantages of abundance of wood, water, coal, and provisions. Iron, too, abounds in large quantities, occurring in tears well roasted in the operations of nature, and shewing veins of the pure metal in its substance.

The people, too, are friendly, though presents are expected for the privelege of working the gold. No difficulty would be experienced by any one of a liberal turn of mind. The present Governor of Tete has put a stop to the war here four times by his well known pacific and liberal character. He has a good opinion of the people who inhabit the gold country to the south-east of this. With presents of cloth, he says, one might go anywhere. The respect which the natives have for a bargain may be seen at Zumbo, where the people told us, 'All this land on the river belongs to the Bazunga'. It is a dear way of getting land to fight for it. The little we have in Caffreland cost several millions sterling.[2]

21st March. The river continues rising, and is not much discoloured.

[1] For Mushinga (Mashinga), see below, p. 434; Abutua (Butua) is 'the Que Que, Gatooma, Hartley goldfield', south-west of Salisbury, S. Rhodesia, and Dambarari was in the vicinity of the modern Jumbo mine, Mazoe district, S. Rhodesia (Axelson, *Portuguese in SE Africa*, 7 n., 69 n.); the Panyanie (Panhame) joins the Zambesi from the south in lat. 15.37 S, long. 30.40 E (GSGS 4355, SD 36/4).

[2] A reference to the cost of the wars against the 'Caffre' (Xhosa) tribes, 1846-7 1850-3, which resulted in the annexation to Great Britain of the territory known as British Kaffraria (cf. *Fam. Letters*, ii. 185; *Lectures*, 169).

This is clearly the water of inundation of the valley. The rise from rains shews water much discoloured, and the rainy season is now pretty well over. The Luenya runs into the Zambesi with so much force the large river is, as it were, held back by it, and at the eddy, which when the river is full is dangerous, much gold is deposited. It never dries, though it becomes low enough to allow of being forded.

Church ceremonies

There was a service in the church which lasted nearly the whole of last night, and on account of the death of Christ.[1] I believe the image was mounted on the cross, for when I went this evening I found the whole as if the image had been left on it, and now the image was taken down and placed in what is intended to look as the sepulchre, and a full-size image of the virgin, as a handsome matron and very good expression of sorrow, was placed with a towel in her hands. The padre gave a sermon on the death of Christ, which, though it contained expressions which sounded strange in Protestant ears, was agreably concluded by a cry for mercy to Him who never disregards the call of the penitent. Candles were then handed to all who would join in procession, and with a bier and image of the virgin, the troops with their arms reversed, and band playing mournfully, the procession moved round the village, which was illuminated with little lamps. On re-entering the church there was some singing, and then all went one by one and, kneeling down, kissed the toe of the virgin and her son.

This bowing down to images was that which shocked my senses most. We cannot help, as religious animals, from looking on with respect and reverence on the religious ceremonies of every portion of humanity. We feel reproved when we see the Mahometan turning his face toward Mecca and praying. And so with the ceremonies of the Roman Catholics. I cannot call them mummery, or speak of them with scorn. In a very short time we shall pass before the tribunal where every man will be awarded strict and unerring justice. We may let others alone till then, and be careful so to live as to exemplify our religion, let our lights shine, and live in love and peace with all mankind. (Witness the Quaker women speaking in church.)

This church was rich, but has lost much of its silver and gold by

---

[1] March 21, 1856, was Good Friday. In *Travels*, 644, DL describes the 'service' very briefly: 'During the period of my stay, a kind of theatrical representation of our Saviour's passion and resurrection was performed. The images and other paraphernalia used were of great value. . . .'

theft. The famous Dr Lacerda who died at Cazembe wrote much, and made many observations on geography and natural history. His notes were stolen by a Jesuit who accompanied him, and death stepped in again and the notes were never heard of. Perhaps they may be found yet in Rome.[1] The Jesuit may not have intended anything wrong, but his effects would probably go to the College and become buried among other papers. Enquire if there are any colleges in Rome devoted to the purposes of preserving documents of defunct Jesuits. The effects of this church were infamously plundered at different times.

22d March 1856. Senhor Candido[2] has sent off negroes to procure different medicinal roots which enter into the composition of a remedy for the wound of a poisoned arrow. It was made by a Jesuit, and is said to be very efficacious.

23d March. ☞ Remember to ask if there is an instrument to purify gold by attracting it as a magnet.

An idea of the trade of Tete may be formed from the fact that 30 brass rings cost here one £, half a sovreign at Quilimane and Senna. In the Interior the same number of rings are valued at £2, or they may purchase one penful of gold of the value of £2. A penful of gold will be purchased here for 24 yards of cotton cloth.

On the opposite bank of the river gold is found in considerable quantity at six places, viz.

Machinga (quartz), Chindundo	Mashinga, Shindundo
Capata, Missal	Missal, Kapat
Mano and Jaua	Mano, Jawa

---

[1] Francisco José de Lacerda e Almeida (1753-98), mathematician, astronomer, and Governor of Rios de Sena, had led a large expedition from Tete in July 1798 with the object of trying to reach the west coast. He died in Kazembe's country on the Luapula in October. The chaplain, Francisco João Pinto (who can hardly have been a Jesuit, since the Order was suppressed 1773-1814) then took command, and after remaining several months with Kazembe brought the expedition back to Tete (November 1799). In *Travels*, 587, DL repeats the statement that Lacerda's papers, 'taken possession of by a Jesuit who accompanied him, were lost to the world'. They had in fact already been fully published, in monthly instalments, in *Annaes maritimos e coloniaes*, vols. iv-v (1844-5).

[2] Cândido José da Costa Cardoso, born in Tete, landed proprietor and trader, president of the local municipal chamber 1853, 'chief captain' of the village 1860, still alive 1868 (Eça, *Guerras*, i. 294, 441; ii. 576, 594, 599; *Expedition*, 167); 'holds the office of judge in all the disputes of the natives and knows their language perfectly' (*Travels*, 641; cf. Gamito, *O Muata Cazembe*, 7); 'a tall man with a grey moustache, a good deal bent, and has a quiet manner' (Stewart, *Zambesi Journal*, 182). For the 'remedy', see below, pp. 441-2.

all east of Tete, chiefly in clay slate.[1] The produce of these parts formerly was one hundred pastos or one hundred & thirty pounds weight,[2] now only eight or ten pounds.

There are three varieties of the senna at Tete, one fedegosa, another called senna, a third a tree. The senna plant is now in flower. It is a shrub with a woody stem, about 3 feet high, having spear-shaped leaves, sharp pointed and bipinnated, on leaf stalks from three to four inches long, 13 or 14 leaves on each. The flower stalks carry bunches of yellow flowers somewhat like broom, 20 or more on each stalk. There are two tiers of petals, one thin & translucent which forms a complete covering to the flower before it bursts into full bloom, and another of deeper yellow. Calyx petals 5, flower petals 5, pistil long and curved, flattened in belly like a pod and tapering to a minute stigma, behind pistil one stamen, in front two with curving round pistils, in front of them 4 shorter stamens, and in front of them again three very short. Fruit thin green pods, through which fiddle-shaped seed may be seen.

24th March 1856. I find that the venereal disease prevails in all its forms in Tete, and among the people lower down the river there are syphilitic ulcers, buboes, syphilis, and gonorrhoea, and very severe. This seems to contradict what I advanced as to the indisposition of the inhabitants of the Interior to syphilitic diseases. But I have no doubt that such is the fact.[3] The cause of the indisposition may be differently accounted for, but of its existence I have not the least doubt. Elevation may be the cause, as even the valley is pretty much elevated. Smallpox too prevails here every few years, while in the Interior it only paid a passing visit about twenty years ago.

A fact showing the degradation to which men may fall has been mentioned both by the Governor and others. A soldier in Senna on

[1] The names in the right-hand column apparently represent an attempt at more phonetic spelling of the Portuguese versions on the left. Described in *Travels*, 637, as 'well-known washing-places' to the east and NE of Tete, they are all in the region now known as Vila Gamito (Sousa, *Distrito de Tete*, 68; cf. *Manual of P.E.A.*, 268, where they are listed among 'the chief gold areas of the Tete district'). Bordalo (*Moçambique*, 1859, p. 223) mentions them as *prazos* (estates), some '60 leagues' from Tete, 'in the district belonging to Pedro Caetano Pereira, commonly known as Chissaka' (see above, p. 428).

[2] The *pasta* = 20 ounces (Bordalo, *Moçambique*, 82).

[3] 'A certain loathsome disease . . . dies out in the interior of Africa without the aid of medicine. . . . It seems incapable of permanence in any form in persons of pure African blood anywhere in the centre of the country' (*Travels*, 128).

obtaining his discharge went and sold himself as a slave, and several natives have done so.[1] A person gives a piece of cotton cloth, and the man, if such deserve the name, is henceforth his slave.

When the slave trade was brisk the Maravi made prisoners and kept them for sale, but now they kill all they can of the enemy–men, woman and children. This is spoken of as if to shew that the slave trade did some good in saving these poor wretches, but it is forgotten that numberless wars were produced for the traffic, and now they occur as the result of heartburnings and vengeance, the direct fruits of the traffic. Upon the whole it is better to have the burnings out of the old fires kindled by the slave trade than to have the everlasting flame of kidnapping, wars, &c, although some of the captives were kept to be used as beasts of burden. There is nothing so thoroughly bad as not to have some element of good in it. The Devil's character has the elements of ability and daring in it.

It is really wonderful where all this vast body of water flows to. The river is still rising; a thousand yards broad, & very deep. At Lupata it is supposed to be a hundred fathoms in depth.

The friars were very laborious when here, and very rich. There were formerly three churches here, now only one. The padre's salary may be about £2.10 per month (=£30 per annum), with a few perquisites and two fields for maintainence. They say it is rare to meet with a really good padre.

The Governor says frankly the cause of the decay of this colony is undoubtedly the slave trade, which withdrew the attention of the colonists from agriculture and every other branch of industry. Cotton, indigo, wheat, coffee, even gold, was neglected for the gambling gains of the hateful traffic, and the ill will of the natives was engendered as well. Here alone are the whites respected. At Senna the Landims (Landins) are exceedingly impudent, and indeed Senna is in ruins.[2]

[1] A specific instance is described in *Narrative*, 49, the purchaser being Major Sicard, 'a notoriously kind master'.

[2] 'The name Landin (=courier) is applied by the Portuguese to all the tribes which are of Zulu origin or have come under Zulu influence' (*Manual of P.E.A.*, 101). Elsewhere (*Expedition*, 73, 104) DL uses it with specific reference to the followers of Manukuza (Soshangane), who *c.* 1820–1 had migrated into the southern parts of Moçambique and there established 'the Gasa empire' between Inhambane and the Zambesi. He not only massacred the Portuguese garrisons of Lourenço Marques, Inhambane, and Sofala, but also (1836) 'attacked Sena, slew fifty-four Portuguese and half-castes, and drove the rest away'. He died in 1856, but his 'empire' was not destroyed by the Portuguese until 1896 (Bryant, *Olden Times in Zululand*, 446–58; cf. Bordalo, *Moçambique*, 129–30).

There is a larger force here than was ever known, 700 soldiers, half or ⅓ whites. Formerly at Dambarari there were 200 white inhabitants, now none, and there are very few here. . . .[1]

Cost of living

25th March 1856. When tea comes here, it is often as high as 3 dollars or 15 shillings per pound, Mocambique 6/6 per pound. Coffee, the arroba of 32 lbs, 12 dollars or £3, Mocambique 10/6 (=4d. per lb). Wheat at Tete, for a panja of about 40 lbs,[2] 1 dollar or 5 shillings (=35 shillings the quarter); Moc. & Senna 3 shillings. 1 panja salt, 5 shillings. 1 arroba of sugar 30 shillings, Moç. 10/10. (Moçambique, 36$000 for arroba of marfim groço,[3] 4/6 per lb; medium 3/9, 30$000; little 24$000 or 3/- per lb.)

June is the best month to come here for supplies, for they are generally in abundance and cheaper than at other seasons. It is also the most healthy season.

The boatswain and steerer of the boats from a certain point of the river where the Quilimane men leave recieve each a piece of fazenda. The paddlers get six braças or 12 yards each,[4] and their food.

A milrei is about a dollar at Moçambique, and 4$500 is a pound sterling. They count chiefly by dollars, 5 of which make £1, then ½ dollar, ¼ do., ⅕ do., ⅛ do.

Carriage up the river puts 10 per cent on goods from Quilimane to Tete. They would probably give 15 for greater speed and safety. The amount of goods now brought up during the last five months were of the value of 30,000 dollars (=£7,500),[5] or annually 60,000 dollars (=£15,000). When traded with, this sum produces 10 per cent more, say 80,000 dollars (£20,000), and this is a mere fraction of what the trade might be.

It would cost from £60 to £80 to live here in a very frugal style,

---

[1] I have here omitted MS 765–6, containing vocabularies of native numerals and other words, copied in part from S. X. Botelho, *Memoria estatistica*, 1835, pp. 391–2.

[2] 'The *panja* was a grain receptacle woven of palmyra fronds' (Stewart, *Zambesi Journal*, 136 n.); its usual content was about 27 litres (Eça, *Guerras*, i. 318 n.).

[3] *Marfim grosso*, tusks of ivory weighing 9 kg. (about 20 lb.), or more; other recognized grades were *meão* (medium), 7–9 kg., and *miudo* (small), 3½–7 kg. (Eça, *Guerras*, ii. 504 n.; Bordalo, *Moçambique*, 85 n.).

[4] *Braça*=fathom; '2 yards of unbleached calico . . . is called 1 braça' (*Travels*, 635).

[5] '30,000 dollars, or about 6000 *l.*' (*Travels*, 635).

with three or four servants, a house, &c. The living is rendered dear by the tea, coffee, and sugar being so very expensive. Country food is all cheap. Quilimane and Senna are cheaper than Tete, =6 fowls for one braça or 2 yds. Wages of laborers (free) for such works as digging coal, gold washing, 1 braça or 2 yds per day. They might be got cheaper, or for 16 yards and their food per moon. For masons, carpenters, &c, the ordinary rate is 2 yards per day, and 4 braças or 8 yards for such tradesmen from Quilimane.

The common price of the land on which a seam of coal exists at Moatizi is 51 dollars (=£12.15.0). They would probably ask more if a wealthy purchaser appeared, but not more than double, because there are lands in the possession of independant tribes with coal in them and they could be purchased for very much less.

There are only a few coffee trees now in the country.

25th. Went to Senhor Fluorindi,[1] who has a good knowledge of native medicines. He recognized most on my list. I shall specify some below. The sweet potato cannot be kept more than two or three days, but the Maravi manage to preserve them during the three months of winter by digging a pit and covering the roots with a good quantity of wood ashes, then making the pit close with earth and beating it down firmly. He met a tribe north of the Loangua called Tambuca, who are emigrants from their own land Camanga.[2] They had plenty of cattle, and a cow could be bought for two or three yards of cloth.

Kurucuru is the name of the red-winged bird[3] in so much esteem in Londa.

I made arrangements with Mr F. to have a little plantation or rather nursery of coffee trees made for me, and also to get the Governor to send seeds to the Cape Garden and get good seeds in return. Gave some seeds to Mr F. & the Govr., which pleased both.

Tuza, a good fruit, Shangoma Port[ugu]ese name. Tasha, a sweet fruit to make aguardiente. Various fruits are employed this way, among others the Morula.[4] The seed inside is used as a sweet meat.

[1] Not identified.

[2] The Tumbuka live between Lake Nyasa and the Luangwa River, south of the N. Rukuru and north of the Dwangwa; Kamanga (Nkamanga), their main 'kingdom', was on the Nyika plateau near the NW shore of the Lake (Tew, *Peoples*, 51–2).

[3] Not identified.

[4] Tuza = *Flaucourtia indica*, 'Batoka plum', and morula = *Sclerocarya caffra* (Wild, *Botanical Dictionary*, 86, 123); tasha, not identified.

The natives distill by means of pots and a gun barrel, and a great variety of wild fruits containing saccharine matter sufficient to yield aguardiente enable them to live in frequent drunkeness.

26th March 1856. The Jesuits have accomplished most in missionary literature, and this was simply because they were always rich and could afford it. Great works of literature have emanated from the English bishops too, because they had ease and time, but to expect a modern missionary, who must be doctor, midwife, smith, mason, carpenter, schoolmaster, and preacher, to attend to literature is simple nonsense. I had the greatest desire to devote some time to keeping up my knowledge & not allow myself to become more ignorant, but had more frequently to scrub at a piece of land, maul iron, or be man midwife, than pursue the path of knowledge.[1] Yet modern missionaries are wondered at because they don't impart more knowledge of the countries they inhabit.

Census of 1850

28th March 1856. The following table of the population of Tete was taken as the return from this district in June 1850.[2]

Baptized	Under 18	Above 18	Above 60 years	
freemen	31	114	8	} 318 baptized free
freewomen	48	84	3	people of all sorts

Unbaptized	Under 18	Above 18	Above 60 years	
freemen	17	5	0	} 30 unbaptized
freewomen	6	2	0	free people unbap.

Unbaptized	Under 18	Above 18	Above 60 years	
slave men	702	1,306	156	} 4,050 slaves
slave women	557	1,147	182	

(Now, 1856, there are more free men than slaves.)

The entire free population of Tete is 348, the entire slave population of Tette is 4,050, total population of this district 4,398. There are

---

[1] Writing to his mother in May 1847, DL mentioned that he had been 'farrier, builder, carpenter, glazier, doctor, minister, man midwife, blacksmith, boardsmith, tinsmith, shoemaker, waggon mender & painter, gunmender, hunter, fisher, and I don't know what else' (*Fam. Letters*, i. 197).

[2] The information that follows is not given in *Travels*.

eleven and a ½ slaves to each of the free population, or the free people are only 8.6 per cent of the population.[1]

In Angola there is about 6 per cent of slaves in the population. Here there is only about 8 per cent of free in it. But it must be borne in mind that there are very many independant tribes living around them, the population of which cannot be counted. They possess slaves too; are so hereditarily. The freemen are very rarely sold; indeed, one of the objects their republicanism has in view is to keep the free class intact. The large proportion of slaves explains the powerlessness of the authorities in case of invasion. A horde of slaves can never be depended on. Even a company of soldiers born quasi-slaves is expected to flee on the approach of danger and leave the officer alone. But the above census was during war.

There is abundance of sugar cane. One field served 4,000 men eating two days.[2] No manufactures now, except some mollasses.

One school to teach writing, private. One church and one padre, Pedro Antonio de Araujo, graduate in dogmatic theology & moral philosophy, native of Goa.[3]

Wheat harvest 1850, & rice, maize, fino, dourrha, earth nuts, beans, yielded the following number of panjos (consumption, & seed of the harvest delivered):

	seed	consumption
Wheat	1,295	1,254
Rice	792	1,561
Caffre corn	6,339	9,670
Maize	1,323	1,681
Dourrha	2,845	2,911
Earth nuts	8,728	8,750
Beans	695	729
Jugo	510	587
? Millet		

The consumption is probably near the mark.

It must be remembered, however, that this statistical report was made when Tete was in a state of seige and most of the free people had

[1] Correctly, 7·9 per cent. DL's figure was reached by taking the 'slave population' as the total.

[2] While plundering Portuguese estates on the north bank of the Zambesi, Kisaka's followers 'came to a field of sugar-cane so large, that 4000 men eating it during two days did not finish the whole' (Travels, 632).

[3] Mentioned by Bordalo (Moçambique, 253, 255) as lessee of three estates in Tete district; died October 1865 (Eça, Guerras, ii. 85).

fled. If present, the free greatly outnumber the slave people. The harvest, too, is as reported by slaves, and incorrect, seeing the consumption exceeds the harvest, and no free man buys the common foods of the country.

Major Secard will collect seeds of fruits and roots for Cape Botanic Garden, and I have written the Commissioner Duprat on the subject for cooperation.[1] It is very surprising how many good kind-hearted people there are in this our wicked world after all. . . .[2]

Captain Castelão went to the Cashan Mountains through the Boers and from Delagoa Bay or Laurenço Marques, which point is in 25° 56′ lat. S.[3] He ascended the river, correctly put down by Com-[mander] Owen as the river of Mangaia, for 3 days N., the river flowing behind a range of hills parallel with the coast. There stands the island of the chief named Mangaia. $1\frac{1}{2}$ days beyond in launches they came to a river named Mongonya or Sabe. They then crossed the Mangaia again, and found [another river] named Incomate. This is clearly the Limpopo, for he passed no other till he came to the Cashan hills, and it enters the sea a few miles north of De Algoa Fort. The Mongonya may be the Lepelole, he having forgot the side from which it comes.[4] [See facsimile map.]

29th March 1856. *Oil of Brother Pedros.* Recieved the following recipe for curing poisoned wounds from Mr Candido. It was invented

---

[1] Dated 26.iii.56, this letter is now in the Grey Collection, S. African Public Library, Cape Town.

[2] I have here omitted a few medical prescriptions (MS 775), the substance of which is published by Gelfand, 110.

[3] Captain Gregório Gomes Castelão, 'of ill fame', born in Portugal, was commandant of Tete for about a month in 1858 (Eça, *Guerras*, i. 242); he was subsequently 'sent prisoner to Mosambique' for administering the poison ordeal to and killing 'a person he suspected of having bewitched his child' (*Expedition*, 167, 250), and died there in 1862, aged 42 (Eça, ii. 66 n.). Lourenço Marques, capital of Moçambique since 1907, is in lat. 25.58 S, long. 32.35 E.

[4] Captain William Fitzwilliam Owen (1774–1857), R.N., commanded a British survey expedition, 1821–6, an account of which was published as *Narrative of Voyages to Explore the Shores of Africa*, 2 vols., 1833. Mangaia (Magaia) is apparently another name for the Manhiça (Manyisa) tribe (cf. Theal, *Records*, ix. 115), who live round the Incomati River above its estuary in northern Delagoa Bay; the river itself was formerly often called after them, and Owen himself has 'Mannees' and 'Manice' (i. 75, 141), not Mangaia. The Sabe (Save) is a tributary of the Incomati, which it joins in lat. 25.19 S, long. 32.16 E. The Limpopo enters the sea in lat. 25.13 S, long. 33.31 E (*Africa Pilot*, III, 211), some distance NE of the Incomati estuary; 'Lepelole' is a native name for the Olifants R., one of its major tributaries (confluence in lat. 24.06 S, long. 32.38 E).

by a padre, and he calls it the Oleo of Frei Pedros. Oil of Ricinus communis, and the following roots: Calumba root, Musheteco do., Abutua do., Batatinya do., Paregecanto do., and root of Itaca or Capande;[1] equal parts to be put into a bottle and kept to be applied to wound as occasion requires. The really effective ingredient may be the

island of the chief named Mangaia. 1½ day beyond in Launches they came to a river named Mongonga or Sabe they then crossed the Mangaia again and found named Incomate This is clearly the Limpopo for he passed no other till he came to the Cashan hills. and it enters the sea a few miles North of Delagoa Fort. The Mongonya may be the Lepelole he crossing forget the side from which it comes.

25° 30′ South

328. 30. Zastsabe R. or Mongonya

Mangaia

321.

Laurenço Marques

25° 56 South Lat
32 35 East Long
Green.

castor oil, for the Bushmen make use of fat only for the cure of these poisoned wounds, administering it internally at the same time. (Wrote Capn. V.)[2]

In West Africa fever is divisible into two kinds only, =remittent

[1] Calumba=*Jatorrhiza palmata*, abutua=*Tiliacora chrysobotrya* (Ficalho, *Plantas úteis*, 80, 82); the other 'roots' I have not identified. Pedro da Trindade (d. 1751) was a Dominican friar who lived at Zumbo for more than twenty-five years; much esteemed by the natives 'for his good works and for his remedy against poisonous wounds or bites', he was also 'chief captain' of the region, monopolized some of its gold diggings, and controlled about 1,600 slaves (Andrade, *Moçambique Setecentista*, 200–3, 265, 281; *Grande Enciclopédia*, art. 'Zumbo'). The 'oleo Fr. Pedros' is mentioned in an account, *c.* 1766, published by Andrade (p. 237).

[2] Possibly Captain Frank Vardon, of the Madras Light Infantry, who had become friendly with DL in 1846 while hunting in Bechuanaland (cf. *Fam. Letters*, i. 181). DL mentions him in a letter to Murchison, 4.iii.56 (*JRGS*, 1857, p. 371).

and intermittent. The remittent may be subdivided into the endemic, epidemic, and contagious. The two former may by local circumstances be converted into contagious, =thus the contagious endemic or contagious epidemic, and both according to persistence attended with yellow skin & sometimes black vomit. (Dr Bryson, p. 250.)[1]

30th March. After service with my own people, I went up the height behind Tete and counted the huts as about 800; $\times 3\frac{1}{2} = 2,800$ souls. The square houses are about 30, and if we say 20 to each = $600 + 2,800 = 3,400$ souls. This must be as much as it contains, for a very great number of slaves are employed in cultivation and now absent on account of the ripening harvest.

One of my men attacked with Sesendi or Lepra. He thinks it is caused by the anger of his barimo or ancestors.

31st March 1856. There is a petition of a Jesuit of Tete, still extant in the office, in which he modestly begs the Portuguese Government to grant him complete power over all the reed in the rivers ajacent to Tete, and all the wands used by the people for their wattle and daub huts. No one was to be allowed to cut either without his licence. As there were at the time more than ten thousand huts, a tax levied on the whole would have brought his reverence in a pretty round sum. It was probably never sent home by the authorities.

Another point of the village, hidden by a ridge, contained 400 huts more   = 1,200 in all

$$\frac{1,200}{} \times 3$$

$$3,600$$
European houses $30 \times 30 =$ 900
$$\overline{}$$
                       4,500 souls

Much of the population is now abroad at harvest operations.

Bread mixed or made into dough by native beer, called Boyaloa or Pombé, alone; allowed to stand, after being well worked, one hour and a half, the temperature being 83° in the shade, the loaves being about twice the size of English buns. They were put into an oven so hot the hand could not hold a thermometer in it, and in twelve minutes were well baked & beautifully risen bread. The juice of the palm or sura[2]

---

[1] See below, p. 456. Alexander Bryson (1802–69), 'medical writer', was a naval surgeon who became 'director-general of the naval medical department, 1864' (*DNB*).

[2] Coconut palm toddy (*Travels*, 639).

does better, and charcoal of a certain tree effects fermentation quickly too. It is put into a bag and suspended in the liquid to be fermented. Probably the charcoal serves as a receptacle merely for the ferment, or as spongy platinum.

Major Secard sent for a specimen of a beautiful kind of wild lint called Buaze,[1] which will do well for ropes; also another, very abundant, of which the natives make bags and even cloth, which may do for paper.

Former Jesuit establishment

1st April 1856. Went to see the site of an establishment of the Jesuits, called Micombo, about 10 miles south of Tete.[2] Like all their places it shews great judgement in the selection. A little stream of mineral water was collected in a tank and led to their house for raising vegetables at times of the year when no rain falls, and it is now in a deep shady grove of mangoes. They were exceedingly industrious. Whoever was lazy they were not, and being wise in their generation were keen traders too in ivory, gold, and everything else. All praise their laboriousness; whatever they did, they did it with their might. Missions were trading expeditions as well as for the advance of their faith and power. We ought to learn something from them.

The Dutch ministers in the [Cape] Colony are mostly Scotchmen,[3] and like such purchase farms whereon to build a church. A good site is chosen, and then every effort made to obtain villagers. All the better parts are let to them, and as the village rises in importance the rents return a handsome revenue to the church. After thus making things snug, with from £200 to £400 per annum from the Government, they are in a position to preach total abstinence from politics, when the prevailing form is unsavoury, & pure spirituality as becoming in all the clergy. This is what deserves the name of worldly wisdom. Give me £600 a year, I think but little else but spirituality would be needed. For such, however, as are content to follow the mode pointed out by

[1] Made from the inner bark of *Securidaca longipedunculata*, violet tree (Miller, *Woody Plants*, 41; Ficalho, *Plantas úteis*, 87).

[2] Not shown on maps consulted.

[3] Owing to a shortage of clergy in Cape Colony, and political objections to employing men from Holland, the Governor (Lord Charles Somerset) had arranged in 1820 for the recruitment of ministers from Scotland, where the 'established church' (Presbyterian) was 'identical in creed and nearly so in form of worship' with the local Dutch Reformed Church; by 1824 six had come, and others followed later (Theal, *History*, v. 369-71).

the saviour of the world, both spiritual and temporal must share their anxieties, and they never can come to the conclusion that the children of God ought to leave the affairs of the state entirely to the children of the devil.

The great-grandfather of the Captain Nunes who kindly accompanied me[1] was a captain too, and recieved a letter from the Marquis of Pombal to be opened on a certain day. When the day arrived, he found therein orders to go with his company and seize all the Jesuits and lead them prisoners to the coast. All their riches fell to the state, and they were immense. Large quantities of gold were often sent from this to Goa, enclosed in images and intended for their superiors. The affair of expulsion must have been well managed. Probably, too, they were odious to the people at large.

2d April 1856. The son of Monomotapa came here yesterday. He was the favourite, and his father expected that he would occupy his place. A strong party, however, placed Katolosa in the chieftainship, and when he dies it is believed there will be a civil war, in order that the party of Katolosa may not continue to hold the chief influence. Probably the offers which the Portuguese have repeatedly recieved of territory, if they would only attend the interment of the chiefs with troops and instal the new chiefs, had this in view. The party they went to instal thus gained influence and probably decided the course of the election, for many would vote on the side of power; and it would be worth while to any man to give a piece of land for the chieftainship, seeing it would not diminish but largely increase his importance to be made a chief thereby. This son of Monomotapa appeared just like an ordinary native. He is named 'Mozungo' or 'white man', and it is believed might in time succeed his father.[2] Has a very narrow tapering

[1] Not identified, unless DL means Captain João de Sousa Nunes de Andrade, a local landowner (Bordalo, Moçambique, 256), who also acted twice (1848, 1854) as commandant of the district (Eça, Guerras, i. 240, 242).

[2] 'Monomotapa' (Mwene Mutapa) was the official name of the chief of the Karanga, a Shona tribe. In the 16th and 17th centuries he controlled much of modern Mashonaland (S. Rhodesia) and the adjoining portions of Moçambique south of the Zambesi. The kingdom subsequently disintegrated, and 'Katolosa' (Katuruza, Mwene-Mutapa XXIV, ruled c. 1835–68) was far less important than the potentate described in early Portuguese records. 'He ruled on the Zambesi, close to Tete, but he was always being opposed by his enemies, and there was no longer a paramount chief to whom everyone paid their respects and showed loyalty. And most of the land belonged to the Portuguese anyway' (Abraham, 'The Monomotapa Dynasty', 1959, pp. 66, 70–1, 82; cf. Eça, Guerras, i. 256, 325,

head. His father had probably more energy. But it is nonsense to call a mere chief an emperor. Katolosa has between one and two hundred wives.

Harris, quoting from Capn. Owen, says, 'How truly has it been remarked by C. Owen that the state of those countries which have been little visited by Europeans is a direct refutation of the theories of poets and philosophers, who would represent the ignorance of the savage as virtuous simplicity, his miserable poverty as frugality and temperance, and his stupid indolence as laudable contempt for wealth; widely different indeed were the facts which came under our observation, and doubtless it will ever be found that uncultivated man is a compound of treachery, cunning, debauchery, gluttony, and idleness.'[1]

Some reach conclusions with wonderful facility. For nearly fifteen years, though living among them, I did not know what to make of their many wonderful good actions and many extraordinary bad ones, and it is only recently that I have come to the conclusion that they are a wonderful compound of good and evil, as man appears to be everywhere else. And intercourse with the lower ranks of our own population always deteriorates their character.

Black sand, like horneblend, has a great affinity for quicksilver.

2d April 1856. The Zambesi flooded again. It is said to have three rises annually, but this year it has four. It is discoloured now.

Besides the igneous effects of igneous rocks on others in the vicinity, there is, everywhere I have seen in Africa, the appearance of all the rocks (with the single exception of soft tufa) having been subjected to the action of an amount of heat not sufficient to melt but to change the colour near the surface. This change of colour is very distinct, and sometimes the action has been upon loose stones; the core of these is generally lighter than the outer portions. In some rocks the heat has

where he is called Catruza). Mozungo (Muzungo) was the son of Nyasoro, Katuruza's 'uncle' and immediate predecessor (c. 1810–35); he never did 'succeed his father' (cf. Abraham, 66, 70–1).

[1] DL's source is W. C. Harris, *The Wild Sports of Southern Africa*, 1839, p. 171. The passage quoted, written by one of Owen's officers about the coastal tribes of S.E. Africa, actually reads as follows (*Narrative of Voyages*, i. 71–2): 'The state of these countries, which have scarcely had any intercourse with civilized nations, is a direct proof in refutation of the theories of poets and philosophers, who represent the ignorance of the savage as virtuous simplicity–his miserable poverty as frugality and temperance–and his stupid indolence as a laudable contempt for wealth. How different are the facts! We ever found uncultivated man a combination of cunning, treachery, drunkenness, and gluttony.'

penetrated only ½ an inch, in others one inch and a half, in others there has been a sort of sweating of the rock and silica stands chrystalized on the surface. Did a comet touch our world at the last destruction of animated beings? It was something sudden, for fishes shew alarm and they have been found in the very act of swallowing others. In this rock of Tete, many oxide of iron looking masses have fallen into it when soft, and coloured the substance around them for 6 inches, as if injected hot. There are also rain drops on the rock as if heavy and coming in a slanting direction, so as to raise out a portion of the sand on the farthest side. I have seen no footprints yet, nor yet shells. Was this only a fresh water delta?

State of the Interior

2d April. The state of the interior of Africa opposite this seems never to have varied much. They are fond of agriculture and settled abodes, have laws and customs which are considered sacred. So far they are a civilized race, and utterly unlike the inhabitants of Tierra de Fuego or (except the Bushmen) the South Australians. They have, too, paramount chiefs, from whom the different chiefs branched off in a friendly manner, and to whom they still owe allegiance. But even these can never attain to anything like a state of civilization without that concentration of power which the knowledge of letters imparts. For as they are now, there is no possibility of governing the more distant population. Though day & night were devoted to the business, no set of men could undertake to hear the interminable talk which all their affairs requires. The more distant chiefs are virtually independant, and the paramount chief weakened in proportion. Literature is therefore one essential ingredient in a high degree of civilization, such as that of China, India, and Mexico.

So far as tradition can inform us, they appear to have lived alternately in a state of peace and war from time immemorial. A chief embued with more ambition than usual begins by overcoming his neighbours, who, fleeing, are set upon by others, and rendered desperate they soon learn their own power, and custom makes them more expert in war. They sweep over a large portion of territory, carrying destruction wherever they go. The death of the chief and principal men leads to a settlement of the tribe in peace. Men breathe, become rich and proud, to be again disturbed, scattered, and peeled, by some other marauder. The Batoka have been thus beaten by one of their own people called Pingola, then by Matibele and Makololo. The real

Caffres have scourged more of South Africa than any other enemy. Successive migrations have taken place of both Zulahs and Basutas. The former, named Landins, keep Senna in awe, and other Portuguese possessions are in danger, as Delgoa Bay. A large party crossed the Zambesi and went north of Tete, to be eaten up by the Maravi.[1] The later wars have all been produced by a sort of backward migration, or from south to north.

Had the powerful chiefs who have from time to time arisen possessed a knowledge of letters, their kingdoms would have remained, but they give themselves up to self-indulgence entirely, and their power slips away from their hands as they become old. The system they adopt is one of espionage, and never engages the affections as a confidential written communication would. The system being perfectly well known, all act on the same principle, and an everlasting undercurrent of intriguing and espionage takes the place [of] the sense of peace and justice.

To impart education is unquestionably a real boon on any nation. So highly do I value a knowledge of letters among a people, I would rejoice to see it imparted by any body of men, even by the Jesuits. There may be a difference where a system of education, in a country like England, would be used as a means [of] exalting an already dominant sect to a position and influence they could not otherwise attain. But in a heathen country education would be a good of unquestionable value, by whomsoever communicated. The work of a missionary among the actual heathen is rendered dreary enough by the daily attempts to convey a knowledge of letters to those who care nothing about it, and who imagine that in looking at the letters they are conferring a favour upon him. Young men who come among the half-christianized, and find the influence of parents and relatives on his side, know nothing of the persevering forcing oneself to act from a sense of duty which the other requires. One must do good without obtaining or even expecting gratitude for spiritual benefits conferred. Yet generally the people are keenly alive to the temporal benefits we bring, and feel kindly toward us on their account. In hope of impressing a conviction of the value of the spiritual, a knowledge of medicine and handicrafts becomes valuable.

[1] This may refer to the Ngoni of Zwangendaba (see p. 369.1), who crossed the Zambesi in 1835; but, far from being 'eaten up by the Maravi', they successfully established several conquest states in what are now Tanganyika, Nyasaland, and N.E. Rhodesia (cf. Tew, Peoples of L. Nyasa, 93–9).

3d April 1856. . . .[1] Mr Candido says that earthquakes have happened several times in the country of the Maravi at no great distance from Tete, or in the region of coal and hot springs. They are named 'Shiwo' in the Maravi tongue, and in that of this side the river 'Shitecoteco' or 'shivering'. They have never been of more than a minute's duration, and never did any damage. Indeed, with huts made with poles stuck in ground it is difficult to concieve what damage could be done unless rocks were rent and waters gushed forth. They have never happened on this side the river. There are many great caverns on the other side of the river, and chiefly in the nearer parts of the Maravi territory, who use them as store houses and places of refuge in time of war. The sea has evidently formed them, as well as the round holes used as cisterns which we have seen.

The natives known to the Portuguese have universally the clear idea of a Supreme God, the maker and governor of all things. He is named Morimo, Molungo, Reza, and Mpambé, in different dialects, but all acknowledge him at once as the ruler. When undergoing the ordeal they swear to their innocence by holding up the left hand to Heaven. When they escape they make a sacrifice of a fowl or sheep, pouring out the blood to the soul of some departed relative. They fully believe in the soul's continued existence apart from the body, and offer food, beer, &c, to those of relatives, and visiting their graves for the purpose. They believe also in the transmigration of souls, and that, too, while persons are still living.

If a man marries and does not pay the principal man of his wife's family a certain amount, the children begotten belong to the family and enter into the heritage of the mother. They are those of the grandmother. If he pays, they enter into the heritage and family of his own father.

On this side the river the sons are said to inherit the chieftainship, but on the other side, as Maravi, Babisa, &c &c, the children of a sister alone, and not those of the chief himself, occupy the chieftainship.

Mr Candido never saw nor heard of any antient inscriptions in this country, nor yet fossils nor shells. Yet a young man from Senna declares that inscriptions do exist at Gorongozo, in the way to Manica, and says they are on large slabs of stone lying flat on the top of a hill. He adds the letters are round, and as he only heard of them from others he cannot tell in what language they are. The Jesuits had an establish-

[1] I have here omitted a quotation from 'Mr Lee on Inflammation of Veins' (MS 790-1).

ment there, and it may have been their work. It is healthy, as their establishments usually are. One might buy an estate without seeing it if only sure of its having been a choice made by them. These inscriptions are eight days from Senna in a westerly direction.[1]

☞ Remember to ask about Chipanga, whence ascent by Shire begins; also the Chronicles of East Africa;[2] also a machine for taking off the seed from maize cobs, American.

Heat of March in shade at Tete, 1856, at 9 a.m. average 84°, at 9 p.m. average 87°, mean 85°; midday 88°. Greatest heat 90° at midday, lowest at sunrise 81°, rainy, cloudy.

Diseases, medicines, &c

4th April 1856. The disease named Maculo exists here as well as in Angola.[3] The end of the bowel becomes affected and the anus does not close. If nothing is done a small ulcer forms and extends up the bowel as gangrene, which is rapidly fatal. The best treatment is a mixture of catechu and lemon juice. This is poured into the open bowel & kept in by a pledget. A grain of the catechu is given 2 or three times a day by mouth. In Angola they insert a suppository of a pounded plant called Herva Santa Maria,[4] mixed with gunpowder, for the same complaint. It seems to affect the constitution, for a remarkable paleness of the palms of the hands and under the eyes is produced by it. Fedigosa is given for syphilis, and is a good substitute for coffee (the seeds).

Went today to visit a cavern. Though probably made by the sea it contains no fossils on its floor. A human skull was lying in it.

Got a plant called Sumsa, which is said to be good for intermittent fever. It is also named the root of Nossa Senhora.[5] Stamena 5 with blue heads, pistil 1, 3 lobed stigma, flower pure white, delicate, petals 2 or 3 double or one on end of other, flower and whole plant very gummy, calyx covered with hairs, each with a little bead of gum on end. A climber. Leaves spear-shaped with broad shoulder.

[1] Gorongosa is a large mountain mass SW of Sena, in lat. 18.25 S, long. 34.05 E (GSGS 4695, sheet 1176). I have found no other reference to 'inscriptions' thereabouts.

[2] Professor C. R. Boxer suggests that DL may have been thinking of J. dos Santos, *Ethiopia Oriental, e varia historia de cousas notaveis do Oriente*, 1609. Chipanga is probably Chupanga (see below, p. 469).

[3] See above, p. 198.

[4] 'Erva de Santa Maria', wormseed, *Chenopodium ambrosioides* (Ficalho, *Plantas úteis*, 240-1, which also mentions its use for treating 'maculo').

[5] Not identified.

5th April 1856. The cedar of Lebanon or one of its kindred exists in large quantity and growth farther down the river, and so does ebony. But there are no camphor trees (Dryobalanops camphora).

6th April 1856. Intend to leave my good friend Major Tito in a day or two, or when the new moon appears. We go down the river quickly with the current.

A lowlying country with a humid atmosphere may act injuriously by allowing the various excreta to remain within the body. As these are given off chiefly by the lungs, pure air in sufficient quantity to oxidize them is needed. If the air is already impregnated with malaria they are not eliminated, and their accumulation may be the cause of fever. When that disease cures itself, it does so by the discharge of much effete matter, salts in urine, and perspiration &c.

7th April 1856. ☞ Major Secard advises me to secure a licence from the Portuguese Government on my return. As many have attempted to ascend the Zambesi and have been prevented, I might come to Mosambique and get the information that I could proceed no farther in that direction. Remember to ask it. I ought to make the representation that having been a missionary for so many years in the Interior, and the path to the point occupied is so long by way of the Cape, I wish to take the much shorter one through the Portuguese possessions.

7th. Recieved the plant named Buaze today. It seems very strong and as if it might prove a good substitute for lint. Very little preparation is needed for reducing it into the proper fibrous state for ropes. This is a great advantage. The Ifi requires to be steeped some time in water, this a very short time, and then it is beaten and makes a white lint by bleaching in the sun. The fine thread which the people make of it seems like catgut in strength. Another of the Aloe family makes a very strong cord. When a fibre is attempted to be broken it almost cuts the finger. It is called Congé,[1] and very fine strong thread and ropes can be made of it, which are strong enough to hold the hippo-potami. I have got specimens of both kinds for experiment.

The lands ajacent to the north bank of the Zambesi are very much more fertile than those on its southern side. Indeed, seeds brought from the country of the Maravi degenerate quickly; yams and other edible roots become less than half the size in a short time. It is very stoney on this side, but the Maravi country is said to be mountainous

---

[1] Cf. *Travels*, 645–6. Elsewhere (MS 741) DL says its Brazilian name is 'pita' (=*Agave americana* and allied spp.).

too. Wheat at Quilimane is not half the size as that of Tete and yields but little meal, and Zumbo gives much larger grains than this part. A hole is made in the ground lately flooded by the river, a few grains dropped in and covered with the foot. With but one weeding a fine crop is ready for the sickle in four months afterwards.

I have never met with a single case of stone in the bladder in the Interior, and in America Professor Gross remarks on their exemption from that complaint. In ten years he never met a single case of either gravel or stone among them in Kentuckey, and Mr Dudley met with only one or two cases. . . .[1]

13th April 1856. A sudden change of temp[eratur]e, occurring at the appearance of the new moon on the fourth, brought fever with it, and laid both Commandant and self, with many others of the village, up of fever. I had two severe fits of intermittent & great internal heat

+ on .4th. 'It is' not like Attest of swift ⹀. beam. And yet this is the

with most vivid waking dreams all night for two or three successive nights. But having made some new pills, the old ones not serving, I got over the fits, and by salts & quinine combined, and the latter in quantity to affect the hearing, I am thank God much better.

☞ Mr Candido sends his broken watch spring to England, that I may purchase another for him. This I have much pleasure in doing, for he has been very kind and obliging to me all along.

☞ Bills of the Bank of Bombay will be best for this service, for though there is some trade with the Cape it is uncertain and irregular. There is much trade between Bombay & this.

The temperature has fallen about 4°, and though the thermometer ranges upwards of 80° the weather feels delightfully cool. The air delicious, calm and clear sky, slight flocculi of clouds still going to the N.W. from south-east, water falling rapidly. In this month we ought

[1] I have here omitted several medical recipes (MS 799) quoted from 'Prof. Gross'. Samuel David Gross (1805–84) was a medical professor at the University of Louisville, Kentucky, 1840–56; Benjamin Winslow Dudley (1785–1870), also a surgeon, grew up in that state (*Dictionary of American Biography*, v. 478–9; viii. 18–20).

to be in Quilimane next year in order to ascend in May. Major Secard offers to furnish me with money if I need it for the way in front of Quilimane, and I might pay it on my return. It is God who influences his heart. May he find mercy of the Lord in that day.

Swallows with pure white belly, black horizontal stripe at eyes, head reddish brown, forked tail, two feathers only, began to repair their nest on 4th. It is not covered in but, like that of swift [*see facsimile*], on the side of a beam. And yet this is the beginning of winter here. Cold seems to [be] the stimulus to procreation in hot countries.

15th April 1856. ☞ It is said that wood ashes mixed with wheat prevent the attack of the weevil, provided the grain is not in the vicinity of common Caffre corn containing many of the insects. Wheat is capable of being preserved too for years in the common small sacks made of palmyra leaves, but not in close proximity to infected maize or other grain. This is a very valuable piece of information for us in the Interior.

17th April. Dr Salis, the late physician of Mosambique,[1] tried the curious experiment of curing fever by depriving the unfortunate patients of water except in very minute quantities. An officer in a fit of raging thirst crawled by night to a large pot of water and drank in long delicious draughts the whole, an enormous quantity between two and three gallons. After returning to his cot he commenced vomiting and purging copiously, and in three days left the hospital quite well. Thus ended the experiment, for no one else would submit to the doctor afterwards.

A bank of clouds rests every afternoon on the hills N.E. of Tete, and in the mornings thin fleecy clouds float away from the S.E. & S.S.E. towards the Interior. Little wind.

The Commandant was dissuaded from taking a brisk purgative after fever began, according to his own custom, the result of experience, and has been very slow in recovering. Only this morning (17th) can he sit up, and I have been about for several days. I intend leaving as soon as he is well. . . .[2]

18th April 1856. A remarkable peculiarity of the Bechuanas often arrested my attention while living among them. Waggons are highly

[1] Jacques Nicolau de Salís di Celerina, 'doctor of medicine, surgery, and obstetrics'; transferred to Angola as chief physician, May 1854; arrived at Luanda, December 1855 (*Boletim official d'Angola*, nos. 532, 539); author of a paper on the diseases of Moçambique (*Annaes maritimos e coloniaes*, vi, 1846, pp. 43–72).

[2] I have here omitted a lengthy quotation (MS 803–7), about yellow and 'bilious' fever, from 'Dr Asabel Smith, in Transactions of New York Academy of Medicine, Vol. I, part 1, 1851'; it is summarized by Gelfand, 113 n.

valued and much sought after as an evidence of respectability, and as old ones are more frequently purchased than new it seems natural to suppose they would wish to be able to mend them. But, so far as I am aware, there is not a single Mochuana who can put in a new spoke, and this though they have had men able and willing to instruct them for more than thirty years. When others mend a waggon they come about it and examine the work as if with the eyes of masters, point out any defect, and seem thoroughly well satisfied with themselves for having reached the eminent knowledge of being able to find fault. It never seems to enter their wooly crania that though the workmanship may be faulty not a man of them could equal it.

I often wondered over this apparent inability to see sequences, till I reflected that a great deal of the present knowledge so much vaunted about in England just amounts to the same ability to find fault. In politics, for instance, how numerous have been the cases in which to hear a candidate one must conclude he would drive all before him – and the very air of the House has muzzled him. So among the Independants. What a multiplicity of faults were found with one who felt it to be his duty to become editor of a newspaper and other periodicals. Like the Bechuanas, they seemed to think if they could find fault they were accomplished men, yet fifty thousand of them could not have done what has been effected by the man whose work was criticised. Has he a successor among the whole crew? I trow not. The fault-finding spirit was notably manifested, too, against the London Missionary Society. And how did it end? In complete vindication of those whose wisdom was impugned.[1]

The men have made a brisk trade for themselves here in carrying firewood from the ajacent country and selling it in Tete. They are delighted with it, and have realized many beads. Thirty or forty have gone to hunt elephants, and the Major gave them two pieces of cloth to buy food in the way. When they kill an elephant they will dry and sell the flesh, which is in much request here on account of all the domestic animals having been lost in the war. The ivory, too, will be sold on their own account. Twenty have been employed by a trader to carry goods for him to Katolosa, and he has paid them well with cloth, &c. I intend to try and get some employed in canoes between this and Senna, as the wages are much better at this than at more common employments.

[1] The editor referred to was Dr John Campbell, of *The Christian Witness* (cf. *Miss. Corr.*, 231 and n.; and, for the attack on the LMS, ibid., 150–1 and notes).

The rapidity of the flow of the Zambesi being $3\frac{3}{4}$ miles per hour cannot be adduced as evidence of great elevation in the Interior, for according to Dr Arnott[1] 3 inches declivity per mile gives a velocity in a smooth straight channel of 3 miles per hour. If we say the Zambesi falls four inches per mile in its sometimes rocky channel in the thousand miles between Quilimane and the Falls, we have only $333\frac{1}{3}$ feet. But if we say 5 inches per mile, which is more than the amount necessary for the velocity of $3\frac{3}{4}$ miles, we have $416\frac{2}{3}$ feet, to which if we add 100 feet for the Falls we have between 500 and 600 feet elevation only.[2]

The Ganges at 1,800 miles from its mouth is only 800 feet above the level of the sea, & takes a month to come that distance. The Chobe is often heard of as flooded forty miles above Linyanti a fortnight or three weeks before it reaches that point, but it is very tortuous. The great River Magdalena falls only 500 feet in a thousand miles. The Rio de la Plata has so gentle a declivity, ships are lifted up by the gradually inclined plane at 1,500 miles distance to heights greater than our loftiest spires. The Ganges descends from a height about equal to that of Arthur's Seat, or twice the height of St Paul's.[3]

18th Ap. The Zambesi has made another slight rise, being the fifth this year. Wheat sowing, $\frac{1}{2}$ panja gave fifty panjas, or 100 fold.

18th April 1856. Mentioned my intention to the Governor to leave Tete on Monday 22d currt. An officer, Lieutenant Miranda,[4] accompanies me to Quilimane, by direction of Major Secard.

[1] Possibly Neil Arnott (1788–1874), 'physician and natural philosopher', author of *Elements of Physics*, 1827 (*DNB*). DL had consulted his work on returning from Angola to Linyanti (*Travels*, 284 n.).

[2] 'The rapid flow of the Leeambye, which once seemed to me evidence of much elevation of the country from which it comes, I now found, by the boiling point of water, was fallacious' (*Travels*, 284). The length of the Zambesi from the Victoria Falls to the Indian Ocean is 900 miles (not 1,000, as stated above, nor 800, as stated in *Travels*, 284 n.), and at the Falls it is slightly under 3,000 feet above sea level (Clark, *The Victoria Falls*, 18, 20).

[3] The Ganges flows through N. India and E. Pakistan into the Bay of Bengal, the Magdalena through Colombia into the Caribbean Sea, and the Rio de la Plata into the Atlantic between Argentina and Uruguay; Arthur's Seat, Edinburgh, is a hill 822 feet high (*Columbia Lippincott Gazetteer*). The cross on the dome of St. Paul's Cathedral, London, is '365 ft. above the ground level, the inner cupola 218 ft. above the floor' (*Whitaker's Almanac*, 1961, p. 497).

[4] Possibly Joaquim Romão de Miranda, born in Lisbon *c.* 1819; ensign and then lieutenant (1855) at Tete; subsequently became a landowner and trader; killed while fighting against Bonga, November 1869 (Eça, *Guerras*, ii. 400, 425–6).

19 April. There exists a great deal of the complaint called spongy or scorbutic gums in Tete. Almost every one suffers from it, and males much more than females. They have limes in abundance, but it may arise from the large consumption of pork & oil.

I leave Boyle & Bryson on Fever, Outlines of Astronomy, two numbers of Medico-Chir. Rev., and Darwin's Naturalist's Voyage, with the Governor.[1] Think an iron house might be brought up the river, if we can manage to come in March and along the Muto[2] in April.

21st April 1856. ☞ Remember to buy the anæsthetic salve allied to chloroform for Major Secard, and also enquire the best thing for strengthening the gums where the teeth are loose from the effects of mercury. Also the best drinks for ardor urinæ.

We intended to have started today, but the Lieutenant Miranda having been up most of the night before in attention on Senhora Goveia he had fever. We shall therefore start early on the morning of Tuesday 22d. This young lady, of twenty years only, had a discharge suppressed by [the] change in weather which affected us, and leeches only were applied. She was seized with convulsions at 3 o'clock yesterday morning, and soon expired. I was called three hours afterwards, and found her bosom as warm as ever I did in a case of fever. This continued for three hours more and then gradually declined. In order to avoid the possibility of trance being mistaken for death, I made an incision on the thigh and another on the temple. She ought to have been bled by the apothecary who attended her. He is a native of Goa. I attended the funeral in the evening. The padre sprinkled plenty of holy water on the body, and sung or chaunted prayers. Poor young lady. She was a widow too, already, & [had] been ten years in Africa.[3]

[1] DL was a regular subscriber to the quarterly *British and Foreign medico-chirurgical review* (cf. *Fam. Letters*, i. 102; ii. 99), and on 12.i.53 had ordered from his bookseller (Snow) copies of 'Boyle's Diseases of Western Africa' and 'Bryson on Diseases of Western Africa', i.e. J. Boyle, *A Practical Medico-Historical Account of the Western Coast of Africa*, 1831, and A. Bryson, *An Account of the Origin, Spread, & Decline of the Epidemic Fevers of Sierra Leone*, 1849. Charles Darwin's *Journal of Researches into the Natural History . . . of the Countries visited during the Voyage of H.M.S. Beagle* was first published in 1839; 'Outlines of Astronomy' may be the work of that title by J. F. W. Herschel, 1849.

[2] See below, p. 471.

[3] She 'had come with her brother from Lisbon' (*Travels*, 652). Eça records the death at Tete, 'in the second quarter of 1856', of D. Carlota Joaquina da Veiga Cabral de Gouveia, aged 22, born in Portugal and sister of Lieut. M. A. de Gouveia (who was in Moçambique by 1849, and at Tete since 1851); but he says nothing about her having been married (*Guerras*, ii. 78, 80 n.).

A gold chain &c has been presented to Agnes by the Major.[1] He is extraordinarily kind. May Almighty God reward him. It is the workmanship of an inhabitant of Tete.

The custom of the country requires the expenditure of a considerable quantity of powder. The slaves fired many times as we accompanied the body to the grave. And when it is one well known in the country, all the surrounding chiefs send deputations to fire over the grave. On one occasion more than thirty barrels of powder were expended. This morning the slaves of the brother of the young lady went round the village making a lamentation, and drums are beat all day now.

It is quite true that the natives in digging for gold do not go deeper than the chin, believing if they do the ground would fall in and kill them. And when they find a piece of gold they bury it again, believing if this is not done the country would soon cease to yield any. It is looked upon as seed.[2]

[1] 'Major Sicard ... presented a rosary made of the gold of the country ... to my little daughter' (*Travels*, 638). Agnes (1847–1912, married A. L. Bruce 1875) was DL's second child and elder (at that time only) daughter.

[2] See above, p. 424.

XX

TO SENA AND QUELIMANE

Descent of the Zambesi

28th [April]. Reached Senna yesterday evening and was well recieved by Sr Ferrão,[1] in the absence of Sr Isidoro, who has gone to Quilimane. I lived with him till Sr Isidoro returned.

I have been favoured with the company of Lieut. Miranda, who is sent by Major Secard with orders to provide everything for both myself and people. I have not often met with more disinterested kindness than that of the Major. He came to the canoes with me and provided every article he could think of for my use, sending the message to Mr Ferrão to treat me as if it were himself, giving orders too to Sr Azevedo[2] to furnish everything at his expence. May my God, who has so bountifully dealt with me, remember him and grant him his blessing.

Sr Miranda having had fever from fatigue on the occasion of the funeral of Sra Goveia, to whom he is related, we waited over Monday 21st and left on Tuesday 22d, arriving in the evening at the garden of Sr Augustino Manoel de Gomes, the son-in-law & nephew of Bonga,[3] who recieved us very graciously. Bonga himself lives in his stockade, and being exceedingly superstitious recieves no one, but Sr

[1] Anselmo Henriques Ferrão, born in Sena, of which his father (a Goanese) was at one time governor; landowner, merchant, brigadier in the local militia, and occasionally acting comandant of the town, he had much influence and prestige among the natives (Eça, 'Inéditos', 19; *Guerras*, i. 355, 362). DL calls him 'large-hearted and hospitable', and praises his 'unbounded' benevolence (*Narrative*, 35–6); Stewart describes him (1862) as 'a little brisk man of about 50, apparently comfortable and happy, and certainly well off' (*Zambesi Journal*, 148). 'Sr Isidoro' was his son-in-law Isidoro Correia Pereira (1817–63), born in Quelimane, a militia colonel, former 'chief captain' of Manica and Quiteve, commandant of Sena, 'upright and esteemed' (Eça, *Guerras*, i. 344; ii. 78, 246 n.); 'a man of considerable energy' (*Travels*, 658).

[2] Francisco Maria de Azevedo, merchant in Quelimane (Eça, *Guerras*, i. 318) and lessee of two large estates in Sena district (Bordalo, *Moçambique*, 259, 260); presented by the Admiralty with 'a gold chronometer watch' for his hospitality 'to all English officers on the east coast' (*Travels*, 667, 671); died December 1860 (*Expedition*, 177).

[3] This description, repeated in *Travels*, 654, is incorrect. According to Eça, who gives a detailed genealogy, Agostinho Manuel Gomes was in fact the brother-in-law (sister's husband) of Bonga; he lived at Marango, on the left bank of the Luenha at its confluence with the Zambesi (*Guerras*, i. 70; ii. 83–4). In *Expedition* (16, 58, etc.) Gomes is called 'Manoel' or 'Sr Manoel'.

458

816

Revubue

Tete

Moendangoma = foot punts grand caract

Nyangoma seen from W.

Mosambique Lat. 17° 34'

Kramatonga

Luenya hills

To East

Lupata as seen from

Mameo

17° 5' 30" N Lunenda

Hotspring

formed for salubrious waters and fruit 17° 26' 30" Lunen

juscriptions

Gorongozo   Nyamonga ant

	hours
Tete to Luenya R.	3
To Golet Mosambique	3
mouth Lupata	2
Shivamba	6½
Nkuesi.	3
Senna	6
	23½

3)16 4 ½ (55 leagues from Tete to Senna.

Manoel recieves and converses with all who come. He is a native of Goa, and the father of Bonga was of Macao and banished thence for theft.[1] Bonga has none of the good properties of his father, and all the bad ones of the natives, among others the belief in the ordeal. Sr Manoel gave us tea and dinner very well prepared, and conversed rationally, but feels a little abashed from being kept at a distance by the Portuguese, or rather he feels it necessary to keep himself so in order not to fall under the suspicion of Bonga. In the morning he came to the canoes after presenting tea and eggs roasted with biscuits, giving also three goats as provisions for the way.[2]

We saw Bonga's stockade after passing the Loenya in the morning,[3] but did not go near it, as he is very suspicious. He has some good houses in it. It seemed strange to see a stockade menacing the whole commerce of the river, and the white man unable to remove it. When the river Luenya is full all canoes must go close to the stockade, or be dashed on opposite bank of Zambesi. [*See facsimile map.*]

On the 24th we came early to the islet called by Dr Lacerda the 'island of Mosambique', from a belief that it lay in lat. 15° 1' south as Mosambique does. I found it to be in 16° 34' south, consequently there must have been some error in the Dr.'s observn. or calculation.[4] The islet lies at the western entrance to the gorge of Lupata, and in two hours we passed through the so-called 'Spine of the World'.[5] It is a range of low hills scarcely 600 feet high as seen from the east, but at the islet of Mosambique, where the hills shew a clear perpen-

[1] DL is mistaken. Bonga's father and grandfather were both born in or near Tete, and his great-grandfather (Nicolau Pascoal da Cruz, born in Siam, 'presumably of pure Mongolian stock') had come to Africa in 1767 as sergeant in a company of sepoys (Eça, *Guerras*, i. 58, 62).

[2] 'After a breakfast of tea, roasted eggs, and biscuits next morning, he presented six fowls and three goats as provisions for the journey' (*Travels*, 655).

[3] The stockade was at Massangano, on the right bank of the Zambesi immediately below the confluence of the Luenha, lat. 16.24 S, long. 33.47 E (GSGS 4355, SE 36/2). It is described and illustrated by Eça, *Guerras*, i. 208, 216–20, and Botelho, *História*, ii. 190–1.

[4] In *Travels*, 655, its location is given as lat. 16.34.46 S, long. 33.51 E; Lacerda (*Travessia da África*, 127) gives lat. 16.30.58 S. DL is mistaken in saying (as he also does in *Travels*, 655) that Lacerda was responsible for naming the island; as early as 1667 Barretto wrote that at the entrance to Lupata there is 'an islet in the middle, which they call Mozambique, because they say it is in the same latitude as the island of Mozambique' (Theal, *Records*, iii. 447, 476).

[5] See above, p. 360. Lupata gorge, 'a natural cutting about 17 miles in length', starts 45 miles below Tete (*Africa Pilot*, III, 241).

dicular section, they appear about the height of Arthur's Seat, Edinburgh. The river is constricted among these hills to about 500 yards, but is very deep and clear of rocks. A steamer could go through it with ease. The western side is of clay slate curiously pressed and contorted, the eastern of porphyry containing large square and rounded chrystals. How it ever came to be called 'the spine of the world' is more than I can guess, for it bends round into the country of the Maganja and then bends to the river again, coming quite close to the left bank before we reach Senna.

25th. Sleep on a small islet. The river is exceedingly broad and full of large reedy islands. It is impossible to give the form of these from a canoe. The mast of a ship alone would enable one to see them. The river itself is several miles wide, and in the parts in which we sailed is always very broad too. A prodigious volume of water is borne along to the ocean. But it is not always so full as now. There is, however, a channel or deep portion which would throughout the year admit a steamer of small draught to work. It has the peculiarity of shifting from year to year, as indeed do the islands, though so very large. Several of the latter are strong enough to bear up against the force of the stream. These were well peopled untill lately, when Landins on one side, and Kisaka on the other with Bonga, attacked and dispersed the population. They were good supplies for Tete and Senna in seasons of scarcity, for the people cultivated largely. Kisaka continues the same system of plundering and murder on the side of the Maganjas, preventing all trade, as he says he has conquered that country, all belongs to him. He can now send to Quilimane, and the Landeens too go there, only visiting Senna occasionally to levy tribute on its impoverished inhabitants.

26th April '56. We breakfasted on Shiramba.[1] This was the choice residence of a worthy brigadeiro, who spent much money in embellishing his residence and gardens. His son destroyed all, and then rebelling with less success than Bonga and Kisaka was seized and sent to Mosambique, a prisoner of war.

When at breakfast the people commenced beating the drum of war. I should not have known the meaning of this but Sr Miranda, being well acquainted with the customs of the country, immediately ordered his people to arm, and sent two soldiers to ask why it was done while we were there. They gave an evasive reply, but the same is done when they wish to collect their neighbours to rob canoes.

[1] Lat. 16.54 S, long. 34.39 E (GSGS 4695, sheet 1176). DL nowhere names its former owner, though he often mentions the place again in *Expedition*.

When the father of Bonga rebelled, an officer and party of soldiers were sent to apprehend him. Nyaode appeared, and asked to be allowed to go into the house to change his clothing. The drum of war began to be beaten and the soldiers said to their officer, 'This is war', but he, disbelieving it, ordered them to allow their arms to stand posted. They were very soon surrounded, disarmed, and put in irons.[1] And there the rebel stockade stands to this day, inviting all the other chiefs of the country to similar acts of rebellion. The two expeditions against Nyaode were badly managed, and when fleeing home to the rescue of their despoiled families the Banyai of Katolosa killed great numbers of them for the sake of their arms. Tete is thus surrounded by enemies.

We spent the night of the 26th on the island Nkuesi, and found our lat. to be 17° 0′ 30″. In the morning the thermometer stood at 70°. It is opposite a saddle-shaped hill & island named   [2]. Having breakfasted at Pita we found that Kisaka is still plundering the country of the Maganjas and exercising despotic sway over other Maravi.

Country round Sena

27th April 1856. We arrived at Senna[3] in the evening and find it in a worse state than Tete, for it is annually visited by the Landeens for purposes of plunder, and rarely by any of the tribes for trade. The fort of sun-dried bricks is overgrown with grass, the walls mended in many parts by palisades, and it is proposed to surround the whole village with these as a protection against their enemies. They foolishly gave tribute or something like it to the Landeens, and are despised by them in consequence, for they go past them to trade in Quilimane. When Major Secard was here, instead of tribute he distributed ammunition, and when the Landeens heard it they fled. He then took possession of the goods intended for them. Sent a party to attack them in their own parts about three days distant. When Sr Miranda reached their villages he found they had fled, leaving vessels on the fires still cooking. They

[1] This happened in 1850; the party consisted of a Goanese ensign and twelve soldiers (Eça, *Guerras*, i. 264–5).

[2] Blank space for name; called 'Kavra misa' in *Expedition*, 37. Nkuesi, which DL locates in lat. 17.01 S, from observations taken on 'April 25' (*Travels*, 687), is about eleven miles from Shiramba (Eça, *Guerras*, ii. 169, where it is called Ancueza), and 'the island of Pita' is 'some miles above Senna' (*Narrative*, 37); neither is named on maps consulted.

[3] Lat. 17.27 S, long. 35.02 E (GSGS 4355, SE 36/3); DL gives the same lat., but long. 35.10 E (*Travels*, 658). First occupied by the Portuguese in 1531 (Theal, *History*, ii. 234).

had been warned by the Senna people of his approach and fled in time. In revenge Sr Miranda burned all the garden huts of their servants.

East of Senna, and about 20 miles distant, there is a large mountain range named Morumbala. It contains a considerable population of Maravi and two fountains, one hot, the other chalybiate. The river Shire flows on the western side of this range to join the Zambesi below Senna. West of the village, and only a few miles distant,[1] there is a double hill named Baramuana.

The situation below so many large reedy islands, and at the commencement of the delta, is not salubrious. The climate is humid, and much dew falls. It is remarkable how little judgement was manifested in the choice of this situation. Morumbala is lofty and very salubrious and fertile. The Shire at its base presents every facility for disembarking cargoes from schooners, and all was completely in the power of the Portuguese, yet they place their village on a flat and beside a multitude of low reedy islands. The people of Morumbala now live as enemies, and though I wish to visit their hot fountain it is impossible. It is said to be sulphurous, smells like gunpowder, and the hot air soon produces perspiration. When drunk it produces either vomiting or purging. The people who have seen it say the rocks near it 'appear as if burned'. Morumbala may be 2,000 feet high.[2]

29th April 1856. Yesterday I ascended Baramuana in order to get a view of the surrounding country. It is about 400 ft. high. Water boils on it at 211°. There is a fort begun on it, and two dismounted pieces of artillery lie on the ground. This was intended for the Landims, who on one occasion killed 150 of the inhabitants of Senna. Morumbala with the conical hills on its north appears beautiful. The Zambesi, full of reedy islands, winds along a dead flat, a few conical hills on the south being the only eminences. West and north all is flat forest, which has a sombre appearance, but very distant and just seen on the S.W. & by S. horizon haze there rises a mountain range, equal in height to Morumbala, called Nyamonga.[3]

[1] '. . . about half a mile' (*JRGS*, 1857, p. 385; *Travels*, 660; cf. Stewart, *Zambesi Journal*, 148). The summit of Mt. Morumbala (Murrumbula) is in lat. 17.28 S, long. 35.22 E, and the Shire joins the Zambesi in lat. 17.42 S, long. 35.19 E (GSGS 4355, SE 36/3).

[2] '. . . probably 3000 or 4000 feet high' (*Travels*, 661); 3,927 feet (GSGS 4355, SE 36/3).

[3] Not named on maps consulted. 'The southern end of the range . . . is at least 60 miles distant. The remotest point . . . is called Nyamonga, and beyond it stands Gorongozo' (23.v.56 Murchison).

In a clear day another range close by & beyond may be seen, which is the Gorongoso of the Jesuits, famed for its clear cold waters and some inscriptions on square slabs on the top. It is remarkably healthy. Belongs to the Portuguese, and is on the way to Manica, which is shortly to be reoccupied. Gorongoso is six days distant, $=1°$. If there were the least probability of the inscriptions being more antient than the Jesuits I certainly would go thither, but they are in Roman characters and probably in Latin.[1] Manica lies three days N.W. of Gorongoso, and the hills of Lupata are said to come round to the latter point, forming a semicircle with Morumbala on the other end. (There is another Ophir mentioned opposite Sofala, or between Manica and that port.)

Fever

30th April 1856. A slight degree of fever, produced by the dampness and cold of the climate here, gives warning to put on warmer clothing. A constant stream of thin vapoury cloud comes from the south, and that is the prevailing direction of the winds here. They are very strong in Septr, Octr. Therm. in morning 70° with rains.

Many boats have been built here by native carpenters without European superintendance, and some are now engaged on a very pretty model (24 feet long) under a tree before my window. They have laid all the ribs themselves. The common name applied to slaves here is bichos (=beasts).

Kisaka's people are plundering on the opposite bank, where most of the provisions for Senna are found. This will reduce this village to straits. The commerce is very small indeed. A few have cattle of a small breed, but the village generally may be said to be in a sad state of decay and ruin.

2d May 1856. I have just got up from an attack of fever, and am not entirely free of it. It is often more persistent here than higher up the river. There is abundance of quinine.

A troublesome complaint often visits Inhambane[2] and other parts on the coast in the winter, and destroyed many, both adults and young,

---

[1] See above, p. 449. 'As [Gorongozo] lies in the direction of a district between Manica and Sofála, which has been conjectured to be the Ophir of King Solomon, the idea that first sprang up in my mind was, that these monuments might be more ancient than the Portuguese; but on questioning some persons who had seen them, I found that they were in Roman characters, and did not deserve a journey of six days to see them' (*Travels*, 661).

[2] Lat. 23.52 S, long. 35.23 E (*Africa Pilot*, III, 218).

before a remedy was discovered by a native. It seems a species of croup or inflammation of the upper part of the trachoea. This man probably derived his information from his progenitors, for he brought a plant, or rather root, with which he scrapes and scoriates the tongue; a piece is then given to chew and swallow the juice, and the patient is soon relieved. He put a split piece round the neck too, which could have but little effect. None have died since the introduction of the remedy. (Note. This croup came with the Dutch the first time they visited Delagoa Bay;[1] unknown before. Though none of the Dutch were suffering they left the disease.)

Another remedy (roots of Inhacanhanha = inyakanyanya,[2] small dark-coloured rather crooked roots of fine aromatic smell and slightly bitter taste), of very potent effects, is well known in Manica. The father of Senhor Ferrão knew many excellent plants, but when he left copious notes of their virtues the papers were all devoured by the white ant in the time of the Landeens attacking Senna.

A large species of bats abounds in all the houses here. They enter by the spaces between the tiles, and last night, while unable to sleep on account of rapid pulse, skin sometimes hot and dry or bathed in perspiration, it was interesting to observe how 6 or 8 of them sallied into the room at 10 o'clock and searched every corner of it for a place of exit to the open air. They often hover close to the face when the eyes are shut and produce a pleasant fanning sensation. I believed they were killing mosquitoes, and had no objection to their familiarity. Having bared the thigh I gave them a fair opportunity of playing the vampyre, but they did nothing. It was interesting to see with what facility they could alight on the bare wall, or part about the door, nearly as horizontal as the roof, with the head either upwards or downwards according to their pleasure. A number live in the balcony of Sr Ferrão's house, and sometimes during the day, often in the evening, unite in a pleasant chorus in the manner of swallows. They are perfectly harmless. A very large species exists in the country which seems to be frugivorous, for it eats a kind of wild fig and is seen on the tree which yields it.

We are waiting for an order from the Commandant of Senna, now at Quilimane, for the dispatch of some goods by sixteen of my people for Tete. Everything is done in this quarter in military style. Other

[1] This refers to a brief visit made by Potgieter and some companions in 1844 (*Travels*, 649; cf. *Fam. Letters*, ii. 69 n.).

[2] Not identified.

sixteen go with me to Quilimane but return with Senhor Miranda, as it is very insalubrious for them and provisions are very dear, the harvest being scarcely ready yet, and during the last year's scarcity many were starved to death.

It would be unpardonable did I not notice the very great kindness shewn to me in sickness, and also in health, by Mr Ferrão. May God remember and bless him and his in their day of need.

Small portions of sulphuret of iron or copper are brought from Manica, which when roasted become red.

Esquinencia root[1] is reported very good for tonsilitis or common sore throat.

3d May 1856. Intend to take a young quinine tree in a box to-morrow, in order to take it to England if possible. The great adulterations to which the remedy is subject may be the reason its virtues are not observed sometimes. By increasing the supply of the real article, less inducement will be held out to adulterate, and good done.

May God grant me to be useful in my day and generation. Promotion comes from him by granting new thoughts to certain of his creatures, and they are thereby enabled to effect much for the amelioration of their fellow men. May he grant me wisdom and guide me with his hands.

4th May 1856. ☞ Remember to have all our boxes if possible of vulcanized iron, as a protection against the white ants. A salve for Mr Ferrão's scorbutic patch on the leg. A little mill which will serve for both wheat & coffee.

The chief person here has a chapel, in which they meet on Sundays to have prayers before the image of our Saviour. They have had no priest for more than 20 years, except occasionally when one comes to baptize, marry, and then go away without attempting to indoctrinate. There is a mighty difference here and where, as in England, they are in the opposition and in the minority. Not much of good is mentioned of them, some being addicted to the use of the bottle and other vices, of which one feels inclined to preserve silence, for religion is wounded both by the perpetration and circulation of the failings of humanity.

The cinchona trees are in abundance close to this, and more in the interior southwards there are forests. The leaves are large, 3 or 4

[1] Not identified. Bordalo (*Moçambique*, 229) mentions 'raiz de esquinencia' as a remedy for 'throat ailments' at Zumbo; *raiz* = root, *esquinência* = quinsy (Taylor, *Dictionary*).

inches long, light green and glistering, the under side paler green, the veins still lighter and not placed opposite each other, the leaves pointed and, though placed opposite to each other on the stalk, each pair takes different sides thereof, so that were four together they would all have their proper positions. The bark is of pale brown colour covered with minute white elevated points arranged irregularly. The fruit is an oblong seed about a quarter or $\frac{1}{2}$ inch long, with a bunch of fine white cotton at one end to assist its dissemination by flight. It is contained in a pod of a foot or fifteen inches long and not a quarter of an inch in diameter. The pods are in pairs at the ends of branches, and are grooved on the inner side. When either pods or trees are wounded, a milky juice exudes which is adhesive. The flowers are said to be white. The roots are covered by a thick soft bark, which is the part chiefly used by the natives for fever, and they know it to be very efficacious. The pods are at present not ripe. Native name, 'Cumbanzo'.[1]

Earthquakes have occurred frequently at Mosambique and a few times at Senna. They have always consisted of a single shock and came from the east, proceeding westward. They shook the windows and doors and made all the glasses of the house tingle. No meteors have been observed to fall.

The hot spring of Morumbala is at its northern end, and on the west side the formation is as if one peaked hill had been packed up against another, & each higher than its fellow, in 9 or 10 lines.

As in Tete have had many applications for medical aid. I could do but little, seeing all my stock was nearly spent, yet some have been cured by the means employed. A case of pericarditis tonight was made better.

5th May 1856. Senhor Isidore Ferrão[2] arrived today, having suffered from fever in the way. Much rain has fallen in Quilimane lately, after the rice harvest on which they depend was spoiled. They have suffered very much from hunger, many having been starved to death, and now another year is before them of the same suffering.

A Hamburgh bark, the Carmelite, was stranded on the bar and sold. An English cruizer came and made enquiries for me in March. Information of my safety will by this means reach England.[3]

---

[1] Not identified; 'apparently an apocyneous plant, very nearly allied to the Malouetia Heudlotii' (Hooker, quoted in *Travels*, 647).

[2] A slip of the pen; as stated below (p. 470) his surname was Pereira (cf. above, p. 458.1).

[3] See below, p. 469. The *Carmelite* is not listed in *Lloyd's Shipping Register*, 1856.

It is interesting to observe how anxious the relatives are respecting their absent friends, and with what joy they are recieved on their return. Unlike the Spanish colonies of South America, and the Boers, they are both here and in Angola all fully alive to the blessings of education, and nearly every family has one of its members absent at some distant school.[1]

☞ Remember to try and get the boxes for books made so as to be capable, when turned on their side, of forming a library, and of iron, as nearly all the books I meet with are destroyed by the white ant and other insects (?). If vulcanized iron can be had, or if that kind which forms with the nails,[2] an electric current can be obtained.

☞ The run after quacks and quack nostrums by those who are well educated and of elevated rank indicates an actual want. Can this be supplied by any remedies yet undiscovered? It is remarkable that some of our most highly esteemed remedies were known to savages before we knew aught about them.

6th May 1856. Senhor Isidore got negroes instructed to build boats and launches. They now make every part of them according to rule, and all from the raw materials growing in the forest. He had some instructed in carpentery in Rio,[3] and they have made him the neatest house in Quilimane. This shews they are not incapable of instruction and excellence in the mechanical arts. A small boat costs £20, a larger one from £30 to £60 or £100. All made of Motondo,[4] a very durable wood.

Senhor Isidore had the goodness to procure for me a few specimens of a fruit I never met with before, and called by the Portuguese 'apples'. It is about the size of small plums, has a stone inside, and tastes exactly as do our apples. It is very abundant both here and at Tete. The native name is Mosau. Has a hooked thorn and, except being light under the leaf, is like the Mokalo.[5]

Impure connection in open air often brings on a disease called Itaca, which seems a 'constipacão', only to be overcome by violent sweating and purging, as by the following of Sr Isidore: Manna 2 or 3 table spoonfuls, cream of tartar one ounce, senna leaves 2 ounces, quinine

[1] 'The European Portuguese value education highly, and send their children to Goa and elsewhere for instruction in the higher branches' (*Travels*, 644).

[2] *Sic*. A word may have been omitted after 'forms'.

[3] 'Rio Janeiro' (*Travels*, 662).

[4] Mutondo, *Cordyla africana* (Ficalho, *Plantas úteis*, 147; Wild, *Botanical Dictionary*, 69).

[5] Mosau = *Zizyphus mauritiana*, jujube (Wild, 139); mokalo (Tswana *mokgalo*) = *Z. mucronata* (Miller, *Woody Plants*, 51).

24 grains, liq. anodyne 18 drops, canella or cinnamon *q.s.*[1] to give aroma. Infuse in one bottle of water; a glass every other hour, with a cup of warm soup between, to be drunk warm. It soon produces copious perspiration and cure. Another method is a spoonful of castor oil in soup without salt, after an hour a cup of same soup, then every alternate hour oil and soup, soup, &c. The root called Root of Ithaca[2] soon produces copious perspiration. Is brought to Quilimane by the Moors, who all know it.

The treatment of the 'fevres' of the Zambesi by observant men who have been often subjected to them is deserving of attention, for it is often effectual and almost always safe. When it partakes of the intermittent form, they wait till the hot stage is well set in, then take bags of hot sand, or of salt and meshueira[3] mixed, and press them on nearly every part of the body, but especially on the joints. This, with warm soup, produces a copious diaphoresis. Or they make a simple vapour bath by covering the body with a sheet and placing under it a small pot of boiling water, keeping it there as long as the patient can bear it. It is sometimes used with aromatic herbs, but the copious perspiration is that which is wished for, and that is effected by the water. After the sweating a purgative is applied, and castor oil answers best of all (2 table spoonfuls). If it returns again, they then use a few grains of quinine.

An irregular intermittent, called 'fimbria', sometimes affects them. In it the patient has chills and heats, with occasional sweating of strongly smelling perspiration, for 24, 48, 72, &c, hours. When a good diaphoresis sets in, he is cured. They remark that those who wear flannel next the skin suffer least from fever.

A native of Quilimane applies a plant to the breasts of women who have long given up suckling, and they have soon a copious supply of milk for any relative who may have lost its mother. It is said the child is not applied untill the mammæ swell and shew milk, the mere act of suckling being otherwise sufficient.

☞ Remember to enquire the name of native d[octo]r at Quilimane. Do. school books for Sr Anselmo's boy & little Caetaino of Tete, son of the Major.

---

[1] *Quantum sufficit* (as much as suffices), a common abbreviation in medical prescriptions.

[2] Not identified.

[3] Bulrush millet; *meixoeira*, 'term used in Mocambique for *Pennisetum typhoideum*' (*Grande Enciclopédia*, xvi. 755; cf. *Narrative*, 278).

Observation rewarded. When the rivers of Manica fill and fall again, they leave a sort of cake of mud on the banks. The natives observe the spots which dry soonest and commence digging there, certain of finding gold.

8th May 1856. Recieved this morning a letter from the Governor De Alpuim of Quilimane,[1] informing me that H.M.'s schooner Dart had touched there in March and recieved my letters with much satisfaction. The schooner went to Mosambique for provisions and promised to return again soon, having previously called twice.[2] I hope to leave this tomorrow morning.

Some of Kisaka's people who have been plundering and murdering the Maganjas on the other side of the river came to sell captives yesterday, and some of the people of Senna went over to buy, and did purchase some. Others thought [it] an unsafe speculation, as they would soon escape. None seemed to think it immoral, though all had misgivings as to the propriety of the merchants of Quilimane selling them powder and arms for some ivory they brought. Some thought buying the poor wretches who had been three days without food might be an act of goodness.

The tree named Mucunducundo[3] gives an antifebrile remedy in its bark. When a decoction is employed it seems to have the same effects as quinine. It is bitter, and is used after the first access of the complaint is over. Grows plentifully in Shupanga[4] and is used as masts for boats.

9th May 1856. Sixteen of my men have gone up the river with goods for Tete. They are well pleased at being employed as boatmen, and as it pays better than gathering wood I hope they will gain something for their return. They left this morning, and we hope to get off tomorrow.

The Commandant has made arrangements to encircle the whole of

---

[1] Col. Joaquim de Azevedo Alpoim, governor of Quelimane 1854–7 (Eça, *Guerras*, i. 236).

[2] HMS *Dart* called again at Quelimane, and left early in May, reaching Simonstown (Cape of Good Hope) on the 25th; the letters she brought from DL ('addressed to any of Her Majesty's ships expected to be' at Quelimane 'on the 1st of April') were the first news his friends received of his safety (*PP England*, 1857, Sess. 2, XLIV, 31; cf. *Miss. Corr.*, 309 n., 317 n.).

[3] '. . . called in the Brazils Pan [Pau] Pereira' (*Expedition*, 41). The Brazilian tree of that name is *Geissospermum vellosii*, family Apocynaceae, 'whose intensely bitter bark . . . is used as a tonic and febrifuge' (Taylor, *Dictionary*, 472).

[4] Chupanga, lat. 18.02 S, long. 35.36 E; 'islet of Shupanga', lat. 17.51.38 S (*Travels*, 687). Mrs Livingstone died and was buried there in 1862 (*Narrative*, 31).

the villa of Senna with palisades as a defence against enemies (Landeens, &c).

Reach Quilimane

14th. Left Senna three days ago, the whole of the inhabitants accompanying us to the boats, the military commandant (Colonel Isidoro Correia Pereira) and Sr Ferrão having supplied provisions abundantly for the journey or voyage down. They were in much sorrow on account of the aforementioned people of Kisaka having come over and behaved in the most insolent manner in the village. This was to be expected seeing they encouraged them, and one of Kisaka's relatives, Ião da Conceicão,[1] lives in the village and treated them abundantly with beer. Sr Miranda would have gone over and routed them with a few slaves, but the Sennaites are very cowardly and feared the consequences. Alferes Ribeiro went with three European soldiers and routed one Marian in his stockade on the Shire.[2] It would be better if the Govt. removed Senna to Mitilone,[3] which is a better port of the Zambesi than Quilimane and not more unhealthy than Senna. Morumbala affords a better site.

36 miles below Senna we came to the mouth of the Shire, 200 yds broad and bringing down large quantities of a water plant which does not require to be rooted in soil. The Portuguese name it Alfaçinya, and it is so abundant higher up the Shire as to prevent the progress of canoes. There is another plant mixed with it and called by the Barotse Njefu, which yields a very pleasant tasted tuber.[4] Sebituane made it a

---

[1] João da Conceição, 'relative and friend' of Kisaka (Eça, *Guerras*, i. 305); called Jão de Concessão in *Expedition*, 43, where DL says he had enough influence at Tete to get 'a friend of the Portuguese' named as Kisaka's successor, 1858.

[2] The *alferes* (ensign) may have been Joaquim Gomes Ribeiro (Eça, *Guerras*, ii. 55). 'Marian' was Mariano Francisco Vaz dos Anjos, 'the notorious bandit of the Zambesi basin' (ibid., i. 311, 346, 363), also known as Matakanya; a half-caste 'slave hunter' and 'rare monster of inhumanity', whose activities brought him into armed conflict with the Portuguese in 1857; died c. 1864, 'from the effects of debauchery' (*Narrative*, 24-6, 578, and passim; cf. also *Expedition*, 49-50, for a description of his stockade; Botelho, *História*, ii. 192-3; Stewart, *Zambesi Journal*, 11).

[3] 'The harbour of Mitilone, which is at one of the mouths of the Zambesi' (*Travels*, 662); probably Mitaone, immediately opposite the modern port of Chinde, lat. 18.34 S, long. 36.28 E (GSGS 4355, SE 37/4; *Africa Pilot*, III, 236-7).

[4] Alfaçinya = *Pistia stratiotes*, 'from its resemblance to a lettuce' (*Travels*, 641); njefu = 'water nut' (Jalla, *Lozi Dictionary*, 216).

part of his tribute. The discharge of these plants in such abundance from the Shire shews it has lakes or large collections of still water above. The mouth of the Zangue is a little higher up and on the other or right bank.[1] A few miles beyond Shire we leave hills entirely and enter on wide flats. The banks seen in the distance are covered with trees.

After sleeping at the place of Senhor Joaquim,[2] we came down to the entrance of the River Mutue, or river of Quilimane, which is not more than ten or twelve yards wide. Farther in N.N.E. it recieves the Pangazi and another river from the N., which enlarges it considerably.[3] The portion near the Zambesi is very small and very tortuous, and even now, when it contains water, we have to carry our goods past the tortuous part to where it is broader. At Quilimane the sea water comes in, but the bar is bad and dangerous. It is remarkable Quilimane should ever have been appointed the capital of the Rivers of Senna,[4] seeing it has so little connection with them. But I am informed the Mutu in days of yore was all large, and admitted of the free passage of large launches all the year round.

Recieved notice from the Govr. De Alpuim that my letters had been delivered to the Dart on 3d May.

25th May 1856. At Quilimane. We were detained a day at Mazaro, which means mouth of Mutu, by rains, and leaving the next I got fever in the way to Mangara.[5] There, too, we had to wait a day in consequence of our carriers not having come up. We have by the

---

[1] The Zangue joins the Zambesi in lat. 17.55 S, long. 35.26 E (GSGS 4355, SE 36/3).

[2] 'A half-caste also, and a very drunken one'; murdered in 1862 by one of his slaves (Stewart, Zambesi Journal, 11, 48); possibly Joaquim Antonio Rodrigues, mentioned by Bordalo (Moçambique, 254) as lessee of two estates on the Zambesi.

[3] The Mutu is a channel, usually dry, connecting Mazaro (see below) with the Cuacua or 'river of Quelimane', which it joins at Mambuxa, lat. 18.04 S, long. 36.06 E; the Pangazi is not named on maps consulted; the 'other river', called Luare in Travels, 670, is the Lualua, which joins the Cuacua in lat. 17.59 S, long. 36.30 E (GSGS 4695, sheet 1175; Eça, Guerras, ii. 168).

[4] Rios de Sena, for some time a separate district, was reunited with that of Quelimane in 1829, after which, owing to the decay and military insecurity of Sena, the administration of the whole district was transferred to Quelimane town (Eça, Guerras, i. 230; Bordalo, Moçambique, 214, 219).

[5] Mazaro is in lat. 18.03 S, long. 35.45 E (GSGS 4695, sheet 1175); DL gives lat. 18.03.37 S, long. 35.57 E (Travels, 687). Mangara, not named on maps consulted, may be 'Mangaua', 16 miles from Mazaro and 57 from Quelimane (Eça, Guerras, ii. 169).

471

filling up of the Mutu from twelve to fifteen miles of land carriage, beginning at Mazaro, and the people being dishonest it is very disagreeable. My fever was a tertian and excessively severe, from travelling in hot sun, and long grass blocking up the path so as to exclude the air. The pulse beat with amazing force, and the stomach swelled enormously, probably because the blood in the cold stage was confined to the internal parts. The swelling is now disappearing, the fever not having returned after my arrival here and use of quinine which I found waiting my arrival.[1]

At Interra[2] we met Mr Azevedo, who very kindly quitted his launch, furnished with a house in the stern, for my accommodation. This was greatly in my favour, with fever upon me, and afforded by anchoring in the middle of the river some rest from mosquitoes at night.

I was recieved into the house of Sr Galdino,[3] one of the best men in Quilimane, and found some letters, but none from my family, none from Hamilton[4] nor from Charles, nor the Directors. But one from Commodore Trotter and a present of port wine and quinine, and a notice that the University of Glasgow had conferred the degree of M.D., and the Royal Geographical Society the Queen's gold medal.[5]

But all my joy in reaching Quilimane was embittered by the information that H.M.'s brigantine Dart had come to pick me up, and the boat containing the commander, two officers, and five men, was lost on the bar. I never felt more poignant sorrow. It seemed as if it would have been better for me to have risked my life for them than as it has happened. May Almighty God pour the balm of consolation into the

---

[1] DL had reached Quelimane on 20 May, 'which wanted only a few days of being four years since I started from Cape Town' (*Travels*, 672). It is in lat. 17.53 S, long. 36.53 E (*Africa Pilot*, III, 245); DL (loc. cit.) gives the same lat., but long. 36.40 E.

[2] Lat. 18.00.30 S, long. 36.27.30 E, on the left bank of the Cuacua and about 40 miles from Quelimane (Eça, *Guerras*, ii. 169, 661).

[3] 'Colonel Galdino Jose Nunes' (*Travels*, 672); a militia officer of high reputation, who had on several occasions acted as commandant of Tete and governor of the district (Eça, *Guerras*, i. 235, 236, 240, 296, 297); often mentioned in *Narrative* and *Expedition*.

[4] The town in Lanarkshire (Scotland) where DL's parents and sisters were living.

[5] Henry Dundas Trotter (1802–59) was commodore of the British naval squadron at the Cape of Good Hope 1854-7 (*DNB*); it was on his instructions that the *Frolic* and *Dart* had called for DL at Quelimane. The honorary degree conferred by Glasgow University (December 1854) was that of LL.D., not M.D., and the RGS award was the Patron's Gold Medal, 1854, 'for his explorations in Central Africa' (cf. *Miss. Corr.*, 276, notes 1 and 2).

bosoms of their relatives. One of them, Lieut. Woodruffe, was a particularly fine young man, and had volunteered to welcome me. He was of the marines.[1]

Recieved intelligence also of the loss by drowning of my nephew David in Canada. Was of a fine disposition, eleven years old.[2] God takes unto himself his own. We must bow to his will in all things.

A Hamburgh barque was lost on the bar here too. The captain and men still here. Indeed, every vessel which enters is in danger of shipwreck. Yet there is a fine port farther south named Bara Catrina. Luaba is the principal arm of the Zambesi.[3]

26th May 1856. Sr Galdino informs me that the common wild vine of this country, Pereira brava,[4] was made tame by a merchant at Zumbo, who doubled down a plant, then, when it had taken root, cut its connection with the main root, and again repeated the process till it shewed good grapes like those cultivated [see facsimile]. The root

[1] The *Dart* (tender to the flagship at Simonstown) had been ordered in January 'to proceed to Quillimane to afford the Rev. Dr. Livingston all the assistance he may require, should he have reached that place; but in the event of his not having arrived . . . to cruize for the suppression of the Slave Trade and the protection of commerce, leaving a letter for Dr. Livingston stating when he [the officer commanding] will be back, and taking care not to be absent from Quillimane for more than three weeks at any one time. Dr. Livingston is to be offered a passage to the Cape of Good Hope in the "Dart" if he wishes it' (*PP England*, 1856, LXII, 159). The accident had presumably occurred when she called at Quelimane at the end of April. Henry Woodruff was a second lieutenant in the Royal Marines, with seniority dating from April 1855 (*Navy List*, October 1856, p. 328).

[2] A son of DL's brother John, he was drowned in a lake about three miles north of Lanark, in Ontario, where his family was then living (information from Mr H. S. Livingstone).

[3] 'Bara Catrina' is at the Rio Catarina mouth of the Zambesi, entered between Inhacombe and Timbue islands; 'Luaba' is the Rio Cuama (Rio Luabo de Este), entered between Timbue and Inhangurue islands, in lat. 18.52 S, long. 36.18 E (*Africa Pilot*, III, 235, and 1959 supplement, 42; GSGS 4355, SE 37/4).

[4] Possibly *Cissampelos pareira* (cf. Ficalho, *Plantas úteis*, 83).

pounded and applied to a fungous ulcer acts as an escharotic, and when the same is steeped in water the latter acts as a purgative.

The women take great pains to instruct the children in the genealogy of the family, and when any dispute arises all are capable of giving opinions founded on a knowledge of remote ancestry. A name is not allowed to die, for when a chief dies his nephew or other relative enters into his place and assumes the name of the departed without losing his own. Hence their lineage is very difficult, and as their goods are slaves only their family concerns are difficult to adjust.

The river of Quilimane, aided by the tide and wind, is eating away the eastern bank or that on which the town stands. A large wall is thrown down at Mr Galdino's house. (Fine house of Mr Isidoro, negro work.)

I thank the gracious God who has spared me thus far and kept me safe in many dangers not mentioned in this book. Accept my thanks, O God, through Jesus Christ.

Quilimane, 26th May 1856

Wrote Sir R. M. on lower Zambesi, & Revd. Dr Tidman on present opening in Interior.[1] Still at Quilimane waiting for a ship to take me south or north, as the case may be. 2d June 1856. Send back some of the men on account of the dearth in Quilimane.

Black swallows in abundance on Mutu R. They seem inclined to build in banks; are pure black, and forked tails. In May.

Good name given by effects of cruizers to all English.

[1] The letter to Murchison, 23.v.56, was published in *JRGS*, 1857, pp. 374–86; for that to Tidman, same date, see *Miss. Corr.*, 306–12. (The entries beginning here are on MS 849, after the list of contents; the preceding entry is on p. 842.)

LIST OF REFERENCES

MANUSCRIPT SOURCES

(*a*) D. Livingstone: letters to Gabriel (British Museum, Add. MS. 37410); Maclear, 13.ix.55, 16.ii.56 (Rhodesian National Archives, LI 1/1, ff. 156–73, 305–75); Murchison, 23.v.56 (ibid., ff. 413–40: draft of version published in *JKGS*, 1857, pp. 374–86).

(*b*) Letters to Livingstone from Maclear, 27.iii.54 (Rhodesian National Archives, LI, 1/1 ff. 82–5), and Murchison, 2.x.55 (ibid., ff. 174–7).

(*c*) Letter from Gabriel to Lord Clarendon, 30.xii. 54 (Public Record Office, FO 84/931).

PUBLISHED WORKS

Abraham, D. P. 'The Monomotapa dynasty'. *Nada*, No. 36 (1959), pp. 58–84.

Admiralty: Hydrographic Department. *Africa Pilot*. Vol. II: *West coast of Africa* (10th ed., 1951, and supplement no. 4, 1960); vol. III: *Southern and eastern coasts of Africa* (11th ed., 1954, and supplement no. 3, 1959).

Allen, W., and Thomson, T. R. H. *A narrative of the expedition sent . . . to the River Niger in 1841*. 2 vols. London, 1848.

Andrade, A. A. de. *Relações de Moçambique setecentista*. Lisbon, 1955.

Annual Register . . . of the year 1854. London, 1855.

Argyle, W. J. 'Historical and oral evidence [about Soli iron-work]'. *J.R Anthrop. Inst.*, vol. 91 (1961), pp. 240 2.

Arnot, F. S. *Garenganze; or, seven years' pioneer mission work in Central Africa*. London, 1889.

—— See Livingstone, *Missionary Travels*.

Axelson, E. *Portuguese in South-East Africa, 1600–1700*. Johannesburg. 1960.

Barotseland Gazetteer, see Northern Rhodesia.

Bastian, A. *Ein Besuch in San Salvador, der Haupstadt des Königreichs Congo*. Bremen, 1859.

Baumann, H. *Lunda: bei Bauern und Jägern in Inner-Angola*. Berlin, 1935.

Bemis, G. *Report of the case of John W. Webster . . . indicted for the murder of George Parkman . . . before the supreme judicial court of Massachusetts*. Boston, 1850.

Blaikie, W. G. *The personal life of David Livingstone*. London, 1880.

Boletim do Conselho ultramarino, vol. iv (1863). Lisbon.

Boletim official do Governo Geral da provincia d'Angola, 1852–6 (weekly). Loanda: Imprensa do Governo.

Bordalo, F. M. *Ensaios sobre a estatistica das possessões portuguezas no ultramar.* Ser. II, livro IV: *Provincia de Moçambique.* Lisbon, 1859.

Botelho, J. J. Teixeira. *História militar e politica dos Portugueses em Moçambique.* Vol. I, 1934; vol. II, revised, 1936 (1st ed., 1921). Lisbon.

Bowdich, T. E. *An account of the discoveries of the Portuguese in the interior of Angola and Mozambique.* London, 1824.

Brelsford, W. V. 'History and customs of the Basala'. *J. R. Anthrop. Inst.*, vol. 65 (1935), pp. 205–15.

Brown, J. T. *Secwana dictionary.* Revised ed. Lobatsi, n.d.

Bryant, A. T. *Olden times in Zululand and Natal.* London, 1929.

Burchell, W. J. *Travels in the interior of Southern Africa.* 2 vols. London, 1822–4.

Cadornega, A. de Oliveira de. *História geral das guerras angolanas,* vol. III (1681). Edited by M. A. da Cunha. Lisbon, 1942.

Cameron, V. L. *Across Africa.* 2 vols. London, 1877.

Campbell, R. J. *Livingstone.* London, 1929.

Capello, H., and Ivens, R. *From Benguella to the territory of Yacca,* ... *1877–1880.* Translated from Portuguese. 2 vols. London, 1882.

Carvalho, H. A. Dias de. *Ethnographia e historia tradicional dos povos da Lunda.* Lisbon, 1890.

—— *Methodo pratico para fallar a lingua da Lunda.* Lisbon, 1890.

Castle, E. B. *Ancient education and today.* Pelican Books, 1961.

Chapman, J. *Travels in the interior of South Africa.* 2 vols. London, 1868.

Chatelain, H. *Folk-Tales of Angola.* Boston, 1894.

Chinyama, T. *Nsaŋu yamawantwa awaLunda* [vernacular history of 'the BaLovale Lunda']. Lusaka, 1945.

Clark, J. D. (ed.). *The Victoria Falls: a handbook.* [Lusaka], 1952.

Colson, Elizabeth. *Life among the cattle-owning Plateau Tonga.* (Rhodes-Livingstone Museum, Occasional Papers, No. 6.) Livingstone, 1949.

—— 'The Plateau Tonga of Northern Rhodesia'. *Seven Tribes of British Central Africa* (ed. E. Colson and M. Gluckman), pp. 94–162. London, 1951.

—— *Social organization of the Gwembe Tonga.* Manchester, 1960.

Coupland, R. *The British anti-slavery movement.* London, 1933.

Courtois, J. V. *Diccionário portuguez-cafre-tetense.* Coimbra, 1899.

Debenham, F. *The way to Ilala: David Livingstone's pilgrimage.* London, 1955.

Dias, G. de Sousa (ed.). *Silva Pôrto e a travessia do continente africano.* Lisbon, 1938.

Diniz, J. de O. Ferreira. *Populações indígenas de Angola.* Coimbra, 1918.

Duffy, J. *Portuguese Africa.* Cambridge, Mass., 1959.

LIST OF REFERENCES

Eça, F. G. de Almeida de. 'Inéditos do Dr. David Livingstone?' [Offprint, pp. 3–24, from] *Moçambique*, No. 73 (March, 1953).

—— *História das guerras no Zambeze; Chicoa e Massangano (1807–1888)*. 2 vols. Lisbon, 1953–4.

Egerton, F. C. C. *Angola in perspective*. London, 1957.

Eldridge, I. M. 'Short history of the Sesheke district'. *Northern Rhodesia J.*, vol. iii, no. 2 (1956), pp. 174–6.

Ellenberger, D. F. *History of the Basuto, ancient and modern*. London, 1912.

Ellerman, J. R., *et al. Southern African mammals . . . a reclassification*. London (British Museum), 1953.

Felgas, H. E. *História do Congo português*. Carmona (Angola), 1958.

Ferreira, F. de Salles. 'Memoria sobre o sertão de Cassange [1853]'. *Annaes do Conselho ultramarino*, vol. i (1854–8), parte não official, pp. 26–8.

Ficalho, Conde de. *Plantas úteis da África portuguesa*. 2nd (revised) ed. Lisbon, 1947. (1st ed., 1884.)

Francina, M. A. de Castro. 'Itinerario de uma jornada de Loanda ao districto de Ambaca [1846]'. *Annaes do Conselho ultramarino*, vol. i (1854–8), parte não official, pp. 3–15.

—— 'Viagem a Cazengo pelo Quanza [1846]'. Ibid., pp. 452–64.

Freeman, J. J. *A Tour in South Africa*. London, 1851.

Galt, A. 'The Livingstone centenary loan exhibition at the Royal Scottish Museum'. *Scottish Geogr. Mag.*, vol. xxix (1913), pp. 242–52.

Gamitto, A. C. P. *O Muata Cazembe . . . Diario da expedição portugueza*. Lisbon, 1854. (New ed., 2 vols., 1937.)

Gelfand, M. *Livingstone the doctor: his life and travels*. Oxford, 1957.

Gluckman, M. 'The Lozi of Barotseland in North-Western Rhodesia'. *Seven Tribes of British Central Africa* (ed. E. Colson and M. Gluckman), pp. 1–93. London, 1951.

Graça, J. Rodrigues. 'Expedição ao Muatayanvua'. *Boletim Soc. Geogr. de Lisboa*, vol. ix (1890), pp. 367–468. (First published as: Descripção da viagem feita de Loanda . . . , *Annaes do Conselho ultramarino*, vol. i (1854–1858), parte não official, pp. 101–14, 117–29, 133–46.)

Grande Enciclopédia Portuguesa e Brasileira. 40 vols. Lisbon & Rio de Janeiro, 1935–60.

Great Britain: Parliamentary Papers
1851, LVI. Correspondence relating to the slave trade.
1854, XLIII. Correspondence relating to the Orange River Territory, 1853–4.
1854–5, LVI. Correspondence relating to the slave trade.
1856, LXII. Slave trade.
1857, Sess. 2, XLIV. Slave trade.
1857–8, LXI. Slave trade.
1861, LXIV. Slave trade.

Gregory, J. W. 'Livingstone as an explorer: an appreciation'. *Scottish Geogr. Mag.*, vol. xxix (1913), pp. 225–42.

Hannan, M. *Standard Shona dictionary.* London, 1959.

Harris, W. C. *The wild sports of Southern Africa; being the narrative of an expedition from the Cape of Good Hope . . . to the Tropic of Capricorn.* London, 1839.

Hiern, W. P., *et al. Catalogue of the African plants collected by Dr. Friedrich Welwitsch in 1853–61.* 2 vols. (6 parts). London (British Museum), 1896–1901.

Horton, A. E. *A Grammar of Luvale.* Johannesburg, 1949.

—— *A Dictionary of Luvale.* El Monte (California), 1953.

Humboldt, A. von. *Cosmos: sketch of a physical description of the universe.* Translated from German. 2 vols. London, 1849 (Bohn's Scientific Library).

Jalla, A. *Dictionary of the Lozi Language.* Vol. I: *Lozi-English.* 2nd ed. London, [1936].

—— *Litaba za Sicaba sa Ma-Lozi* [vernacular history of the Lozi people]. 5th ed. (corrected), Cape Town, 1954. (1st ed., 1909.)

Johnson, F. *A Standard Swahili-English dictionary.* London, 1939.

Lacerda e Almeida, F. J. de. *Travessia da África* [1798–9]. Ed. by M. Múrias. Lisbon, 1936. (First published in *Annaes maritimos e coloniaes*, vols. iv and v, 1844–5; English trans., by R. F. Burton, *The Lands of Cazembe*, London, 1873.)

Lane Poole, E. H. *Native tribes of the Eastern Province of Northern Rhodesia.* 3rd ed. Lusaka, 1949. (1st ed., 1934.)

Lichtenstein, M. H. C. *Travels in Southern Africa in the years 1803 . . . 1806.* Translated from German, 2 vols. London, 1812–15.

Livermore, H. V. *History of Portugal.* Cambridge, 1947.

Livingstone, D. 'Explorations into the interior of Africa'. *J.R. Geogr. Soc.*, vols. xxv (1855), pp. 218–37; xxvi (1856), pp. 78–84; xxvii (1857), pp. 349–87.

—— *Missionary Travels and Researches in South Africa.* London, 1857; new ed., with notes by F. S. Arnot, 1899.

—— See Monk, Schapera, Wallis.

Livingstone, D. and C. *Narrative of an expedition to the Zambesi and its tributaries.* London, 1865.

London Missionary Society. *A register of missionaries . . . from 1796 to 1923.* 4th ed., by J. Sibree. London, 1923.

Lopes de Lima, J. J. *Ensaios sobre a statistica das possessões portuguezas no ultramar.* Livro III: *De Angola e Benguella e suas dependencias.* 2 parts. Lisbon, 1846.

MacNair, J. I. *Livingstone the liberator.* London, 1940.

McCulloch, Merran. *The Southern Lunda and related peoples.* (International

African Institute: Ethnographic Survey of Africa, West Central Africa, Part I.) London, 1951.

Manual of Portuguese East Africa. London, 1920 (Naval Staff, Admiralty, I.D. 1189).

Miller, O. B. *The woody plants of the Bechuanaland Protectorate*. (Reprinted from *Journal of South African Botany*, vol. 18, pp. 1–100.) Kirstenbosch, C. P., 1952.

Moffat, R. See Wallis.

Monk, W. (ed.). *Dr. Livingstone's Cambridge Lectures*. 2nd (enlarged) ed. Cambridge, 1860. (1st ed., 1858.)

Monteiro, J. J. *Angola and the River Congo*. 2 vols. London, 1875.

Mupatu, Y. W. *Mulambwa Santulu u amuhela bo Mwene* [vernacular history of the Mbunda]. London, 1958. (1st ed., 1954.)

Navy List, June 1854; October 1856. London.

Neves, A. R. *Memoria da expedição a Cassange . . . em 1850*. Lisbon, 1854.

Northern Rhodesia Government. *General List of Chiefs, January 1954*. Lusaka, 1954.

—— *Gazetteer of geographical names in the Barotseland Protectorate*. Lusaka, 1959.

Owen, W. F. *Narrative of voyages to explore the shores of Africa, Arabia, and Madagascar*. 2 vols. London, 1833.

Paias, D. 'Efemérides angolanas'. *Mensário administrativo* (*Angola*), Nos. 17–28 (1949, monthly). Luanda.

Pereira, J. M. 'O coronel Borges'. *Boletim Soc. Geogr. de Lisboa*, vol. xi (1892), pp. 731–40.

Pettman, C. *Africanderisms: a glossary of South African colloquial words and phrases*. London, 1913.

Pogge, P. *Im Reiche des Muata Jamwo*. Berlin, 1880.

Posselt, F. W. T. *Fact and fiction: a short account of the natives of Southern Rhodesia*. Bulawayo, 1935.

Ravenstein, E. G. (ed.). *The strange adventures of Andrew Battell . . . in Angola and the adjoining regions*. London, 1901.

Redinha, J. *Campanha etnográfica ao Tchiboco (Alto-Tchicapa): notas de viagem*. Lisbon, 1953.

Rita-Ferreira, A. *Agrupamento e caracterização étnica dos indígenas de Moçambique*. Lisbon, 1958.

Roberts, A. *The birds of South Africa*. Revised ed. [Cape Town], 1957. (1st ed., London, 1940.)

—— *The mammals of South Africa*. Johannesburg, 1951.

Santos Júnior, J. R. dos. *Contribuição para o estudo da antropologia de Moçambique: algumas tribus do distrito de Tete*. Pôrto, 1944.

Schapera, I. *The ethnic composition of Tswana tribes*. (L.S.E. Monographs on Social Anthropology, No. 11.) London, 1952.

—— *The Tswana.* (International African Institute: Ethnographic Survey of Africa, Southern Africa, Part III.) London, 1953.

—— *Government and Politics in tribal societies.* London, 1956.

—— (ed.) *David Livingstone : Family Letters, 1841–1856.* 2 vols. London, 1959.

—— (ed.) *Livingstone's Private Journals 1851–1853.* London, 1960.

—— (ed.) *Livingstone's Missionary Correspondence 1841–1856.* London, 1961.

Scott, D. C. *A cyclopædic dictionary of the Mang'anja language.* Edinburgh, 1892.

Seaver, G. *David Livingstone: his life and letters.* London, 1957.'

Selous, F. C. *Travel and adventure in South-East Africa.* London, 1893.

Sillery, A. *The Bechuanaland Protectorate.* Cape Town, 1952.

Silva Pôrto, A. F. F. da. *Viagens e apontamentos de um Portuense em África.* Lisbon, 1942.

Simmons, J. *Livingstone and Africa.* London, 1955.

Smith, E. W. 'Sebetwane and the Makololo'. *African Studies,* vol. xv (1956), pp. 49–74.

Smith, E. W., and Dale, A. M. *The Ila-speaking peoples of Northern Rhodesia.* 2 vols. London, 1920.

Soares, A. L. 'Esboço histórico sobre a extinta circunscrição civil do Golungo Alto'. *Mensário administrativo (Angola),* No. 14 (Oct. 1948), pp. 29–31.

Sousa e Silva, P. A. de. *Distrito de Tete (Alta Zambesia): caracteristicos, historia, fomento.* Lisbon, 1927.

Stewart, J. See Wallis (ed.).

Tams, G. *Visit to the Portuguese possessions in South-Western Africa.* Translated from German. 2 vols. London, 1845.

Taylor, J. L. *A Portuguese-English Dictionary.* London, 1959.

Teixeira, A. de Almeida. *Lunda: sua organização e occupação.* Lisbon, 1948.

Tew, Mary. *Peoples of the Lake Nyasa region.* (International African Institute: Ethnographic Survey of Africa, East Central Africa, Part I.) London, 1950.

Theal, G. M. *Records of South-Eastern Africa.* 9 vols. Cape Town, 1898–1903.

—— *History of South Africa.* 4th ed. Vols. II (1927), V (1915). London.

Torrend, J. *An English-vernacular dictionary of the Bantu-Botatwe dialects of Northern Rhodesia.* London, 1931.

Trapnell, C. G., and Clothier, J. N. *The soils, vegetation and agricultural systems of North-Western Rhodesia.* 2nd (revised) ed. Lusaka, 1957. (1st ed., 1937.)

Trimen, H. 'Friedrich Welwitsch'. *Journal of Botany,* vol. xi (1873), pp. 1–11.

Turner, V. W. *Lunda rites and ceremonies.* (Rhodes-Livingstone Museum, Occasional Papers, No. 10.) Livingstone, 1953.

—— 'A Lunda love story and its consequences: selected texts from traditions collected by . . . Carvalho . . . in 1887'. *Rhodes-Livingstone Journal*, No. 19 (1955), pp. 1–26.

—— *Schism and continuity in an African society: a study of Ndembu village life*. Manchester, 1957.

Valdez, F. T. *Six years of a traveller's life in Western Africa*. 2 vols. London, 1861.

Verhulpen, E. *Baluba et Balubäises du Katanga*. Antwerp, 1936.

Wallis, J. P. R. (ed.). *The Matabele journals of Robert Moffat 1829–1860*. 2 vols. London, 1945.

—— *The Zambesi journal of James Stewart 1862–1863*. London, 1952.

—— *The Zambesi expedition of David Livingstone 1858–1863*. 2 vols. London, 1956.

White, C. M. N. *Lwena-English vocabulary*. London, 1944.

—— *The material culture of the Lunda-Lovale peoples*. (Rhodes-Livingstone Museum, Occasional Papers, No. 3.) Livingstone, 1948.

—— 'The Balovale peoples and their historical background'. *Rhodes-Livingstone Journal*, No. 8 (1949), pp. 26–41.

Wild, H. *A Southern Rhodesian botanical dictionary of native and English plant names*. Salisbury (S. Rhod.), 1953.

Willoughby, W. C. *The soul of the Bantu: . . . magico-religious practices and beliefs of the Bantu tribes of Africa*. London, 1928.

MAPS

Angola, 1912: Esboço da Carta de Angola, 1 : 2,000,000. Lisbon.

Angola, 1917: ibid., revised ed.

Gibbons, 1904: Map of North Western Rhodesia, 1 : 1,230,000, by A. St. H. Gibbons. London.

GSGS 2465: Africa, 1 : 1,000,000 (published by War Office: Geographical Section, General Staff).
  SC 34: Dilolo (1st ed., 1949).
  SD 34: Cassambo (1st ed., 1949).
  SE 35: Livingstone (1st ed., 1948).

GSGS 4355: Yard Grid (South Africa), Africa: 1 : 500,000 (War Office: Geographical Section, General Staff).
  SD 36/4: Zumbo (2nd ed., 1947).
  SD 36/5: Chicoa (3rd ed., 1949).
  SE 36/2: Tete (3rd ed., 1946).
  SE 36/3: Port Herald (4th ed., 1946).
  SE 37/4: Chinde (3rd ed., 1946).

GSGS 4646: World 1 : 1,000,000 (War Office: Geographical Section, General Staff).
  SB 34: Lusambo (1st ed., 1942).

SC 33: Loanda (1st ed., 1943).
SD 35: Lusaka-Sakania (2nd ed., 1942).

GSGS 4648: World Aeronautical Chart, ICAO, 1 : 1,000,000 (War Office: Geographical Section, General Staff).
sheet 3152: Busango Swamp (1st ed., 1952).

GSGS 4695: R.A.F. 1 : 1,000,000 Aeronautical Chart (War Office: Geographical Section, General Staff).
sheet 1175: Zambesi Delta (1st ed., 1951).
sheet 1176: Mazoe River (1st ed., 1953).
sheet 1177: Victoria Falls (1st ed., 1956).

Rhodesia and Nyasaland, 1 : 500,000 (Survey Dept., Office of the Surveyor-General, Lusaka, N. Rhodesia).
Livingstone SE–35 NW (1st ed., 1957).
Lusaka SD–35 SE (1st ed., 1957).

WAC: World Aeronautical Chart, ICAO, 1 : 1,000,000 (Trigonometrical Survey Office, Pretoria).
3177: Livingstone (1st ed., January 1955).
3274: Kalahari (1st ed., February 1952).
3300: Johannesburg (1st ed., August 1953).

INDEX

INDEX

INDEX